Psychoanalysis
AND THE
Education of the Child

Books by Gerald H. J. Pearson, M.D.

EMOTIONAL DISORDERS OF CHILDREN

PSYCHOANALYSIS AND THE EDUCATION OF THE CHILD

—with O. Spurgeon English, M.D.

EMOTIONAL PROBLEMS OF LIVING

COMMON NEUROSES OF CHILDREN AND ADULTS

Psychoanalysis
AND THE
Education of the Child

GERALD H. J. PEARSON, M.D.

DEAN, INSTITUTE OF THE PHILADELPHIA ASSOCIATION FOR PSYCHOANALYSIS

W · W · NORTON & COMPANY · INC · *New York*

FIRST EDITION

PRINTED IN THE UNITED STATES OF AMERICA
FOR THE PUBLISHERS BY THE VAIL-BALLOU PRESS

TO

My Wife

Contents

PART TWO

Ego Psychology and the Education of the Child

PART THREE

Psychoanalysis and the Development of the Moral Sense

Preface

THE ORIGINAL purpose of this book was to collect and present the contributions psychoanalytic research has been able to make to the field of education, but I found as the book progressed that it included both the contributions of psychoanalysis and my own philosophy of education. The inevitability of this change in purpose became clear when I realized that many of the notes from which this book was written went back fifteen or twenty years. For that length of time at least I have been turning over various problems of education in my mind. It is natural, therefore, that some of my philosophy should enter into this book.

The longer I live the better I understand the fact that the people with whom the young child is libidinally connected and the circumstances of the young child's life leave ineradicable effects on his personality and on his adult pursuits, both vocational and avocational. I can see now why I have been interested in education and also why I did not become an educator but became a physician instead.

I wish to express my indebtedness to my own analyst, who first started me on the road to understanding my own past, and to those other friends and teachers who have helped me to understand myself and other persons. Of course such a book as this implicitly acknowledges indebtedness to Freud and to his early and later followers, who for the first time opened up all of the areas of the human mind to scientific investigation.

I am indebted also for having had the privilege of participating for two years in a seminar group consisting of Miss Esther Mason, Head of the Elementary Education Department at Temple University, Mr. John Niemeyer, Headmaster of Oak Lane Country Day School, Dr. Ralph Preston, Professor of Education at the University of Pennsylvania, Dr. Robert Waelder, Dr. G. Henry Katz, and Dr. Sydney G. Biddle, which met monthly to discuss the relationship between the contributions to education made by psychoanalysis and those made by educators and educational psychologists. My interest did not begin with this group but the discussion stimulated a great deal of my thinking.

I am indebted to Mr. Charles Clisby, Headmaster of the Miquon School, and to many of his teachers, past and present. I am indebted also to the many teachers with whom I have talked and even more so to the many child patients who have taught me the most about the learning process and about education.

I wish to thank Dr. George S. Sprague for the many suggestions and corrections he advised after a careful reading of the manuscript. Finally, I wish to express my gratitude to Mrs. Samuel D. Auerbach and Miss Virginia Helensky, who have helped me in its preparation.

Psychoanalysis
AND THE
Education of the Child

Introduction

As THE reader observes the title of this book he well may ask, "What has psychoanalysis to do with the education of children?" Psychoanalysis is a medical technic used for the purpose of curing individuals who suffer from psychoneurotic symptoms. Its aim is to bring the unconscious into consciousness. By so doing the patient is made aware that his symptoms are an attempt to solve a conflict in his unconscious mind between his antagonisms and revulsions against his instinctual desires and the demands of his instinctual desires for discharge and gratification. When he becomes conscious of the presence of a conflict in his mind, and of the two sides of the conflict, he realizes that through his conscious judgment he can find a solution for the conflict which is more satisfactory than leaving it buried but unsolved in his unconscious mind.

At first glance this seems to have little relation to education, which the dictionary defines as "the imparting or acquisition of knowledge; mental or moral learning; cultivation of the mind, feelings and manners. Education in a broad sense, with reference to man, comprehends all that disciplines and enlightens the understanding, corrects the temper, cultivates the taste and forms the manners and habits; in a narrower sense, it is the special course of training pursued, as by parents or teachers, to secure any one or all of these results." Russell [1] says:

> Education has three kinds of purposes: technical, intellectual and moral. It teaches certain skills—of which reading, writing and arithmetic are

[1] Bertrand Russell, "As School Opens—The Educators Examined," *The New York Times Magazine,* September 7, 1952.

the most elementary and the most indispensable. From these as a basis it can advance to the most delicate and difficult kinds of technique. But such training does not of necessity involve any education of either mind or heart. Intellectual education has two purposes: to enable the pupil to understand things that are difficult and to put him in relation to things outside his personal life. I do not wish to underestimate the importance of the first of these, but it is of the second that I especially wish to speak. A human mind is like a lantern on a dark night; things that are close at hand it shows with a certain clarity, but with increasing distance there is increasing dimness, and beyond a certain radius there is total blackness. Mental education should increase the brightness of the lantern and the extent of the area over which it sheds light. Left totally without education, a peasant will know nothing, or almost nothing, beyond the confines of the village. The educated man, on the contrary, knows something of foreign countries, of past times, of the sun and the planets, and even of the millions of unimaginably distant nebulae. It is this enlargement of the area of awareness that is the great intellectual merit of education; and it is not *merely* an intellectual merit, since it enables a man to be aware of distant dangers and hopes that are not immediate. The moral gains to be expected from education are a more difficult and debatable matter. Education may turn a man into a mental slave, as Fichte thought it should, and as Communists see to it that it does. It may, on the contrary, loosen the bonds of traditional morality and make a man feel justified in any villainy, provided it is successful. This kind of effect is associated with the name of Machiavelli, but it has at times dominated whole communities with disastrous results. Between slavery and anarchy a middle ground has to be sought in matters of intellect as elsewhere. Education, if it can find this middle ground, can give form and discipline to impulse without destroying it. And it is in giving this form and discipline that its *moral* value consists.

From these definitions it would appear that the aims and the purposes of education and psychoanalysis are so very different that they have little in common with each other. In fact it would seem that only the latter part of Russell's description has any relation at all to the aims and purposes of psychoanalysis. Even there it would seem that psychoanalysis and education are basically opposites, for education gives form and discipline to the expression of the instinctual drives, while the purpose of psychoanalysis is to make the person aware that they exist as part of himself.

As the two disciplines seemed so unrelated, psychoanalysts for a long time were not very sure whether what they had learned about the human psyche could be applied in the field of education. Some attempts were made, but because of the improper application of psychoanalytic concepts, they did not accomplish the desired results. In fact, the results were disastrous, as I will show later on. The two disciplines do have a relation because they have the same end in view—to enable the person to live comfortably with himself and in a social group—although they go about attaining this end in diametrically opposed ways. Also, a careful study of the definitions of education reveals that the two disciplines are more closely related than at first is apparent. In ordinary usage the term "education" has two definitions. In the first it is applied to the process and methods by which a child or adult is taught skills. It means the learning process. This is more commonly the American and English meaning of the term. In the second, "education" is applied to the process and methods of learning to live with other people. It means the training process, or what is often called "character building." This is more commonly the European meaning of the word. In all countries the word has both meanings, although in some countries the emphasis falls more on the learning aspect, in others, on the training aspect. This second definition of education—as the training process—is closely related to the knowledge of the human psyche which has been obtained by psychoanalytic researches.

When Freud first began to be concerned with the problem of understanding the psychoneuroses in order to cure them he found that the patient's illness was the result of a conflict in the patient's mind. This conflict lay between the demands for gratification by the patient's instincts and his unwillingness to permit himself this type of gratification or even to know that he had instinctual desires which were demanding gratification. Freud first thought the conflict lay between the conscious part of the patient's mind and the unconscious part, and postulated that the patient would be relieved of his illness if he could know, i.e., become conscious of, the desires in his unconscious mind. In order to learn what thoughts, feelings, desires, and wishes were in his patient's unconscious mind, so that he might help the patient to know them, Freud first used hypnotism. Later, as he found that with many patients this method did not give satisfactory results, he began to use the technical procedure of psychoanalysis—free association—which he found to be a much better method than hypnosis for making the unconscious conscious. He found that desires were kept in the unconscious through repression because the patient feared that he would be punished or disliked in the present, or that he would suffer pangs from his conscious conscience if he allowed himself to know what he really wanted to do. As Freud understood it, the patient's basic conflict was between the demands of his instincts (his libidinal desires) and his fear of real punishment or ostracism in the present (his need for self-preservation).

He had thought originally that the patient would be able to solve his dilemma if he knew what his unconscious desires were. However, he soon found that another factor was present in this conflict. A man who has sexual desires toward a married woman may repress these desires into the unconscious and develop impotence as an added protection lest he suffer the jealous retaliation of her husband if he actually attempted to seduce the woman. But an explanation like this cannot account for the impotence of a married man with his own wife. The psychoanalysis of such situations reveals that the patient's fear of punishment has originated in a part of his mind which has been unconscious since the age of six or seven and is compounded of the little boy's fear of his father, of the terror-ridden fantasies of what his father would do to him in punishment if he had sexual wishes, of the projection of his own feelings of jealousy onto his father ("I feel jealous and would like to destroy my rival. I am a male human being; therefore all males, especially Father, must feel the same way I do."), and of the memory of certain actual occurrences during his early life. All of these combined together are intermingled with his real knowledge of his father. In order to be able to get along with his real father, he incorporates them into his mind as a new part, which stands as a threatening reminder that he had better not allow himself to have sexual wishes if he wishes to remain alive and intact. The conflict that produces the impotence of the married man with his own wife therefore is a conflict between his sexual desires and his forgotten childhood fear of his father's punishment, which was partly real and partly the result of his own fantasies. Freud [2] designated this incorporated fear of the father the superego. The superego has the same functions as the conscious conscience. It reminds the individual of what he should or should not do or *think*, but it is unconscious.

Freud found also that in certain instances the real attitude and behavior of the father to the little boy forms an important part of the superego. If he really is very severe, very punitive, or very cruel, or if he is very opinionated as to what is permissible behavior in a little boy and what is not—especially with regard to the childish manifestations of sexuality or the childish manifestations of hatred—the little boy's fear of his father increases and therefore the incorporated superego becomes very prohibitive and very cruel, particularly toward the expression or the conscious recognition of the specific instinctual desires of which the father disapproves. There is a similar result if the father is very weak, very indulgent, and overpermissive. This latter discovery did not make as deep an impression on the thinking of many of Freud's pupils as the former did. Freud found, and all psychoanalysts since have found, that those neurotic patients whose illness is the result mainly of a conflict between their instinctual desires and an oversevere and prohibitive unconscious superego respond best to psychoanalytic therapy and achieve the most permanent cures.

The discovery and delineation of the unconscious superego and of the fact that its behavior in the adult is the result partly of the early rearing of the child by his parents—particularly by the parent of the same sex—was an important addition to the knowledge of the psychodynamics of neurotic illnesses and of the human mind.

Freud was a scientist and did not jump to the conclusion that because a certain number of male patients with neurotic symptoms were ill because their superego was too prohibitive, and because its severity reflected the actual prohibitive severity of their fathers to them in childhood, all boys who had severely prohibitive fathers inevitably would become psychoneurotics. He was too much of a scientist to believe that one swallow makes a summer or to suppose that he could intrude into fields—like education—with which he was not well ac-

[2] Sigmund Freud, *The Ego and the Id*, London, Hogarth Press and the Institute of Psycho-Analysis, 1927.

quainted. He did write one paper [3] in which he pointed out that the "civilized" repudiation of sexuality increased the tendency to neurotic illnesses, and in his monograph *Three Contributions to the Theory of Sex* [4] he stated:

> It is during this period of total or at least partial (sexual) latency that the psychic forces develop which later act as inhibitions in the sexual life. . . . These psychic forces are loathing, shame and moral and esthetic ideal demands. We may gain the impression that the erection of these dams in the civilized child is the product of education and surely education contributes much to it. In reality, however, this development is organically determined and can occasionally be produced without the help of education. Indeed education remains properly within its assigned realm only if it limits itself to additional education of organically predetermined processes and impresses them somewhat clearer and deeper.

Certain of Freud's pupils were not as meticulously scientific as Freud, and they with their followers began to teach that if children were educated less strictly and if parents were less severe and prohibitive, the frequency of neurotic illnesses would be decreased. As is always the case with new ideas, this concept was misapplied, particularly by educators who did not understand what the psychoanalytic findings really were. There have been two main misapplications. First, there was the conclusion that if undesirable consequences have resulted from too strict training, then children should be given complete freedom to do as they like. Not many years elapsed before the disastrous results of this misapplication were evident. Children brought up in this way actually did not learn, nor did they become civilized, capable human beings. There was also the misapplication of what Freud had said in his paper on "'Civilized' Sexual Morality and Modern Nervousness" and, especially, of what he had said so carefully in his case history of little Hans: [5]

[3] Sigmund Freud, "'Civilized' Sexual Morality and Modern Nervousness," *Collected Papers,* Vol. II, London, Hogarth Press and the Institute of Psycho-Analysis, 1933.

[4] Sigmund Freud, *Three Contributions to the Theory of Sex,* New York and Washington, Nervous and Mental Disease Publishing Company, 1930.

[5] Sigmund Freud, "Analysis of a Phobia in a Five-Year-Old Boy," *Collected Papers,* Vol. III, London, Hogarth Press and the Institute of Psycho-Analysis, 1933.

Hitherto education has only set itself the task of controlling, or, it would often be more proper to say, of suppressing the instincts. The results have been by no means gratifying, and where the process has succeeded it has only been to the advantage of a small number of favored individuals who have not been required to suppress their instincts. Nor has anyone inquired by what means and at what cost the suppression of the inconvenient instincts has been achieved. Supposing now that we substitute another task for this one, and aim instead at making the individual capable of becoming a civilized and useful member of society with the least possible sacrifice of his own activity; in that case the information gained by psychoanalysis, upon the origin of pathogenic complexes and upon the nucleus of every nervous affection, can claim with justice that it deserves to be regarded by educators as an invaluable guide in their conduct toward children. What practical conclusions may follow from this, and how far experience may justify the application of these conclusions within our present social system, are matters which I leave to the examination and decision of others.

In speaking of "the origin of pathogenic complexes" he referred to the conflicts in the mind of every human being between the needs for expression of the instinctual desires and the repressing forces, particularly when, during childhood, the latter are reinforced too strongly by the dislike of the parents and other adults for the child's expression of his sexual feelings and his sexual curiosity.

Certain educators who did not understand the real implication of what Freud reported, because they had had no personal experience through psychoanalysis with the intrapsychic problems that revolve around the instincts, thought that neurotic development could be prevented by arranging that the child's sexual curiosity and sexual desires should never be frustrated. I know of one instance which I think caricatures this basic philosophy by reducing it to an absurdity. An intelligent woman happened to open the door of a bedroom where her eight-year-old son and the daughter of a neighbor were playing. She found them attempting intercourse and very quietly she shut the door and tiptoed away lest she damage the future sexual life of both children.

To the surprise of those who had advocated it, psychoanalytically based sex education did not yield satisfactory results. Many children brought up along these lines developed character disturbances and behavior disorders. It is true that in comparison with children reared in the conventional way, they appeared less inhibited. They were brighter and showed a variety of interests and talents, but they were often less curious about the more complicated world of objects. They had no perseverance, and readily relapsed into daydreaming, which made them appear introverted. They clung to many infantile habits which gave them cheap consolation in the face of disappointments. They very readily gave vent to emotions that vanished as quickly as they appeared. Some showed periodical lack of control of bodily functions and suffered from enuresis or soiling. The expected changes during the latency period did not occur. Instead they showed only a limited reduction of instinctual expression. Ordinary school life put a great strain on these children and their teachers. Even in progressive schools they showed comparatively little spontaneity, and their concentration was disturbed. They seemed egocentric and were affected very little by the demands of the group. They had little respect for the rights of adults and were extremely intolerant of their demands. Timetables, meal times, table manners, and routine hygienic measures, even if leniently handled, became sources of conflict. Traffic policemen and park keepers were regarded as public enemies. To the psychoanalytically trained observer these children showed an unexpected degree of irritability, a tendency to obsessions and depression, and certain peculiarities which during subsequent analytic treatment usually proved to be symptoms of concealed anxiety. It became clear that their education did not enable them to live in harmony with the restraints of civilization. Instead, they were involved in a constant struggle against the demands and duties required by the real world. When these children reached the period of latency, educational procedures did not help their development, and the threatened deterioration of their character had to be offset by psychoanalytic therapy.

These unfortunate results of psychoanalytic sex education were caused not by an erroneous application of analytic principles but by an incomplete one. The paramount importance of the lack of early sex education in the elaboration of neurotic conflicts had indeed been demonstrated through the results of adult analysis, but the desirable alternative to the old-fashioned neglect or denial of infantile sexuality is not to admit that infantile sexuality exists and then leave the child alone to manage his various drives as best he can. This is merely another way of neglecting the immature organism.

Despite the disastrous results of these misapplications, all psychoanalysts today realize that the early training of the child does have an effect on the type of superego which he will develop. The discoveries concerning the unconscious superego which have been made by psychoanalytic research are a distinct contribution to the field of education. This data is of greater importance for parents than for teachers because teachers usually do not have the management of the child till close to the final stages of the formation of the superego, which occur at about six or seven years of age. I intend to devote part of this book to a discussion of the application of psychoanalytic knowledge concerning the formation and functions of the superego to the field of education.

It is interesting to observe that Freud's discoveries of the effects of too severe rearing of the child occurred about the time when John Dewey began to teach his—then—revolutionary theories of education. I do not know whether he was influenced at all by Freud's discoveries. I am inclined to believe that both Freud and he arrived at similar conclusions independently. This seems most likely because the end of the nineteenth and the beginning of the twentieth centuries was an era of change. As Zilboorg [6] says, this period was one of protest against a culture which seemed to be forgetting the human personality.

Just as people who were not informed misapplied Freud's discoveries, so many educators have misapplied Dewey's concepts of education. Since Dewey first promulgated his theories of education in America there have been two opposing methods of education. In the traditional method, attention is directed mostly to the learning of skills. However, it should not be forgotten, as it often is, that the educators of the traditional school are concerned also with character building. They believe that it is advisable for the pupil to learn Latin partly because such knowledge helps him to reach a better understanding of English and makes the acquisition of the Romance languages easier and partly because such learning imposes an important

[6] Gregory Zilboorg and George W. Henry, *A History of Medical Psychology*, New York, W. W. Norton & Company, 1941.

discipline on the faculties and teaches the pupil how to study. It helps to develop a character which can subject itself to hard work. Thus the learning process goes hand in hand with the process of training, although the emphasis is placed on learning. The pupil learns because it is necessary for him to learn and also because learning develops his character.

There are other educational measures used to develop character. The aim of traditionalism has not been solely to enforce on the child submission to the father and to the past. The traditionalistic philosophy has held that the child comes from corrupt flesh, is weak, and ought to be chastised. This is perhaps best illustrated by the philosophy of the English public school, which has always stressed the worship not of human authority but of the authority of a code whose main emphasis is on the repression of instincts. The man who has not been chastised has not been educated.

Against this philosophy, and against the old-fashioned techniques and goals, the educators of the progressive method rebelled. This rebellion occurred because the traditional type of education did not accomplish what it purported to do and because the changes in culture changed the goals of education. The progressive educators believe that if people are left free what comes out will be good. They believe that skills are taught better through utilizing the child's curiosity about the world around him and his desire to do what adults do. The simple rules of arithmetic can be learned through buying and selling transactions in a play store—a procedure which calls into action the child's great desire to be like the adult. Learning to read can be stimulated by his need to obtain information—obtainable only by reading—necessary for his projects. In this way, an attempt is made to utilize his curiosity in getting him to learn to read. They believe that the training process, particularly training in interpersonal relationships, so-called character building, is more important than the mere acquisition of skills and that it takes place best when the child is not forced by chastisement or otherwise to conform to certain rules, but is encouraged through freedom to develop his own standards.

One of the best statements of the aims of progressive education is the following: [7]

[7] From a statement by the Faculty of the educational philosophy of the Oak Lane Country Day School of Temple University, Philadelphia, Pennsylvania.

We are attempting to create a safe, healthful environment in which children learn responsibleness appropriate to their development, and acquire the knowledge necessary for effective living now and in the future, with the least possible sacrifice of their individual needs for expression. The best way for children to become socially sensitive, responsible, and intelligent in the future, we believe, is to live now in a school community which requires and encourages these qualities. Consequently, we try to provide in our program as many opportunities as possible for social living, with children facing and finding solutions for problems which they feel are theirs, planning together, experiencing success and failure, and evaluating their own endeavors. We believe that such a program not only stimulates desirable socialization of the individual, but provides meaningful opportunities for academic work. Although we recognize the need for separate periods of work on such skills as arithmetic and spelling, and accept the desirability in the upper grades of more specialized subject-area organization, a major portion of our "academic" curriculum emerges from—or at least is related to—the problems and activities of the classroom and school communities. Learnings, therefore, often cut across subject-area lines, and are functional.

We believe, also, that a program should include many activities, should offer many opportunities for free expression. Cooking, painting, modeling, dramatizing, building, playing, dancing, singing, talking—all of these are given importance.

In this type of program, we believe, the role of the teacher is extremely important. For the teacher must not only give "instruction" in the traditional sense of that word, but must help children to understand their responsibilities and solve their problems, provide the security of reasonable limits, give the warmth of adult friendship, and establish a pattern of fairness, reasonableness, honesty, self-control, and intellectual curiosity which children will want to emulate.

We believe that the evaluation of each child's growth in relation to his own capacities and to the achievement of others should be a continuous and integral part of the program, and should be carried on by the child, his teachers, and his parents. We oppose "marks" and awards because we find them unnecessary for motivation, and misleading in that they direct attention away from primary goals.

We believe that a child's education is the joint concern of the school and the home. We, therefore, encourage active participation in the school by the parents and maintain close contact with parents so that the home and the school may supplement and understand each other more adequately.

Finally, we feel that the attitudes, the ideals, and the interests—acquisitions which we might well call "spiritual"—which a child develops in school are his most important learnings. For if we give a child competence of a high order, but do not help him develop love of learning, respect for himself and his fellow human beings, courage, the desire for the beautiful, and the zest for living—then we fail in our most important responsibility.

Progressive education tends to neglect the mechanical skills, such as writing, spelling, and arithmetic, and it tends, in its emphasis on learning about the world around the pupils, to ignore the lore of the past. It is interesting that many students from progressive schools after they leave school are highly critical of their education in writing and spelling. They seem to feel guilty about their schooling and condemn it even in ways which are rather nonsensical. This is due in part to the fact that it was different from the more common type of schooling. It was a violation of the cultural pattern.

The traditional schools which try partly to imitate the progressive methods often show by a species of caricature some of the faults in the progressive concepts and, getting the kind of result to be expected from lip service, leave the pupil to fall between two stools, actually learning neither the fundamentals of the present nor the lore of the past. Illustrations of this cover a wide range of situations. Student government is supposed to have the purpose of teaching the students to reach decisions which contribute to the welfare of the social group. One principal stated that his school was administered entirely through student government. In the next breath he went on to say naïvely that the school had a splendid orchestra. "Of course they never play jazz because I do not approve of jazz music." Schools very often require junior-high-school students to select for themselves the courses which they wish to take in high school. The student may select courses which will not give him sufficient credits for college entrance and be allowed to take them until, in the senior year, he finds to his amazement that he will have to take perhaps another year of high-school work before he can be admitted to a college. In some grammar schools entire emphasis for several years may be placed on learning about Pennsylvania or China—because the students have temporarily become enamored with the particular subject—and so eventually they miss any opportunity to learn about the rest of the world.

The report in *The New York Times* [8] of a recent meeting of the National Conference on Life Adjustment Education for Youth, which represented many of the nation's important educational organizations, highlights very well this species of caricature. For instance, in one part of the discussion it was suggested that instead of depending on marks in courses as the means of evaluating the progress of high-school pupils, the teacher also grade the pupil on his practical competence in shopping and buying wisely, caring for children, and driving a car, and on his health knowledge, self-confidence and poise, good health habits, honesty and responsibility, friendly relations with others, and ability to accept majority decisions.

Enlightened as this discussion seems, a careful study of its content shows that it illustrates some of the misapplications of Dewey's concepts. From time to time I intend to refer to some of the theories of progressive educators and to point out also the need for them to subject these theories to the light of the knowledge that has been gained through psychoanalytic researches.

In his researches into the psychopathology of the neuroses Freud's first and greatest contribution was the discovery of the unconscious. Psychoanalysis was developed as a technical procedure for investigating the unconscious part of the mind and especially the conflicts that existed there between the psychic representations of the instinctual desires and the forces which caused these representations to be kept unconscious. It did not concern itself with the conscious mind or with those parts of the psychic apparatus which were not involved in conflicts. These already had been and are being adequately studied by the psychologists. It was found, however, that there were certain neurotic manifestations which could not be understood as the result of conflict between the instincts and the superego. These manifestations occurred in people who seemed to have an inadequate ability to understand reality. The ability to test reality was not part of the instinctual life or of the superego. It had been observed for a long time that there was a part of the mind which separated the external world, the superego, and the instincts, and whose function was to determine in the light

[8] "Education in Review," *The New York Times,* October 12, 1952.

of the prohibitory demands of the superego whether instinct representations could be admitted to conscious thinking or not. This part of the psychical apparatus was not the conscious mind, for often this whole process occurred in the unconscious. Freud [9] chose to call this part of the mind the ego. Thereafter, psychoanalysts turned their attention more and more to understanding the functions of the ego—particularly its unconscious components.

The ego is a part of the personality which is partly conscious and partly unconscious and which is defined best by its functions. It is in contact with the external world through the perceptive systems and so is aware of external stimuli and stores up memories of them. It avoids excessive stimuli by flight and remembers the perception of moderate stimuli for future use. It has control of voluntary movements and it performs the task of self-preservation. Instead of mere motor discharge it produces action and thinking, which is trial action. It learns to bring about through activity appropriate modifications of the external world to its own advantage. It is in contact with the inner world of the instincts, maintains control over their demands, and decides whether they shall be allowed gratification. For some it postpones satisfaction to times and situations favorable in the external world. In other instances it represses completely the instinctual excitations. It is governed in its activity by consideration of the tensions produced by stimuli present within it or introduced into it. It feels the raising of these tensions as unpleasure and their lowering as pleasure. It feels any expected and foreseen increase of displeasure as anxiety and regards whatever causes an increase of displeasure as a danger. From time to time it gives up its connection with the external world and withdraws into the condition of sleep. It has the function of integrating and synthesizing these various functions. As a result of the long period of childhood dependence, there is left behind in the ego a precipitate of the influence of all of the developing child's life experiences, and particularly of the influence of the parents' personalities and the racial, national, and family traditions handed on by them.

Researches into the development and the dynamics of the ego have been fruitful in the last fifteen years and have brought the knowledge

[9] Sigmund Freud, *The Ego and the Id,* London, Hogarth Press and the Institute of Psycho-Analysis, 1927.

of the psyche developed through psychoanalytic research into closer connection with the data discovered by psychologists and educational psychologists. Therefore psychoanalysis can now make a further contribution to the field of education. Fifteen years ago I would have felt doubtful as to whether it had any such contribution to make. But with our greater knowledge of so-called ego psychology, the findings of psychoanalysis can be brought into a real connection with the field of education. I intend to show the contributions which the knowledge of the ego gained by psychoanalytic research can make to the field of education.

Freud found that certain of his patients suffered from a neurotic inhibition in their ability to learn. In his case of the so-called wolf-man [10] he mentions that the patient, although of good intelligence, had difficulty in learning. Since then many neurotic disturbances in learning have been studied and considerable data has been collected on the effect of intrapsychic conflicts on the learning process. The learning process is a part of the functions of the ego and the psychoanalytic studies on the ego have given data which are important in understanding how the child learns. I intend to discuss these psychoanalytic contributions to the knowledge of the learning process.

Educators in Western civilization, and particularly now in America, for some time have engaged in a controversy as to what subject matter should be taught in the schools—what percentage of the curriculum should be devoted to the practical problems of daily living and what to the humanities. I believe that a fair estimation of the problem appeared recently on the editorial page of *The New York Times*.[11] The author first quoted from a discussion by Matthew Arnold on the relation between literature and science, in which Arnold predicted that humane letters were not in much danger of losing their leading place in education, and followed this by the story of the contest between Huxley and the academic educators of his time. He concluded his article as follows:

> Since that remote time seventy years ago when the defenders of *belles-lettres* sought merely to retain leadership for the humane letters the

[10] Sigmund Freud, "From the History of an Infantile Neurosis," *Collected Papers*, Vol. III, London, Hogarth Press and the Institute of Psycho-Analysis, 1933.

[11] *The New York Times*, August 31, 1952.

picture has changed considerably. Today the humanities must fight to obtain any place in the curriculum, and sometimes the fight is in vain. The engineering sciences have ensconced themselves in "the leading place in education," and there seems little likelihood of an eviction in the near future. The twentieth century concept of education lays greatest stress on utilitarianism. One does not enter a university to obtain a broad background in matters cultural and scientific, but rather one enters to learn a trade. Today's freshman enrolls one week and must decide the next if he wishes to take pre-law, pre-medicine or pre-engineering. No matter which he chooses, it is certain that his only traffic with *belles-lettres* will come in a general literature course designed to familiarize him with the great names in letters from the time of Homer to the present.

What, then, is the future and function of the humanities in this era of technological specialization? It seems clear that there will always be men, no matter how small their number, who will be interested in the best that has been thought and said in recorded history. These are the men who will make our laws and change our statutes as changes become necessary. These are the men who will not lose sight of the fundamental social, economic, and spiritual problems which increase in importance with the rapid advance of science. Humane letters may never again attain that position of pre-eminence which Matthew Arnold foolishly predicted they could maintain indefinitely, but as long as men must live together and work together the experience and wisdom of the past will remain the irreplaceable guide to actions in the present and future.

Russell [12] says, "Education officials have always tended to overvalue what is definite. In the old days they liked Latin grammar because if the pupil made a mistake there could be no doubt about it. In modern times, they like arithmetic for the same reason. I do not know how it may be in America, but in elementary schools in England there is undoubtedly an overemphasis upon arithmetic. The ordinary person can get through life fairly successfully with no more arithmetic than is needed for keeping accounts, and I do not think it could be said that facility in doing complicated sums is a quality of very high intrinsic value." I intend to discuss whether psychoanalysis has any contribution to make to this problem.

[12] Bertrand Russell, "As School Opens—The Educators Examined," *The New York Times Magazine,* September 7, 1952.

This book therefore will be devoted to discussing the contributions of psychoanalytic research to understanding of the learning process and knowledge of the development of the various functions of the ego, particularly the integrating and synthesizing functions, of the relation of the ego to reality, and of the development of the superego. These topics will be dealt with in this order. I am not attempting to write a treatise on education; such a treatise would be entirely out of my field. My contribution will be simply to add the pertinent results of psychoanalytic research to the vast body of knowledge which has been obtained by educators and educational psychologists concerning the education of children, in the hope that educators will incorporate it into their philosophy and practice.

PART ONE

Psychoanalysis and the Learning Process

CHAPTER I*

Disorders of the Learning Process I: When the Learning Process Is Not Involved in the Neurotic Conflict

THE LEARNING process is one of the functions of the central nervous system. Over a long period of time neurologists, neuroanatomists, neurophysiologists, and neuropathologists have been studying the central nervous system through various avenues of investigation. Some of the data has been obtained through phylogenetic and ontogenetic observations. Some has been obtained from experiments on animals, some by direct electrical stimulation of parts of the central nervous system in both animals and man, the most, by the study of the effect of disease and injury, which has yielded important knowledge about the function of one part when it has been released from the controlling function of another part, now diseased. The correlation of all of these data, particularly those obtained from the study of diseased conditions, has given us our present extensive knowledge of the functions of the central nervous system, and particularly of its integrative functions.

On the basis of this knowledge, educational psychologists and educators have approached the study of the learning process in the child. There have been many experimental studies on the learning process in man and in animals, and the results of these experiments

* Much of the material presented in this and the following chapter is taken from a previous publication of mine: Gerald H. J. Pearson, "A Survey of Learning Difficulties in Children," *The Psychoanalytic Study of the Child,* Vol. VII, New York, International Universities Press, 1952.

have been correlated with studies of the functions of the central nervous system. There have been many detailed day-to-day observations on how children appear to learn and whether they learn better through one method of teaching than through another. The various functions through which learning takes place—perception, attention, memory, and the recall of memorized material—have been the subject of experimental and observational studies which have revealed a good deal concerning the effect of conscious feelings and of conscious emotions on the learning process. Many studies have also been made on children who have difficulty in learning. All of these observations have been correlated with each other and also with the conclusions of the neurological studies, and as a result there has developed a definite system of educational procedures. As I am neither an educator nor a psychologist, and have not studied theories of education or the results of these psychological investigations, I am not capable of discussing critically these theories of education or their practical application.

In recent years psychologists and educators have felt that their technical methods of investigation are not sufficient to understand certain problems of education, particularly the cases of children who seem to have difficulty in learning their school work. They tend to believe that many such children are suffering from neurotic problems, and they are sending them to psychiatrists and to psychoanalysts who specialize in the treatment of children. This is a step in the right direction. Liss [1] states that every child who shows any form of steeple-like or valleylike learning pattern requires an evaluation by a psychoanalyst.

I mentioned earlier that much of our knowledge of the functions of the central nervous system has been obtained from studies made of conditions which result from disease or injury. In presenting what I consider to be the psychoanalytic contributions to the knowledge of the ego and hence to the theory and practice of education, I intend to follow a similar method. For over fifty years the technic of psychoanalysis has been used to investigate the human mind, with particular emphasis on intrapsychic conflicts, conscious and unconscious—espe-

[1] Edward Liss, "Psychiatric Implications of the Failing Student," *American Journal of Orthopsychiatry*, 19, 1949.

cially the latter. Originally psychoanalysts were interested largely in studying the unconscious, the vicissitudes of instincts and the psychosexual development of the child. In the last thirty years, however, they have been forced by their patients to direct their attention to a study of the resistances and methods of defense which the patient uses to prevent himself from becoming conscious of his unconscious. Out of the study of these defense mechanisms they have learned a great deal about the functions and dynamic structure of the ego. It seems to me, therefore, that the time has come to attempt to bring together the data obtained through psychoanalytic research on the structure and functions of the ego, and the influences which other parts of the mind exert on it, which I believe constitutes the main psychoanalytic contribution to the knowledge of the learning process, so that the educator can begin to correlate these findings with the results of his own extensive and intensive investigations into the process of learning. I will begin my presentation with what I have learned from a survey of the literature [2] and from my experience with a large number of such

[2] The most important articles on learning difficulties in children are as follows (I am indebted to Dr. Mahler's 1942 paper for the references marked *):

* Karl Landauer, "Zur Psychosexuellen Genese der Dummheit," *Zeitschrift fuer Sexualwissenschaften und Sexualpolitik,* 16, 1929.

* Berta Bornstein, "Zur Psychogenese der Pseudodebilitaet," *Internationale Zeitschrift fuer Psychoanalyse,* 16, 1930.

* Edmund Bergler, "Zur Problematik der Pseudodebilitaet," *Internationale Zeitschrift fuer Psychoanalyse,* 18, 1932.

Edward Liss, "Libidinal Fixations as Pedagogic Determinants," *American Journal of Orthopsychiatry,* 5, 1935.

* Anna Maenchen, "Denkhemmung und Aggression," *Zeitschrift fuer Psychoanalytische Paedagogik,* 10, 1936.

Edward Liss, "Emotional and Biological Factors Involved in Learning Processes," *American Journal of Orthopsychiatry,* 7, 1937.

Melitta Schmideberg, "Intellectual Inhibition and Disturbances in Eating," *International Journal of Psychoanalysis,* 19, 1938.

C. P. Oberndorf, "The Feeling of Stupidity," *International Journal of Psychoanalysis,* 20, 1939.

Edward Liss, "Learning—Its Sadistic and Masochistic Manifestations," *American Journal of Orthopsychiatry,* 10, 1940.

Edward Liss, "Learning Difficulties. Unresolved Anxiety and Resultant Learning Patterns," *American Journal of Orthopsychiatry,* 11, 1941.

Margaret S. Mahler, "Pseudoimbecility: A Magic Cap of Invisibility," *Psychoanalytic Quarterly,* 11, 1942.

Otto Fenichel, *The Psychoanalytic Theory of Neurosis,* New York, W. W. Norton & Company, 1945.

[*notes continued overleaf*]

cases about the reasons certain children have difficulty in learning academic work in school.

I have received the impression that in the last few years an increasing number of children are having difficulties in learning their school work. In the course of the discussions in the seminar group mentioned in the Preface, Dr. Preston said that 10 per cent of the children in private schools had reading disabilities. He believed that this retardation resulted because they were pushed too early in learning to read or they suffered from strephosymbolia. The large percentage may also be explained by the fact that some were sent to private school because they were failures in public school. The increase in problems of learning may be real or it may be only apparent. Perhaps teachers are now more aware that difficulties in learning may not be due to the child's laziness or stubbornness. I have been informed that such difficulties are encountered only occasionally in Europe, with the exception of England, so that some of them, particularly reading problems, may actually be difficulties in learning to read, write, and spell the English language. The increase in the number of problems may be due to changes in the methods of education that have occurred in the last few years. In the seminar discussion I mentioned earlier Dr. Preston cited Robinson's studies at the University of Chicago on reading difficulties. He attributed 50 per cent to home conditions and 20 per cent to visual weaknesses, and believed that poor teaching was only a minor factor. The increase may be due to the fact that parental pressure for education is stronger now than it used to be, or it may be due to the changes in the laws concerning compulsory education. Whether or not this rise in the number of cases of learning difficulties is real or apparent, more and more cases of learning difficulties are being referred to psychoanalysts who treat children, and it is hoped that increased knowledge of the learning process and its application in the technics of education will soon result from their studies of these children.

Clinical studies indicate that the various factors which hinder the

---

Anna Freud, *The Ego and the Mechanisms of Defense,* New York, International Universities Press, 1946.

Emanuel Klein, "Psychoanalytic Aspects of School Problems," *The Psychoanalytic Study of the Child,* Vols. III–IV, New York, International Universities Press, 1949.

ego in its ability to learn may occur as a result of influences on the ego from the external world, as the result of influences on the ego which emanate from the superego or the instinctual life, or as a result of a disorder in the ego itself. This may be a disorder in the function of the ego or in the organic substratum of the ego—the central nervous system.

DIMINISHED CAPACITY TO LEARN DUE TO DISORDERS OF THE EGO WHICH ARE THE RESULT OF ORGANIC DISTURBANCES

DIFFERENCES IN INTELLIGENCE

A child may have difficulty in learning because his intellectual endowment is different from that of the average child. It may be lower or higher. In the child whose intellectual endowment is lower than average, the cortical centers and the association pathways are less capable of functioning than those of the average child, as the result of lack of development or of disease or injury to the central nervous system. The causes, symptomatology, diagnosis, and treatment of intellectual deficiency are so well known to educators and psychologists that they do not need to be reviewed here. However, an intellectually defective child labors under a difficulty beyond the organic one. He is slow in developing and is not able to identify with his parents as rapidly and as efficiently as the average child. As a result, his infantile anxieties are prolonged because he has less capacity to deal with them, and the constant pressure of anxiety further weakens the development of his ego. His parents also cannot have as much real affection for him as they would for an average child because his defectiveness is a severe blow to their pride in themselves—their narcissism. In order to avoid this hurt, most parents refuse to recognize that the child is defective intellectually. They try, inadvertently, to distort the history of the child's development and may even go so far as to try to convince the psychiatrist that the child is psychotic instead of feeble-minded. This lack of parental affection further interferes with the development of the child's ego and with his acquisition of the skills for which he may really have the capacity. His contact with the real world, therefore, is made with an ego weakened organically and weakened also by a defect in the ability to identify and by the inadequacy of the amount of love he receives. I have discussed this more fully elsewhere.[3]

Differences among individuals exist not only in generalized intellectual ability but also in certain special lines of intellectual endowment. I will discuss this fact in detail in a later chapter. All children do not develop the same capacities at the same time. In some there is a lag in the development of auditory sensation; in others, in visual discrimination. Similarly the ability to learn to read, write, and do arithmetic develops as part of a maturational process. Until a certain age all children are unable to learn any of these skills. As they grow older this ability becomes manifest. Educators have shown empirically that there is no use in trying to teach a child to learn to read until he is *ready* to do so. This empirical observation is explained usually by the assumption that only when certain associational pathways have become myelinized, and therefore usable, is the ability to learn to read possible. This has not been proven by anatomical studies, but the assumption seems to be correct. Similarly there must be a time when the child is incapable of learning to write or to do arithmetic, and a time when through certain anatomical and physiological maturational processes he becomes capable of doing so. In some children this maturational process is completed later than in others, without any pathology being present. The knowledge of this, however, is very necessary to educators, who then can spare the child the secondary emotional conflicts which would arise if he were forced to *try* to read before he was physiologically able to do so. Such conflicts might result in the child's losing all desire to learn to read, write, or do arithmetic.

Children whose total intellectual endowment is very superior may find difficulty in learning in the average educational setup, as Terman pointed out long ago. Their failure is the result of boredom. Children whose I.Q.'s are average or slightly above may take about one hour to understand and master a particular problem which the child in the same class with very superior intelligence may be able to learn in fifteen minutes. For the remaining three quarters of an hour such a

[3] Gerald H. J. Pearson, "The Psychopathology of Mental Defect," *The Nervous Child,* 2, 1942.

child has nothing to do, and in order not to be restless and disturbing, he will spend his time in daydreaming. The daydreams soon become more interesting than was the unsolved problem of the first fifteen minutes, and instead of occupying only the unemployed time they begin to occupy the whole hour. Consequently such children learn little or nothing, and at the end of several months their achievements are far lower than those of the other members of the class. On the basis of their poor school work the teacher may believe they are intellectually retarded. Furthermore, they have not learned certain basic fundamentals, so that now when confronted by more complex problems, which the rest of the class have the basic skills to solve, they fail utterly. This secondary failure drives them into more intensive daydreaming.

DEFECTS RESULTING FROM ILLNESSES

It is a well-known fact that children who are always fatigued because of lack of sleep, overstimulation, and overexertion do not learn as quickly and as effectively as unfatigued children do. (I am referring here to children whose fatigue is not the result of conscious or unconscious emotional conflicts. It has been proven abundantly, particularly during the years of World War II, that abnormal fatigue in *adults* is most commonly the result of such conflicts. However, the adult does not suffer, as the child does, from a constant expenditure of energy in the simple process of growing. In the child, therefore, actual physical causes produce fatigue more readily and more frequently than they do in the adult.)

The psychophysiology of the inability to learn in the physically fatigued child is as follows: Steady exercise rushes the venous blood too rapidly through the veins so that it is imperfectly oxygenated. This reduced oxygen tension adversely affects the cortical centers, inducing a sense of fatigue, and impairs the efficiency of the heart so that the circulation becomes inadequate for the bodily and particularly the cortical needs. The cortical functions are depressed also by the slight rise in H-ion concentration.[4] The central nervous system, particularly the cortex, of the child requires more oxygen than that of

[4] Sanson Wright, *Applied Physiology,* New York, Oxford University Press, 1940.

the adult because part of the oxygen is used by the former for the purposes of growth, so that any decrease in the oxygen supply to the cortex results in diminished function.

Even in those children whose fatigue results not from excessive physical exertion but from insoluble intrapsychic conflicts, and in adults whose fatigue arises from the latter cause, the physiological basis for the feeling of fatigue and its associated symptomatology is the result of excessive muscular action. Anxiety, the sign of an insoluble intrapsychic conflict, produces tension in the muscles. The muscular stimulation, however, results not in movement but in constant submovement contractions which cause the same circulatory disturbances as I have described above.[5]

Chronic illnesses, particularly those in which toxic substances circulate in the blood or in which the oxygen-carrying power of the blood is decreased, as in anemia, result in an impairment of the functions of the cortex, and therefore the child with an average or better-than-average intelligence has an impaired ability to learn. Intellectual and neurological changes may also result from a vitamin deficiency. In certain cases the child's difficulty in learning is the result of chronic avitaminosis.

Vision and hearing are the sensory organs most used in the learning of academic subjects; therefore, any defect in them—lens defects, partial or total deafness, and the like—will interfere with the child's capacity to learn. Often in little children gross defects of this kind pass unnoticed for a number of years. This is less common today than it was several years ago, because there has been a steady, desirable indoctrination of the public on this subject. However, the effect of slow eye movements on the capacity to learn to read is not yet well known. Educators are aware that a good reader usually reads rapidly, i.e., his eye movements are rapid, while poor readers often read very slowly as a result of slowness in their eye movements and they need exercise to speed up the rapidity of these movements.

The ability to learn to write, draw, model, and make things, i.e., the ability to learn to use the hands in creative ways, may also be disturbed by physical factors. Some of these, like chronic illnesses, fatigue,

[5] Otto Fenichel, *The Psychoanalytic Theory of Neurosis,* New York, W. W. Norton & Company, 1945.

and avitaminosis, have already been pointed out. The effects of gross motor disturbances due to major cortical insults are so obvious that they need only be mentioned. However, certain cortical or subcortical lesions involving particularly the cerebellum and the cerebellar association pathways may occur, as the result of birth anoxia, birth hemorrhage, physical trauma, or some type of encephalitis. These may not be evident on clinical examination but they lessen the capacity to learn the finer uses of the hands and fingers.

The ability to learn, therefore, has a structural basis in the central nervous system. If this structural basis differs from the average through constitutional inheritance or as a result of disease or injury, or if the structural capacity to function is diminished by physiological disturbances, the ability to learn is affected. This structural basis, which is the result of hereditary endowment, and which provides general intelligence and particular abilities, recently has been considered a part of the ego by Hartmann.[6] He calls it the nonconflictual part of the ego. By this he means that the other parts of the organized ego are formed as a result of the conflict between the instinctual drives and external reality (which includes the relationship with the parents) while this part has a different origin. Although it is not formed as the result of conflict, its efficient functioning may be disturbed secondarily by the conflicts in the other parts of the ego.

DIMINISHED CAPACITY TO LEARN DUE TO CONFLICTS IN THE EGO

Recently Bettelheim [7] has discussed certain reasons why some children show an active aversion to attending school. The many reasons he found for this symptom serve to indicate the many types of conflict in the ego which can result in a diminished capacity to learn even if the child attends school. He states that a child may refuse to attend school because of learning difficulties, because of an inability to get on with other children, or because of tensions within the child himself. These tensions, which arise from many sources, may occur on the

[6] Heinz Hartmann, "Psychoanalysis and Developmental Psychology," *The Psychoanalytic Study of the Child,* Vol. V, New York, International Universities Press, 1950.

[7] Bruno Bettelheim, *Love Is Not Enough,* Glencoe, Ill., The Free Press, 1950.

way to school and result in a need to run away or may be worked out by violent activity before school starts. Every child suffering from fears about school goes through an intermediate period where he is trying to adjust to the classroom but is not yet adjusted to it. He needs special help in convincing himself that he need not run away or be afraid. The tensions themselves may occur for a number of reasons. There may be an association of school with the loss of a love object, or the school may represent the losing of freedom and of independence. There may be a fear of exploring, which is really a fear to learn, lest the child discover horrible facts—usually, forbidden family secrets. There may be a fear to learn about sex, lest the child get into trouble from having such knowledge. (To overcome these fears the teacher has to establish her trustworthiness and her willingness to protect the child from the parents' anger.) The symbolic function of reading is often affected by the child's fear of exploration. A reading inhibition may follow a threat against exploring his own or others' genitals. Learning itself may mean the giving up of primitive pleasures. The child may fear the classroom because he fears competition after many defeats or because he has guilt lest competition mean the destruction of dangerous rivals. Bettelheim cites the case of a boy who refused to learn because he feared his hostility would bring him to the electric chair, but he might get off if he was so dumb he could not learn. (This solution to a conflict is seen frequently in psychoanalytic practice. A patient who fears his murderous hatred of his father, in his actual life as well as in his psychoanalysis, may tend to idle his time away waiting for his father to die so he can grow up without killing him.) The symbolic material presented to the child in his academic work may be personalized by him and then regarded as a real enemy. There may be no need to learn because the child believes when he becomes an adult he can use magic to divine things. There are certain children who feel that knowledge comes by magic and that therefore they have no need to recall anything they have learned. All of these tensions interfere with the child's desire to attend school and often give him an active aversion for it.

Bettelheim's book illustrates very well that the aversion to attending school may be an attempt to solve a number of different interpersonal and intrapsychic conflicts, of most of which the child is unconscious but which if stimulated by his being forced to attend school would result in an overwhelming conscious feeling of fear. Also, he shows that it is possible to be very specific as to the nature of these conflicts. Similar conflicts interfere with the learning process and it is just as possible to be specific as to their nature. Among them are conflicts resulting from unsatisfactory conditioning experiences.

IMPROPER OR UNPLEASANT CONDITIONING EXPERIENCES

It is well known that the human being turns to anything which gives him pleasure and away from anything which gives him pain. Educators have developed methods of utilizing this pleasure-pain principle to encourage the child to learn academic subjects in which, at the time, he has no interest because they mean little or nothing to him. In some instances they use his desire for pleasure, either bribing him with rewards or presenting the subject to be learned in such a fashion that its learning in itself is accompanied by a feeling of pleasure. On the other hand, they may use his desire to avoid pain. This method has been employed for many centuries in the use of punishment, i.e., the infliction of pain, for not learning. If the child does not learn as quickly and as completely as the teacher feels he should, he suffers real pain, so that he quickly comes to associate not learning with pain.

This method often miscarries. The child may associate the teacher with the pain and come rapidly to hate him. Then he will not learn. Again, he may associate the pain with the subject matter to be learned.

Case 1. A ten-year-old boy did well in all his school subjects except mathematics. In this subject he persistently failed. Careful study of his mathematics revealed that he did all arithmetical processes correctly regardless of their difficulty if the number 3 was excluded. He consistently made errors in the simplest computations when the number 3 was included. In the first grade the teacher had become provoked with him because of his slowness in learning how to write a 3. She hit him over the hands many times to force him to form it properly. As a result he associated the number 3 with pain and so could not use it in his computations.

This case was never investigated fully enough to exclude without some doubt the possibility that this patient had a phobia for the number 3. Wegrocki [8] reported the case of a patient who had a phobia for even numbers, particularly 2, 14, and 18. He was indifferent to odd numbers, except 21 and 23. He first began to be afraid of the number 2 because it was unlucky, and if he did something twice he had to avoid the ill luck by repeating it a third time. The numbers 2, 14, and 18 symbolized certain intrapsychic edipal conflicts. For example 2 was equated with the idea of a "couple" and with his unconscious sexual feelings for his mother and his desire to be coupled with her. The number 14 was equated with ideas of his vengeful father on one side and two couples on the other. The 1 in 21 was equated with ideas of his vengeful father, whom he desired to be rid of, and the 2 was equated with his longings for his mother.

The following case is a good example of the results of a conditioning experience.

Case 2. A girl of fourteen seemed quite unable to do any problem which required the use of long division. One day during the time when she was being instructed in this process she had been kept after school because she had misbehaved. In order to keep her occupied during her period of punishment she was given several long-division sums to do. The teacher did not know that the patient had an exaggerated repulsion against using any toilet except the one at home. Consequently, every day the girl contained herself and therefore had to hurry home immediately after school to relieve herself. She became more and more uncomfortable as she sat in detention, and at last she asked the teacher if she might go home, but did not state the reason. The teacher refused. The patient's discomfort increased as she struggled with the long division, and at last she wet herself, to her intense shame. After this episode the concept of long division was associated with intense feelings of shame and mortification. These unpleasant feelings were so strong that she could not learn long division. Even when the feelings were repressed they remained associated in the unconscious with the concept of long division, and so this skill could not be learned.

[8] Henry J. Wegrocki, "A Case of Number Phobia," *International Journal of Psychoanalysis,* 19, 1938.

DISTURBED CURRENT OBJECT RELATIONS

The need to learn, i.e., to acquire ego skills and particularly the ego skills of an academic nature, arises from a number of sources. One important one is the need to identify with the adult. The child envies the power, self-sufficiency, and apparent freedom from fear of the adult and desires to be like him so as not to be tormented with his ever-present feelings of fear, inadequacy, and incapability. This psychic mechanism is one of the most important in the process of education. Among primitive peoples and in cultures where the child can easily see the connection between particular grown-up activities and their goals, it retains its position of importance in motivating education. However, in our own complicated civilization, the small boy cannot see the relationship between his father's mysterious work activities and his own studies at school, and so he does not connect them with his desire to identify with his father. This motive to learn academic skills is lacking to him and must be replaced by other motives.

The child of school age wishes to do whatever he sees the other children doing. If they are learning to read, he also wishes to learn to read. This competitive envy, which is a real intrapsychic motive in learning skills, exists even if the adult, particularly when he is attempting to be progressive, tries to make the learning situation noncompetitive. Even more important in motivating learning is the child's relationship with his teacher. The child who loves the teacher tries to please him by doing what he asks, by being like him. He identifies himself with the teacher just as he formerly identified himself with his parents, and in making this identification he learns the academic skills which he observes the teacher knows. This identification takes place only if the child loves the teacher; therefore if he reacts to the teacher in a different way, with hate, anger, or fear, for instance, the learning process will be interrupted. A certain number of learning difficulties arise because the child hates or fears the teacher either because of the teacher's attitude to him or because he displaces these feelings from another adult to the teacher.

DEFLECTION OF ATTENTION

The centering of the attention on the academic subjects to be learned and the inhibition of the deflection of the attention to other internal or external situations is necessary for a successful learning process. This is interfered with if attention is drawn to other external situations which the child finds important because they can serve as a means of gratification for some pressing instinctual desire or because certain instinctual desires are forcibly attracting the child's attention to themselves.

Intrapsychic conflicts, whether perceived consciously as worries, feelings of guilt, shame and embarrassment, or daydreams, or occurring in the unconscious portions of the ego, attract the child's attention to themselves and deflect it to a greater or less extent from all other external or intrapsychic constellations. These "worries" may be classified into several groups.

Dangers to Security

Case 3. A boy of ten could hardly bear to remain a full day in school. Usually he ran home after a short period of classes. During the time he was in school he could pay no attention to what was being taught. His parents quarreled constantly, and his mother, to whom he was much attached, threatened verbally almost every day to pack up and leave the family. He really never knew when he left the house in the morning whether he would find her at home when he returned. When he sat in school he worried lest she had left already, and when the worry became unbearable he ran home to assure himself she was still there. In itself the situation at home was sufficient to cause the patient a great deal of real worry, but he also had an intrapsychic conflict, which was joined to the real situation.

In this case the patient's attention was centered on the real situation, with great apprehension of what might really happen to him, and on the intrapsychic conflict; therefore it could not be centered on learning academic subjects.

Guilt, Shame, and Embarrassment

Case 4. A boy of thirteen was deeply in love with a girl in his class. The love affair was a fantasy one, as is usual at this age, and he expressed his feelings only very occasionally, in private, to the girl, who reciprocated only slightly. He did express his feelings of love through writing verse, which he never showed to her or to anyone.

One day a friend of his found the book in which he kept his poetry and read a verse or two aloud, mockingly. The author became overwhelmed with shame and embarrassment and for several days was tormented by these feelings to such a degree that he was unable to do any of his school work. Before his friend's betrayal the boy had been constantly reproved by his superego for his feelings of heterosexual love but the strength of the love caused him to attempt to ignore the reproof. His friend's ridicule reinforced the reproof of the superego, and the combination of dread of further external ridicule and of dread of ridicule from his superego centered his attention on his feelings of shame in order to activate his defense against his instinctual desires. The focusing of his attention on his feelings of shame deflected it from his learning tasks.

The focusing of attention on superego manifestations is usually quite marked, and the consequent deflection of attention from the task of learning is indicated by a quite serious, although perhaps short-lived, decrease in academic achievement. It is unfortunate that these deflections of attention, from whatever cause, result in the child's not learning the particular sections of the subjects being taught at the time the attention is deflected. This interruption of learning, however short-lived it may be, results in difficulties in mastering later aspects of the same subjects, and the individual may labor under inadequate skills in these subjects for the rest of his life unless he receives special tutoring in the parts he did not learn. It is the duty of the educator to see that this special tutoring is provided in these cases, after the conflict has been solved.

Horror and Fear

Case 5. A girl of twelve began to fail in her school work. Shortly before the failure began she had been told by her friend about the phenomenon of childbirth, the friend depicting vividly and with much exaggeration the painfulness and bloodiness of labor. The patient formerly had been quite satisfied with her feminine role and had looked forward with eager anticipation to the time when she could be married and have many children. Now these desires and anticipations became terrifying. In order that the synthetic function of the ego could be used to make these two incompatible ideas compatible, she had to focus her whole attention on this conscious conflict so that she had no capacity to attend to her academic work, and this made it impossible for her to learn anything.

Instinctual Desires

Case 6. A girl of fourteen rather suddenly began to fail in her school work. At this time she had become aware of a strong desire to masturbate, to which she succumbed at intervals. After each time, however, she experienced remorse and fear so great that she preferred to walk the floor all night lest in getting into bed and trying to go to sleep she might succumb again. Of course the fatigue on the next day interfered with her ability to learn. Her attention was focused night and day on the problem of whether she would masturbate or not and so was deflected from her task of learning. In this case the conflict was due to the strength of her instinctual desires and their demands for gratification. These desires were opposed by her ego fears of the results of the act and by her feeling, derived from superego prohibitions against the unconscious fantasies during masturbation, that masturbation was morally wrong.

Daydreams

In the cases I have discussed so far the attention of the patient has been focused on unpleasant conscious feelings and therefore deflected from the task of learning academic skills. In the next group of cases the learning failure results from the deflection of attention from the feeling of worry, which is not then recognized, to fantasies which may be conscious or unconscious and which serve to comfort the child about some feeling of unpleasantness. Freud [9] has discussed the dynamics of daydreaming. He says:

> There is a general tendency of our mental apparatus which we can trace back to the economic principle of saving in expenditure; it seems to find expression in the tendency with which we hold on to the sources of

[9] Sigmund Freud, "Formulations Regarding the Two Principles in Mental Functioning," *Collected Papers,* Vol. IV, London, Hogarth Press and the Institute of Psycho-Analysis, 1934.

pleasures at our disposal, and in the difficulty with which we renounce them. With the introduction of the reality principle one mode of thought activity was split off; it was kept free from reality testing and remained subordinated to the pleasure principle alone. This is the act of fantasy making which begins already in the games of children, and later, continued as daydreaming, abandons its dependence on real objects.

During the first few days or few weeks at boarding school the learning ability of a child often decreases. If he is questioned it will be found that he is centering his attention on daydreams about his home and his family and has deflected it from the task of learning. He may not feel unhappy or anxious, unlike other children in the same situation who may be obviously homesick on the first day or so at school or camp, because he is focusing his attention on pleasant memories, but his ability to learn suffers during this time. In this instance the child is conscious that he is daydreaming.

During World War II, a condition known as "cryptic nostalgia" [10] was reported. Certain soldiers, shortly after their induction, apparently were unable to obey orders, to follow even the most simple instructions, to remember anything for even a short period of time; they behaved as if they were quite feeble-minded. Their induction records, intelligence and aptitude tests and the like, usually showed their intelligence to be above the average. The patients themselves did not understand what was the matter with them and were unaware of any feelings of dislike for the service, their colleagues, or their superiors, or of any feeling of homesickness. Careful investigation, however, revealed that they were thinking constantly about home but were not aware that they were doing so till the fact was brought to their attention; hence the name "cryptic nostalgia." Here the individual was not conscious that his attention was focused on thoughts of home and therefore was deflected from his daily tasks. Conditions of this type, in which escape from unpleasant intrapsychic conflicts results in a focusing of the attention on fantasy, produce learning difficulties in children.

There is another way of focusing attention, also pathological, which results in an increased ability to learn instead of a failure in learning.

[10] C. L. Wittson, H. I. Harris, and W. A. Hunt, "Cryptic Nostalgia," *War Medicine*, 3, 1943.

Case 7. A boy of nineteen explained that when he was younger he had found that if he felt deeply and expressed his feelings he was exposed to rebuffs by his parents, who favored his younger brother and who seemed to dislike him. About the age of nine he decided that he would not allow himself to feel anything again, but would only allow himself to think. In this he was caricaturing the old adage, Look before you leap. Instead of responding to a situation with feeling, he thought the whole situation through very carefully before he acted. He focused all his attention on the process of thinking and of learning academic skills to increase his thinking ability. As he devoted all his time to studying, his school grades were excellent. However, in his adolescence he began to notice that he had no friends, that his colleagues seemed to avoid him and ridiculed his scientific interest. It was this loneliness and unhappiness that brought him to treatment. In this case, he focused his attention entirely on learning academic skills in order to avoid deep-seated and painful intrapsychic conflicts and the feelings that are inherently a part of daydreaming.

The child who is *too* interested in his school work and strains too hard at it is often a more pathological case than the one who fails because his attention is deflected away from learning.

CHAPTER II

Disorders of the Learning Process II: When the Learning Process Is Involved in the Neurotic Conflict

IT MAY appear that I have already discussed all of the types and causes of learning disorders, particularly since I have included the deflection of attention from the task of learning because of conscious and unconscious intrapsychic conflicts. However, the question arises, Does the concept of deflection of attention account for all types of learning difficulties based on intrapsychic conflicts? Certainly it plays a part as a mechanism that interferes with learning, but in itself it does not seem to account for certain cases of learning difficulties, encountered particularly in adolescents, nor does it take into account the possibility of the actual involvement of the learning process itself in specific types of conflicts between the ego, the superego, and the instinctual life. Learning of any kind, but particularly the learning of scholastic skills, is a function of the ego. The energy utilized by the ego and by the superego emanates basically from the instincts. It would seem probable that certain learning difficulties arise because the learning process itself becomes part of whatever intrapsychic conflicts are proceeding between the three parts of the personality, rather than simply because the attention has been deflected from the subject to be learned to the intrapsychic conflict.

Freud [1] pointed out long ago that the functions of the ego in the

[1] Sigmund Freud, *Three Contributions to the Theory of Sex,* New York and Washington, Nervous and Mental Disease Publishing Co., 1930.

psychic sphere have their prototype in the functions of the ego in the physical sphere. The digestive activity of the body ego is the prototype of learning as a psychic ego function. The digestive activity consists of four parts:

1. The taking of food into the body through a special organ, the mouth, and the upper part of the gastrointestinal tract.
2. The digestion and assimilation of the food by a complex of special organs and their activities.
3. The putting out of the results of the digestive process, part being put out immediately as energy, part being stored for future production of energy, and part being excreted as unusable.
4. The use by the ego of the energy formed through digestion in the functioning of the total individual.

Similarly the learning function consists of four parts:

1. The intaking of information through the special senses and other parts of the sensory nervous system.
2. The correlation and association of these sensory impressions among themselves and with the memories of previous sensory impressions through the association pathways of the cortex and subcortex.
3. The putting out of the end products of these association processes through motor activities such as writing and speech.
4. The use of these end products by the ego in the successful functioning of the total individual.

Therefore, just as nutritive disorders may arise because of disturbances in the organs and their functions at any one of the four steps, and just as disorders of the organs and the function of the gastrointestinal tract may result from organic changes or from the influence of emotional conflicts, so, in the same way, the learning process may be disturbed. In gastrointestinal disorders, a disturbance in the function at one step is bound to result in some degree of disturbance at all the other steps. The same effect characterizes disorders of learning.

DIMINISHED CAPACITY TO LEARN DUE TO DISORDERS OF THE *USE* OF LEARNING

The acquirement of knowledge and skills is used in life to fulfill three desires: 1. successful competition with contemporary rivals; 2. successful advancement in the chosen sphere of life; 3. the attainment of ultimate success, i.e., of power, money, position, or prestige.

Each of these human desires exists throughout the whole of life, but each is given somewhat different conscious connotations at different periods of life. In the period of early childhood the desires are expressed in purely physical concepts. The little child wishes to be grown-up and do all the things that adults do. In order to achieve this he has to be more capable physically, and he tries to accomplish this result as quickly as possible. If he could be more competent physically he could compete more successfully with his rivals. In short, for the small child success is a matter of increasing the size and power of his body. In his mind, his body is equated with his penis, so during this period his wishes and endeavors are to make his penis bigger and more powerful in accomplishing his desires in life and in competing with his rivals. With the onset of the latency period such concepts are repressed to some extent and the wishes are attached to fields of endeavor much broader than the purely physical and sexual. The equation between the body and the penis becomes more-or-less unconscious, but the ambition to be more capable physically still remains.

Although the desire to be more capable physically persists during the latter part of the latency period and in adolescence, it is increasingly replaced by the desire to be successful in vocational and erotic ventures; the individual wishes to master the skills which will enable him to attain prestige and wealth and attract the desired members of the opposite sex. (I am speaking here of the male; the criteria of success for the female are somewhat different.)

Sometimes the use of the acquirement of knowledge and skills becomes disordered. In my experience disorders of the use of learning are seen more commonly in adolescence than during the latency period. They are more readily observed then because the adolescent, more than the child of the latency period, is expected to take responsibility for his school work, and therefore his shortcomings are more glaringly evident. Furthermore, the reactivation of sexual activity in adolescence reactivates the unsolved edipal conflicts, and the defense mechanisms which were used to make temporary peace with these conflicts are reactivated at the same time and become more apparent, whereas during the latency period both the unsolved edipal conflicts and the defense measures exist at a lower level of activity.

The most common disorder of the use of learning is an inhibition of the function. Freud [2] states that "inhibition in the field of occupation" (and learning is the occupation of the child), "which so often becomes a matter of treatment as an isolated symptom, is evidenced in diminished pleasure in work, or in its poor execution, or in such reactive manifestations as fatigue (vertigo, vomiting) if the subject forces himself to go on working." He defines an inhibition as the expression of a functional limitation of the ego. The ego renounces the functions proper to it for one of three main reasons:

1. In order not to have to undertake a fresh effort of repression which will mean a further conflict with the id.
2. In order not to become involved in conflicts with the superego. Here the inhibition evidently subserves a desire for self-punishment, as, for example, inhibitions in the sphere of vocational activity frequently do.
3. Because it is so impoverished with respect to the energy available to it that it is driven to restrict its expenditure in many places at the same time.

The reasons for the inhibition of the use of learning are of the second type. Here the ability to take in knowledge, to digest the knowledge, and to give it out all function perfectly. The difficulty lies in the inhibition of the use of the learning. In this the disorder very closely resembles sexual impotence, and therefore I would like to designate it as "learning impotence." Disorders in the use of learned knowledge usually are an expression of the fear of sibling rivalry or the result of feelings of guilt or the dread of castration.

[2] Sigmund Freud, *The Problem of Anxiety,* New York, W. W. Norton & Company, 1936.

FEAR OF SIBLING RIVALRY

Case 8. A girl of thirteen for several years had done extremely well in her school work and was interested in academic subjects and academic accomplishments practically to the exclusion of all else. She looked upon parties, clothes, boy or girl friends, sports, movies, and all other things which usually interest girls of her age as very boring, and she regarded with disdain her associates who had such interests. Her ambition was to be a writer, and she spent a great deal of her time writing essays. Shortly before this intense interest developed, she had been rather indifferent to her school work, even to the point of telling her mother that she saw no point in learning anything about history. Her mother had replied that whether she saw any point in it or not she was going to learn it. Her behavior was in marked contrast to that of her sister, who was three years older. This sister did just enough work to get by in school but was vitally interested in boys, parties, clothes, and so on. This sister was the favorite in the family, somewhat spoiled because she could always get her own way if she had a temper tantrum, and intensely jealous of and cruel toward the patient. The latter, in order to avoid the pain and humiliation of the sister's attitude to her, developed a strong passive homosexual attachment to her almost to the point of overt homosexuality. It was interesting that shortly after the older girl learned to read, she made the patient sit down and remain quiet for long periods while she read to her and taught her to read. This was her method of bossing and controlling her. Frequently the younger child tried to rebel, but the sister always punished these rebellious attempts severely. Reading and learning therefore became a way for the patient to avoid the older girl's jealousy and cruelty. Intense devotion to scholastic pursuits allowed her to have some individuality because it did not bring her into actual rivalry with her sister, as would have been the case had she allowed herself to have her sister's interests. Learning, for her, became a way of establishing her individuality, a way of expressing her rivalry with her sister, a way of obtaining her parents' love in a field that would not arouse her sister's jealousy, and a method of avoiding her sister's jealous hostility. (Her homosexual attachment to her sister had the same basis. It said emphatically that she was not her sister's rival: she loved her sister, was not jealous of her, and did not hate her.)

In her mind, learning and interest in learning became her penis, for behind the rivalry with the sister lay a deeper rivalry with her older brothers, and her desire to be a boy.

In this case there was not a defect in the use of learning but a disorder of learning because the patient centered all her interests in one direction. As long as this direction was satisfactory in reality, she would have no difficulty, but when she met rivals who were as capable intellectually as herself or when she became more aware of her repressed heterosexual interests, she would begin to have difficulty with her school work.

FEELINGS OF GUILT OR DREAD OF CASTRATION

Examination Anxiety

Perhaps the simplest example of the effect of feelings of guilt and of dread of castration on the use of learning is found in the universal examination anxiety, severe instances of which are seen fairly frequently. Psychoanalysts have seen many examples of the dynamics of examination anxiety in recent years during the processing interviews of applicants for admission to the psychoanalytic training institutes. Even among these experienced psychiatrists, examination anxiety is as universal and severe as it is among grammar-school, high-school and college students. During the personal psychoanalysis of a student in training to become a psychoanalyst, examination anxiety is also seen frequently. Such a student feels and really has a sword of Damocles hanging over his head. He is expected to tell *all* his thoughts to his analyst, who, in many institutes, will pass on his graduation as a psychoanalyst. There is such a strong realistic situation underlying this anxiety that many institutes now are attempting to determine the capabilities of the student without asking for the opinion of his psychoanalyst.

Rosenberg [3] points out that the physical and mental manifestations of examination anxiety are closely related to those of fear, which are

[3] Elizabeth Rosenberg, "Anxiety and the Capacity to Bear It," *International Journal of Psychoanalysis*, 30, 1949.

preparatory for action. An individual anxious in this way will be conscious of some feeling of anticipatory dread, mental alertness, and tension. Physically he will produce some or all of the bodily changes which in an external danger situation would equip him to either fight or take flight. These have been studied by Brown and Gelder.[4] They consist of an increase in systolic blood pressure, in pulse and respiratory rates, and in the amount of blood sugar, which sometimes reaches the point of glycosuria. Rosenberg goes on to say that in the situation associated with examinations there are two types of anxiety. The first type has a stimulatory effect. This type causes the student to strive toward success. If it brings success the anxiety is replaced by a definite feeling of pleasure. If the anxiety is not consciously perceived there is no incentive to drive for accomplishment and no subsequent pleasure in success. In fact there is often a feeling that the success is unreal. The second type has an inhibitory effect. In this type of anxiety, the person is like a helpless infant: his mind becomes blank, he is tremulous and distressed and unable to use his resources in a purposive way. Too much anxiety produces a paralysis of action and slowness in doing the examination. The inhibitory factor can be used as a weapon to retaliate against the parents.

Long ago Freud[5] drew attention to the fact that when a person dreams he has failed in an examination, it is usually in a subject in which he really did well while at school, never in a subject in which he really failed. Such a dream tends to occur on the eve of a day on which the dreamer is faced with a responsible task which could end in his disgrace. The dream comforts him about this possibility by saying, "See, you don't need to dread the task tomorrow; don't you remember that you felt you might be disgraced on this particular examination but instead you came through with flying colors?" From this example we can see that one cause of examination anxiety is the fear of disgrace. The child dreads that his teachers and parents will find out that he has not applied himself diligently, will discover his shortcomings, and will humiliate him. If this fear is connected associatively

[4] C. H. Brown and Dean Gelder, "Emotional Reactions before Examinations," *Journal of Psychology*, 5, 1938.

[5] Sigmund Freud, *The Interpretation of Dreams*, New York, The Macmillan Co., 1913.

in the unconscious with the memory of the humiliation the child suffered earlier when he discovered how much smaller his genitals were than those of his father, the examination anxiety will be enormously increased, even though he has applied himself diligently to his pre-examination studies.

Anna Freud [6] says that restriction of the ego is a turning away from a task it can do in order to avoid the pain or disappointment that would be felt because someone else would do it better. This goes back to the comparison by the boy of his genitals with those of his father or his hopeless edipus rivalry. In the girl the feeling of disappointment is due to her awareness of her genital differences from the male. The ego restriction is a fear of narcissistic mortification. If associatively the fear is connected in the unconscious with strong feminine desires, which are kept unconscious because they conflict with masculine pride, the examination anxiety will be increased because it will represent at the conscious level an unconscious wish to fail.

Instead of the fear of disgrace, examination anxiety may arise from the fear of being found out and punished for lack of diligence. Fluegel [7] states that Freud says the general fear of examination is a revival of infantile guilt and anxiety in which the examiners take over the role of parents who judge and punish the misdemeanors of children. Bergler [8] points out that an examination is like being brought before a court of justice, and fear of failure may be due to the fear of punishment or may equal a need for punishment. Redl [9] states that there are different levels of examination anxiety. There really may be a justified fear because of genuine absence of knowledge and insufficient preparation. There may be a fear of the consequences of failing which is a fear of the displeasure of the parents or the teacher because the student has let them down, or a fear of losing something of value for personal development. There may be a fear depending on specific features of

[6] Anna Freud, *The Ego and the Mechanisms of Defense,* New York, International Universities Press, 1946.

[7] J. C. Fluegel, "The Examination as Initiation Rite and Anxiety Situation," *International Journal of Psychoanalysis,* 20, 1939.

[8] Edmund Bergler, "Psychoanalyse eines Falles von Pruefungsangst," *Zentralblatt fuer Psychotherapie,* 6, 1933.

[9] Fritz Redl, "Wir Lehrer und die Pruefungsangst," *Zeitschrift fuer Psychoanalytische Paedagogik,* 7, 1933.

the examination—its form, oral or written, its place, its subject, the personality of the examiners—and there may be logically groundless fears attached to the examination situation. Blum [10] points out that there are two phases of difficulty connected with examinations. There is first the psychology of studying for examinations. This is done to acquire knowledge, to learn forbidden things, to express love (because the examinee unconsciously expects by learning to receive a better penis). If the examinee is a girl she unconsciously may expect to receive a penis by learning. Studying for examinations may be a sublimation of a number of unconscious desires—to become pregnant with thought, to take the mother's breast in love, or to consume the mother's genitals in hatred. Passing examinations may mean, in the unconscious, to express love for the analyst and the father, to give out orally and anally, to acquire a penis and be a boy, to give birth, or to be born, so as to be independent of the mother. If the fear of disgrace is associatively connected in the unconscious with strong fears of punishment by castration for masturbation, the examination anxiety will be increased because examinations are identified with proof of sexual capacity and failure is equated with impotence and castration. There is another cause for greatly increased examination anxiety. To be successful in the examination is to progress onward in ambition. If this idea is connected associatively in the unconscious with the edipus fantasies of killing the father and taking his place, and these fantasies are not yet solved, but still dreaded lest the father retaliate in kind, then there will develop fear of succeeding and perhaps also a desire to fail. Both of these appear in consciousness as greatly increased examination anxiety.

There are two aspects of examination anxiety to be considered. On the one hand there is the attitude—conscious and unconscious—of the examinee to the examiner, and on the other there is the attitude—conscious and unconscious—of the examiner to the examinee. Both are important. For instance, a student whom I observed felt he could learn better from one of his instructors than from another. The former only occasionally asked him what his conclusions were. Instead he usually acquainted him with what he saw in the material. This was done not

[10] Ernst Blum, "The Psychology of Study and Examinations," *International Journal of Psychoanalysis*, 7, 1926.

in a critical way but simply as the presentation of another point of view, supported by the data as understood by the instructor. The second constantly asked him what he thought and made him give more minute attention to the data presented. The student had need for a friendly father. Because of his strongly positive feeling to the first instructor and a slight desire to ingratiate himself, he was willing to listen, to consider, and to act on his advice—if it seemed advisable to him—or to try to act on it if he did not agree. He was passively receptive in order to please and be liked. With the second instructor his learning was interfered with by the hostile element in his ambivalence, which was aroused by what he felt was a searching, critical attitude. This example makes apparent the two-sidedness of examinations.

Stengel [11] points out that examinations are a testing, a tormenting, of the younger by the older. If assessment of knowledge were the logical motive for examinations, such procedures would continue to be demanded as time went on, but actually the attainment of the highest grades in professional life never depends on examinations. Fluegel [12] compares examinations to initiation ceremonies which express the elders' envy and jealousy mixed with love and the youngsters' fear mixed with reverence and gratitude. Rashdall [13] points out that the examination ceremony gratifies the bullying instinct, the social instinct, and the desire to find an excuse and means for a carouse. It consists of two unconscious elements, castration—anal purging as is found in medieval confession of sins and in extortion of money, and guilt—for the examination is the equivalent of an ordeal. He notes that examiners are amenable to personal and sometimes to financial influences. Sloane [14] says that according to Reik, the purpose of initiation rites is to preserve the privileges of the fathers. The chief principles of the totemistic system are exogamy and preservation of the

[11] Erwin Stengel, "Pruefungsangst und Pruefungsneurose," *Zeitschrift fuer Psychoanalytische Paedagogik,* 10, 1936.

[12] J. C. Fluegel, "The Examination as Initiation Rite and Anxiety Situation," *International Journal of Psychoanalysis,* 20, 1939.

[13] Hastings Rashdall, *Universities of Europe in the Middle Ages,* edited by F. M. Powicke and A. B. Emden, New York, Oxford University Press, 1936.

[14] Paul Sloane, "Analytic Training and Initiation Rites," an unpublished seminar discussion.

totem—in other words, the prevention of incest and parricide. The initiation rites consist in the main of the ritual of circumcision and the representation of the idea of rebirth. The process is characterized by terrifying experiences which are intended to serve as a foretaste of what is to come in case the sons do not heed the warnings of their elders. Circumcision is a token castration and is considered an expiation for the unconscious incestuous impulses of the youth. Once the candidates submit to the rites, they are received into the community of elders, but they must avoid the company of their near female relatives and must marry outside the tribe. The cruel practices of the elders are largely motivated by their ambivalence toward the youngsters. As a matter of fact the men are not quite trusted by the women of the tribe, who suspect them of wanting to harm the youths, and in case an initiate dies as a result of circumcision, the women hold the men responsible for it.

The hostility against the young men is based on the fear of retaliation which stems from the elder's guilt toward his own parents. "I rebelled against my parents and therefore anticipate that I will be paid back in kind by having my children rebel against me." According to Reik, "The son who feels hostile impulses against his father and must repress them as soon as he himself becomes a father will fear the same attitude on the part of his son out of the same unconscious complex." While inflicting the cruelties, the elders also attempt to appease the youngsters and thus to forestall any retaliation. This is accomplished by impressing the initiates with the awesomeness and secrecy of the proceedings and by imposing upon them vows of silence concerning the rites, thus binding them in a bond of secrecy from which the women are excluded. Thus strong homosexual tendencies dominate all the aspects of the puberty rites. All this points to the universality of the motivations behind initiation rites and indicates how they aim to solve some of the basic problems of mankind. It would seem that uncertainties in regard to the fundamental questions of life and death are based on man's ambivalence in regard to the relationships of the family romance, an ambivalence which he is probably destined never to solve.

It is therefore not surprising that the same tendencies should stand out in the relationship between the student and the teacher and examiner. A dream reported by Sloane of a patient who was in the midst of an examination indicated clearly the parallelism between initiation rites and the examination process. Stengel [15] says that the neurotic examiner may make himself a severe, overstrict father or a loving and overlenient father, he may narcissistically insist that a student's views and methods of expression be like his own or he may fear the candidate.

Learning Impotence

Case 9. A fourteen-year-old boy was referred for treatment because he was failing in his school work although his intelligence was above average. He was just passing in mathematics and science and was failing in social studies, English, and art. In the classroom he either did no work at all, or defiantly disturbed the routine by reading books during the class period and mimicking and ridiculing the teacher.

He had done extremely well in the first two grades. He did less well in the third grade, but this might have been because he had changed schools. In the fourth grade he improved. In the fifth grade, when he was ten, his teacher began to complain of his behavior. He was fascinated by matches and fires and once started a fire under his desk. However, this behavior was temporary and he had little trouble during the next two years. His real school difficulty began when he was thirteen. He failed at the second report period and was so apprehensive about his failure that he altered his report and truanted for two days. He was able to make up his work and was promoted. During the next year his achievement and behavior were as I have described.

At home he seemed to be obstinately lazy. He disliked getting up in the morning, having to be called a great many times. He dawdled in the bathroom, sometimes perhaps for as long as an hour, in dressing, in eating his breakfast, in doing chores or errands, in doing his homework, in coming to meals, and in going to bed. His mother tried to hurry him by constant reminders which soon turned into angry nagging, so that breakfast ended in a flood of angry weeping on the mother's part and sullen unhappiness on his.

[15] Erwin Stengel, "Pruefungsangst und Pruefungsneurose," *Zeitschrift fuer Psychoanalytische Paedagogik*, 10, 1936.

Part of the mother's angry nagging seemed somewhat justified by the boy's tendency to dawdle, but the greater part of it did not seem so, because there was more nagging about nonessentials than about essentials. She was an uninterested, unhappy woman, and everything that happened in the home got on her nerves. She also suffered from migraine. She was overprotective and overrestrictive to both of her sons but much more so to the patient than to his brother.

The father, whose hours of work were long and often necessitated his rising at 3 A.M., tried to keep the peace between his wife and his son by being consistently on his wife's side, severely condemning the boy even when he was obviously not in the wrong. He maintained this attitude not because parental differences of opinion were harmful to the children but because he wanted some peace and quietness in his home.

The patient was the older child, having a brother four years his junior. Both parents seemed to love and respect the younger boy more than the elder. The patient dated his difficulties from the birth of his younger brother, and although he quarreled with his brother and often picked on him, he was unconscious of his feelings of jealous hatred to him. His feelings of jealousy, more marked than the situation justified, were conscious in his relation to his schoolmates. At the time of his brother's birth and for a number of years afterward, the family, who were Jewish, lived in a non-Jewish neighborhood, and the patient was ostracized by the non-Jewish boys, so that he was reduced to playing either with girls or with his brother. In order not to lose his brother as a playmate he repressed his hatred of him and displaced it onto his schoolmates. He also tried to overcompensate for his hatred by seducing his brother into sexual play with him.

The mother's pregnancy with this child had been the cause of the parents' marriage, which seemed to be quite an unhappy and loveless one. At the age of one year the patient suffered a compound fracture of the elbow which caused him great pain and demanded a great deal of his mother's attention. He was very frightened of the doctor who had to reduce the fracture and dress the wound, and for some time after the fracture healed, he screamed with fear whenever he saw a strange man. Shortly after the fracture healed, the mother, who had breast-fed him up to this time, decided to wean him and in order to do so sent him to her mother-in-law's. He was toilet-trained completely by the age of eighteen months. His mother restricted his physical activities; in fact he was not permitted to play much on the streets till he was about ten. When he was eleven, his mother, dissatisfied with her role as a housewife, started to work and the children were left unsupervised.

The patient's presenting problem was his difficulty in getting along with his mother and his complaint that his father did not support him against her.

He had a phobia of bodily injury and of developing heart trouble. He became conscious of this when he was about eleven. At this time a girl in his class at school died of a heart lesion. He believed consciously that part of his school difficulty was caused by the fact that his hands got tired easily, so that either he could no longer write or, if he did, his writing was illegible. He told me that he would rather be considered lazy than be angry. He denied any interest in girls. He stated that since he had reached the age of thirteen he had felt differently toward girls than other boys did. He disliked them and particularly disliked a girl who was rather maternal. He denied any conscious feeling of love for his mother.

He had two main unconscious conflicts. His fear of bodily injury, his castration fear, more intense and therefore crippling to him because of the unconscious memory of his pain and terror at the compound fracture, caused him to repress his heterosexual desires and his tender feelings toward his mother. It caused him to repress his jealous hatred of his father and brother and to overcompensate for this by extreme dependence on his father. This made him feel very inferior to his father. It caused him to repress all hostile feelings, such as anger, hatred, and the desire to compete, and so interfered with his competitive drives to achieve success in his school work. In the same way, fear of conflict with rivals at school made him unable to work to the best of his ability. He wanted to run away, and he had several dreams in which he went to far distant places. However, these dreams often ended in a conflict with rivals in the new situation. It was this fact that unconsciously prevented him carrying out his conscious inclinations to run away, for he would be no better off in the new situation.

In order to supplement his efforts at repression he inhibited his desire to use the knowledge he had learned to make himself successful, lest he suffer the punishment of bodily injury at the hands of his rivals.

A second unconscious motivation in his lack of scholastic achievement was the desire to spite his mother, who was interested in having him do well in school. His truancy from school also got her into trouble with the school authorities and was done partly for that reason. His conscious fantasies of suicide always ended in his mother's being very sorry for the way she had treated him and in her deep grief for his loss. The purpose of this spitefulness was to punish her for not loving him as he desired. It contributed also to his desire to avoid his castration fear, by changing his active love toward her into a passive wish for her love. Both his poor scholastic achievement and the way in which he spent his money were unconscious attempts to attract his mother's sadistic interest and love.

A great deal of the trouble with his mother centered around his attempts to deny his strong unconscious wishes to be fed by her. For many years, although he ate well he had a marked distaste for milk. His conscious masturbation fantasies were largely about breasts and girls with large breasts. Part of the motivation in not using learning was an unconscious wish to be the baby he was before his mother weaned him and part was his attempt, by refusing to take in knowledge, to punish her for the weaning.

His denial of his love for his mother because of his castration fear caused his object love for her to regress to identification with her. Several of his dreams showed a wish to be a man who fed people and gave them liquids to drink. Here he identified himself with the nursing mother. Although he smoked and stole money from his mother (who objected to his smoking) to buy cigarettes, he objected vigorously to my smoking. This was an obvious identification with the aggressor, i.e., the weaning, depriving mother.

Besides the oral fixation to his mother, this patient had regressed somewhat from the phallic to the anal sadomasochistic level in order to avoid his fear of castration. This was indicated by his great interest in fires and explosives and by his character trait of procrastinating and then suddenly having a desire to work. The accentuation of his sadism was shown in his spitefulness toward his mother and his masochistic attitude to her, which caused him to force her to nag him and fight with him. This regression was not a very deep one and had not reached the stage where he really had identified himself with her in order to receive passive anal masochistic gratification from his father. He was not completely oriented to want his father to love him in the way his father loved his mother.

His main problem was an active phallic desire for his mother and his fear of castration if he gratified it. His school failure was an attempt to inhibit his use of knowledge lest he be castrated by his father and was also motivated, to a lesser degree, by the need for taking revenge on his mother for not loving him.

This case illustrates the usual dynamics in boys who suffer from a diminished capacity to learn because the use of learning is inhibited by feelings of guilt and fear of castration. In these cases the use of knowledge is equated unconsciously with the use of the penis. The disorder of the use of learning usually begins in early adolescence. Previous to this, the patient has suffered from severe phobias but has never told anyone about them. At this time his school achievement is good. By some means he has been able successfully to repress the phobias, as in the case I have described elsewhere.[16] Shortly after the repression of the phobias, the school failure begins. Usually, as in this case, little or no real regression has taken place.

In the next case the dynamics are the same but a major regression has taken place and the use of knowledge has become equated with an anal penis or with early concepts about feces.

Case 10. A fourteen-year-old boy was referred because he was failing in his school work. He was attaining grades very much lower than his ability justified, was inattentive in class, and took no responsibility for completing his required work. Often his mother had to compel him to do his work, at which times his marks improved. He had been ill as a child and had had to live in several different climates, and therefore had changed schools a number of times. He started his school career in a good, traditional, private school where he did well and received some merited prizes. When he was ten he attended an

[16] Gerald H. J. Pearson, *Emotional Disorders of Children,* New York, W. W. Norton & Company, 1949.

outdoor school in Florida, where his achievement was better than fair. At eleven he entered boarding school, where he received marks which were just passing. The next year he went to Arizona. There he did little work in school until his mother forced him, at which time his marks improved. At thirteen he entered another good private school, which he was attending at the time of his referral, but shortly thereafter he was expelled. A little while after this the mother moved to another town and the patient entered public school, where his achievements varied. Sometimes he did well, sometimes very poorly. After a year of this his mother moved again and he entered a boarding school, from which he was eventually expelled because of his grades and his constant breaking of rules. These were usually minor infractions, but were very frequent. Here he was inattentive and had very inadequate routines of studying and doing his school work. Often he would listen to the radio instead of doing his assigned work. He did not seem to flout rules deliberately but was late constantly and failed to complete requirements. Typically, at one time he failed in algebra but received a national award for an essay, while at another, he failed in English but obtained high marks in algebra. His I.Q. was 120.

Socially he had some degree of popularity with boys but usually selected friends who were not in his natural social group or were somewhat antisocial. He seemed to dislike girls.

His behavior at home resembled his behavior in school. Although he had many illnesses in his life, he took no care of his health. He deliberately exposed himself to poison ivy. He ate irregularly and unwisely. He would fall or jump into the lake when he had a cold. He seldom brushed his teeth. He consistently went to bed very late. He refused to sleep in pajamas—instead he slept in his underpants, which he wore during the day and rarely changed. He seldom lifted the toilet seat when he urinated and seldom flushed the toilet after defecation. He never used toilet paper and therefore his shorts were always stained with feces. He went on hikes through rain and wind in his best clothes. He never untied his shoes, so that they soon had broken backs from being put on while tied. He used his mother's best linen for various chemical and biological experiments. He would throw bloody rags, old swabs, fishhooks, dirty socks, into drawers of clean clothes. He would put cigarette ashes into lamp bases or magazine racks instead of into ash trays. He never shined his shoes, and he put off getting his hair cut as long as possible. As a result his slightly peculiar appearance was made very peculiar by his unkempt hair, face, and nails. There were constant difficulties over his use of money and the size of his phone bills. He would start a household chore but never finish it.

He was the older of two children, having a sister who was born when he was two. She was two inches taller than he was. The parents had been divorced when the patient was five. The mother preferred the patient's sister, who, however, also showed some antisocial traits. The father was a man whose behavior was unpredictable. He was cruel to his wife and did everything possible to annoy her. As an example, he encouraged the patient at the age of three or four to play with loaded guns. He stuttered and the patient when three started to imitate his father's stuttering. The patient was very much afraid of his father because he was so rough, but in boarding school he became very resentful of any housefather who seemed to favor another boy. His mother was very apprehensive lest the patient become like his father. The patient had not seen his father for years.

The mother was a timid woman who suffered from a phobia. She had been indecisive in her management of both children but particularly of the patient. She had attempted to be "modern" and had allowed them to criticize her openly and constantly. (The children were encouraged by the paternal relatives to do this.) She had often allowed the patient to do as he liked, whether it was advisable or not, and then, when she became exasperated by the discrepancy between his behavior and her standards, had nagged and pleaded with him. She seemed to be afraid of the patient, would argue with him and then give in, would make promises she could not fulfill, and would even make promises she could fulfill and then not carry them out. When he was twelve he wanted a rifle, although there were no real opportunities for shooting except in situations where it would be dangerous. She refused, he persisted, she refused. When he bought a rifle, she allowed him to keep and use it. He wished to drive the car although he was under the legal age. She refused. He persisted, so she had him taught and then permitted him to drive her around. (In many cases of this type of scholastic failure, the mother is found to object to some wish of her son which really would break the law, but then to give in and actually participate in the illegal procedure.)

The mother herself wished to be a physician and was hopeful that the patient would become one. The patient on his own initiative got a job assisting a veterinarian. He was so responsible for a while that the management of the treatment of the animals was left in his hands. After a time he became somewhat careless, quarreled with the veterinarian and refused to work for him any more.

The patient's acute difficulties started at the same time as the mother's acute neurosis. He wanted his mother to do his work for him, even to keeping him clean. He stated that he was ashamed of his mother's unconventional behavior, and in conversation gave the impression that his ideals were very conventional. He intruded constantly on his mother's privacy.

At the time of his referral the family was living with the maternal grandmother. The mother disliked her mother, and the patient got along very poorly with his grandmother.

The mother had been very angry when she discovered she was pregnant with this child, the conception having been an accident. Her health was good throughout the pregnancy. The use of high forceps at his birth resulted in a temporary partial paralysis of the right side of his face. He was circumcised while in the hospital and screamed continuously for twenty-four hours after the operation; in fact, he screamed almost constantly for the first six months. He was breast-fed for six weeks, and there were no weaning difficulties. His mother stated that his bowel training was completed by the age of five months and his bladder training by eighteen months. Following this he was constipated and was given many enemas. When he was two his sister was born and he exhibited great resentment toward her from the day she was brought home. He had a tonsillectomy at the age of two and one half, and the mother could not come near him for several days after the operation because the smell of the ether made her ill. At three he was started in nursery school. Between three and five the father tried very hard to estrange the child from the mother. When the parents separated, the mother took the children to live with the maternal grandparents. The next year she employed a very strict governess and during this regime the patient's social attitude changed from shyness to "poise." At seven he had a severe attack of pneumonia. To prevent a recurrence he lived with his mother in Arizona and Florida. At ten he developed insomnia because he was afraid of his dreams.

The patient's capacity to use his learned knowledge successfully had been inhibited out of a sense of guilt and a need for punishment. In order not to feel guilty he had to inhibit his desire to learn, and in order to assuage whatever feelings of guilt he suffered he had to punish himself by failing. The sense of guilt and the need for punishment indicated the presence of a very severe superego of a primitive type. This primitive severity was caused by three factors. The father had actually been a cruel man. The patient had been absent from his father since he was five years of age, and so there had been no opportunity for him to temper his edipal fantasies of the father's cruelty by comparing them with the real father. Because of this separation there had been no father with whom to identify. His school failure occurred to avoid the punishment at the hands of his superego.

His sense of guilt and unconscious need for punishment arose from his ego fear of the superego's resentment against his marked unconscious incestuous attachment to his mother. If he was successful in accomplishing his ambitions and in pleasing his mother by learning knowledge and skills, he might be able to possess her; he dreaded this lest it result in his castration and death at the hands of his fantasied cruel father.

The unconscious need for punishment caused him to project his superego onto external authorities, and he frequently actually did make them punish him. Part of his need for punishment by an external authority was an expression of a passive longing for a firm, consistent father who would prevent him from getting into trouble when he acted in ways that really were forbidden. This passive longing for a father was increased by his fear that if he possessed his mother she would send him away, as she had sent away his father. He felt that if he took his father's place he would be punished by ostracism.

His capacity to use his learned knowledge also was inhibited in order to express his spite toward his mother, who wanted him to learn, for favoring his sister and for sending his father away.

Desiring his mother's love, he endeavored to circumvent the severity of his superego by an unconscious fantasy. If he could be a girl then his mother might love him more; he would be favored as his sister was. This again interfered with his ability to learn, because if he learned, he would be more masculine and so would not be favored by the mother. At the same time, his masculine pride revolted at the idea of being a girl because it entailed castration, so he had to regress to another unconscious fantasy, that of being a baby. This unconscious wish to be a baby interfered with his ability to learn. The regression was mostly to the anal-sadistic stage, although there were oral elements, and it indicated that he had accepted the idea of being a girl. He had identified himself with his mother and sister, but at the same time he was able to retain his penis. Now his orientation was to have a penis but to be passive and masochistic toward men, that is, toward external authorities. This anal passivity also interfered with his ability to learn, which is an active process. Consciously, of course, he reacted violently against his strong unconscious passive-masochistic desires, but his reactions were of the kind that again would gratify his passive masochism. They were antisocial and caused the external world to become punitive toward him. This indicated again that the conflict had regressed from the phallic level, where learning represented the successful use of the penis, to the anal sadomasochistic level, where learning could be disregarded because the only importance of the penis was its possession, not its use. He possessed knowledge, but he did not use it.

In this case the use of learned knowledge, which in the unconscious represented the use of the penis, was inhibited. This defense was not sufficient to placate the primitive severity of the superego, so the regression to the anal-sadistic level took place. The superego would not tolerate the sadism at this level, because it represented the phallic activity before the regression took place and so was still connected with the use of learned knowledge. As a further defense the active sadism had to be changed into passive masochism. He would now unconsciously be a girl and a baby and demonstrate that he had no capacity to use learned knowledge. Still, he would possess knowledge, which unconsciously no longer represented a penis but the feces of the little child.

In cases where there is a disorder of the use of learning accompanied by regression and acceptance of castration, the history of earlier severe phobias which have disappeared due to the substitution of the inhibition of the use of learning for the phobic mechanism is not found. It appears as if the inhibition of the use of learned knowledge was not a sufficient defense. The further defenses of regression, changing activity into passivity and sadism into masochism with the acceptance of a passive-masochistic orientation, i.e., of castration, have to be introduced. Against this unconscious orientation the masculine pride of the patient struggles. The passive-masochistic orientation forbids the active use of learning and so an inhibition of the use of learning results.

There are many references to cases like this in the psychoanalytic literature. Freud [17] found in a patient suffering from an obsessional neurosis that the chief result of his illness was an obstinate incapacity for work which enabled him to postpone the completion of his education for years. Liss [18] points out that there may be a rejection of the use of learning because this signifies maturity. As a result there is seeming stupidity and immaturity. He [19] states also that where hostility and rivalry remain the major content of the use of knowledge the subject matter is colored by the hostile content and is accepted or rejected, depending upon guilt or regression. Fenichel [20] says that people become stupid when they do not want to understand because understanding would cause castration anxiety (the ego being dominated by a severe superego) or feelings of guilt (loss of love from the superego because the ego is dominated by a severe superego), or would endanger an existing neurotic equilibrium. There are two main reasons why the ego may be induced to keep its intellect perma-

[17] Sigmund Freud, "Notes upon a Case of Obsessional Neurosis," *Collected Papers*, Vol. III, London, Hogarth Press and the Institute of Psycho-Analysis, 1933.

[18] Edward Liss, "Learning Difficulties. Unresolved Anxiety and Resultant Learning Patterns," *American Journal of Orthopsychiatry*, 11, 1941.

[19] Edward Liss, "Emotional and Biological Factors Involved in Learning Processes," *American Journal of Orthopsychiatry*, 7, 1937.

[20] Otto Fenichel, *The Psychoanalytic Theory of Neurosis*, New York, W. W. Norton & Company, 1945.

nently in abeyance. First, there may be repression of sexual curiosity which may correspond to intense unconscious scoptophilia or may have an intimate relationship with sadistic impulses. The consequent stupidity may represent obedience to parents who have frustrated sexual curiosity, rebellion against similar parents, or an endeavor to gain access to forbidden knowledge. The impulse to know is related genetically to oral pleasure, manual grasping of pleasure, and to anal mastery. Second, it may be that the inhibited intellectual functions may have been more strictly sexualized. The function of thinking may have been equated with sexual functions and therefore inhibited because of fear of castration, or it may have acquired special anal connotations. Indeed, whenever the sexualization of thinking occurs, the sexuality attached to the thinking has an anal quality.

In Case 10, and other cases of this type, the regression to the anal-sadistic stage does not seem to have been followed by the secondary defenses of an obsessional neurosis. In the wolf-man there was an inhibition of learning as part of a character disorder resulting from a remission of an obsessional neurosis, and Freud [21] points out that an obsessional neurosis may recover or remit and be followed by a decrease in the ability to learn. From Freud's case it might be argued that my patient's primary illness might be an obsessional neurosis with regression from the phallic to the anal-sadistic stage. The obsessional neurosis would be of a severe type in that not only was there regression, but activity had been replaced by passivity, sadism by masochism, and any phallic strivings by the acceptance of castration. In order to maintain the passive-masochistic orientation, an inhibition of the use of learning occurred secondarily. It is difficult to decide in these cases whether the inhibition in the use of learning is the final result of a remission of an obsessional neurosis, or whether, as I have described, the capacity to use learned knowledge itself is involved in the unconscious fantasies of the neurosis. This may be true also of the cases in which there is a disorder of the use of learning without regression. In the latter the disorder of the use of learning is an inhibition which seems to be the result of an attempt at self-cure of an anxiety hysteria.

[21] Sigmund Freud, "From the History of an Infantile Neurosis," *Collected Papers*, Vol. III, London, Hogarth Press and the Institute of Psycho-Analysis, 1933.

The symptoms of anxiety hysteria have been controlled and replaced by inhibitions falling on the capacity to use learned knowledge and by changes in the character.

I believe that Case 10, and others of this type, are character neuroses, consisting of the defenses of inhibition and ego restriction, and are not the result of a remitted obsessional neurosis. It may be that there are really two varieties of disorders of the use of learning accompanied by regression. In one there is an obsessional neurosis, the acute stage of which recovers by producing a decrease in the ability to learn and character changes which are the result of an attempt at cure. In the other, no acute obsessional neurosis occurs, but the capacity to use learned knowledge becomes involved in the regression and the associated mechanisms, along with character alterations, and any obsessional symptoms which occur are secondary.

In cases like Case 10 the regression has caused the concept of the penis to be replaced by the earlier concept of an anal penis. This concept is regularly associated with the concept that sexual gratification is obtained through a fight in which one partner, the male, masters, hurts, and destroys the other, the female. Through the regression the use of knowledge becomes associated with the anal penis, and therefore the pleasure in its use becomes a sadistic pleasure. The patient feels very frightened and guilty about this and has to change his desires to use knowledge in a sadistic way into a masochistic apparent lack of knowledge. In some cases this apparent lack of knowledge may make the child appear almost feeble-minded in the use he seems to make of his knowledge.

All of the patients who have diminished capacity in the use of knowledge show also a lack of ambition. One of the sources of ambition is a sublimation of urethral erotism. If this sublimation fails, the individual is not as ambitious as he otherwise could be, and an interference with ambition disturbs the need and desire to learn.

In the cases of boys who have diminished capacity to use learned knowledge, there is an inhibition of the use of knowledge because in the unconscious it is equated with the use of the penis. In girls the use of learned knowledge may be inhibited because it is equated with the use of the vagina. They are afraid that their genitals will be injured if they admit their feminine role. In this they are behaving as the counterpart of the boys whose learning difficulty lies in the fear that their genitals will be injured if they use their knowledge. They are ashamed of their penisless state, which increases their dreaded passive-receptive wishes. They feel they are defective as compared with boys and strive to overcome this feeling by enhancing their passive receptiveness, which they dread.

Frigidity in the female is the equivalent of impotence in the male. The impotent male dreads his active-aggressive sexual impulses and so inhibits the genital functions through which he normally would express them. The aims of the sexual impulses and the genital functions by which the woman normally would express them are inhibited in the frigid woman by the inhibition of her orgasm, with more or less anesthesia of her genitals for pleasurable sensations. Therefore, the inhibition in the case of frigidity falls on the pleasure of the dreaded passive-receptive impulses. The dread is of the active aggression in the feminine passive-receptive desires. The frigid woman is afraid unconsciously that she will be injured by the penetration of the penis or that she will injure or destroy her partner's penis and in turn will be punished according to the talion law.

When the ego functions of learning and of using the knowledge so obtained are equated in the unconscious with the passive-receptive vaginal desires, they will be inhibited if these are feared, and the girl will not learn lest she find herself a grown-up and capable woman.

REPUDIATION OF LEARNING BECAUSE IT IS ASSOCIATED WITH MASCULINITY OR FEMININITY

Learning of academic subjects and the use of such learning may have acquired for the child a specific masculine or feminine flavor as the result of the parental attitudes toward learning. Oberndorf[22] points out that the development of intellectual precocity or psychogenic stupidity may be caused by the choice of identification (superego formation) with the intellectual attributes of one of the parents. Sometimes the person has been rebuffed and emotionally traumatized by the stupid parent of the same sex and so flees to an identification with the thinking parent of the opposite sex. On the other hand, in a

[22] C. P. Oberndorf, "The Feeling of Stupidity," *International Journal of Psycho-analysis*, 20, 1939.

specific family, if the mother is very interested in learning while the father is indifferent, the boy may come to regard the desire to learn academic subjects as a feminine attribute. In this way the desire to learn becomes connected with the passive-receptive feminine desires which he dreads lest their gratification result in castration. As a result, such a desire has to be repudiated. If the child is a girl whose mother is not interested in learning and whose father is, learning may become a masculine attribute and be used as a conscious substitute for the unconscious wish to have a penis.

Case 11. A girl of eleven did very poor work in arithmetic. She objected to learning the use of a protractor, but she was extremely envious of the slide rule used by her much older brother. This brother, who was very good in mathematics, was her hero, whom she respected and envied; he and his slide rule represented perfection in mathematics. She was certain that boys had a peculiar innate ability in mathematics which girls did not possess. When arithmetic demanded from her some energy in learning she felt inadequate because she did not possess the particular ability (slide rule, penis) which her brother had and which she envied. Therefore as she did not have the equipment necessary to learn arithmetic, she had to fail.

If an individual unconsciously considers not knowing as a sign of unmanliness and weakness, his ability to learn may be interfered with. Such an individual feels it is necessary for him to know before he really has learned, lest he be considered unmanly. Therefore he does not learn but supplies his lack of knowledge through the use of omnipotence, by trick information, and the like.

The effects of the association in a child's mind between his sex and the sex of the parent who is most interested in learning form the basis of many more learning disabilities than educators are aware of at present.

DIMINISHED CAPACITY TO LEARN DUE TO DISORDER IN THE FUNCTION OF TAKING IN KNOWLEDGE

Curiosity, the desire to know by taking in through the avenues of sensory intake, is an important basis for learning. This psychic faculty is closely related to the need of the young baby to take in food through the mouth and to get pleasure from putting articles in the mouth. In fact, the former may be a partial displacement of the latter. Curiosity may be injured directly if the child is punished for his curiosity or becomes frightened or upset by what he learns through his inquisitiveness. It can be injured also indirectly if adverse influences cause the child to suffer fear, pain, or displeasure as a result of his mouth activities during his very early life.

Schmideberg [23] points out that instinctual conflicts can inhibit or favor the function of sense organs if the conflicts relate to libidinal instinctual aims (inhibition of sexual curiosity) or if they disturb libidinal trends which become amalgamated secondarily with the function of sense organs or thought. If seeing, smelling and thinking are perceived as oral, inhibitions in eating can be replaced by inhibitions affecting sight, smell, and thought. Intellectual inhibitions when analyzed are seen to be due to an earlier inhibition in eating. The inhibiting factors against oral-intellectual ingestion are fear of the envy of others, fear of one's own sadism, numerous incorporations, or oral defiance. There may be a refusal to take in knowledge because the individual was not given enough food as a child.

Liss [24] points out that there are two types of oral difficulties which occur early in life—difficulties in oral processes involved in learning and difficulties in talking, reading, and singing. These are, first, idiosyncrasies toward food, either gluttony or, more usually, anorexia. In these children all innovations in foods are met with active or passive antipathy. When food is ingested there is either rumination, regurgitation, or in extreme cases, vomiting. Often they need substitute oral gratifications such as thumbsucking. The young child with the second type of difficulty has frequent upper respiratory infections, has difficulties in dentition, or shows a delayed speech development.

Ungratified excessive oral needs in infancy, and the fear of the results of oral gratification, often will affect the future learning ability of the child. One result of such a conflict may be a simple inhibition in the taking in of knowledge.

[23] Melitta Schmideberg, "Intellectual Inhibition and Disturbances in Eating," *International Journal of Psychoanalysis,* 19, 1938.

[24] Edward Liss, "Libidinal Fixations as Pedagogic Determinants," *American Journal of Orthopsychiatry,* 5, 1935.

Case 12. A twelve-year-old boy, whose intelligence and whose musical ability were very great, was referred because a dispute had arisen between him and his music teacher. His I.Q. was 166. At the age of ten he had been regarded as one of the greatest of child violinists and as a pianist of distinction. He wanted to play the musical works he was studying in his own way, which he said and felt was more truly musical than the way in which the composer wrote them or the way in which his teacher insisted they be played. As a result of this attitude the patient was refusing to practice. His refusal was jeopardizing the scholarship under which his training to be a concert musician was taking place. His musical education had been paramount in his life, so he had not attended the usual schools but had been tutored or had attended special half-day classes. His educational achievement was slightly superior to that of boys who had had the usual school experiences.

It is not necessary here to describe and discuss all of the personality problems which this boy showed. One important element in his desire to do things his own way and his refusal to accept his teacher's and his mother's advice was revealed in a dream. He dreamed that cannibals came into his home and started to devour his sister, while his mother, his father, his grandmother, and he hid between the springs and mattress of his bed.

In this dream the patient expressed his hatred of his sister. This hatred was conscious, so it was curious that he had to dream about it and also to dream about it as a projection. The hatred directed to the sister in the dream was displaced from the mother, father, and grandmother, all of whom he protected in the dream text. He was not aware of this hatred in his waking life. He protected himself from knowledge of his feelings toward them by his general inactivity. This inactivity was a punishment for his guilt about his sexual desires for his mother and his competitive hatred of his father. It not only protected him but was also a means of expressing unconsciously his edipal hatred of his father and his spite at his mother for her restrictions on him and for depriving him of the babying care she had given him when he was a small child until she weaned him and until she bore his sister. He showed some regression to the anal-sadistic stage of development by his interest in maps, cataloguing, and collecting, by his personal untidiness and disorderliness, and by his reaction formations of unwillingness to take exercise and his stubbornness and rigid independence. Through this regression he was able to get his mother and his father to nag him. He consciously disliked this, but unconsciously it gratified in a passive-masochistic way his unconscious sexual love for his mother and his desire for his father's love.

His learning difficulty was partly the result of his character traits. More largely it resulted from the inhibition of his devouring oral aggression. His tendency to eat up those objects whom he loved and whom he hated had to be inhibited lest he suffer the punishment (and gratify his unconscious desire) to be eaten up himself. The cannibals in the dream represented oral hatred. The displacement from his parents and grandmother to his sister did not suffice to defend him against the fear of retribution in kind, so he had to project it. The severity of the oral hatred was the result of the fact that he had been breast-fed for only three months and after he was weaned from the breast had become a feeding problem.

This inhibition of his oral aggression prevented his being able to learn from his parents or from his teacher, for if he responded to them with either love or hatred he would eat them up. He preferred, therefore, to do things his own way so as not to be in any close emotional relationship with them. He inhibited his desire to take in and to learn because of his dread of the unconscious fantasy of devouring and being devoured. In certain patients who have difficulty in learning there is an excessive need for oral incorporation which has resulted from severe feeding difficulties in early infancy. They have an intense need to devour in order not to suffer again the pains of starvation. This is based on the organic memory trace of the infantile starvation experiences. This excessive need is feared because they dread the results of its gratification and so they inhibit it lest they devour the mother and so destroy and lose her. In these patients the degree of ambivalence to the mother is very great, and every desire to incorporate has both a strong desire to retain and keep the object and a very strong desire to destroy the object. In order to keep the ambivalence to the mother unconscious, the patients have to repress a great deal of the knowledge which they have incorporated, so that they may learn but develop amnesia for what they have learned.

The presence of a fixation at the oral level which produces either an excessive need for oral incorporation or an excessive fear of the ability to incorporate orally interferes with the ability to learn and may result in amnesia for what has been learned, an inhibition of the ability to learn, an active repudiation of the ability to learn, or an increased ability to learn, but only nonuseful information.

DIMINISHED CAPACITY TO LEARN DUE TO DISTURBANCES IN THE ASSIMILATION AND DIGESTION OF KNOWLEDGE

Difficulties in learning arise not only from disturbances in the ability to take in knowledge, a disturbance of the mechanism of oral incorporation, but also from disturbances in the ability to associate, correlate, and assimilate the incorporated knowledge, i.e., in the ability to digest it. This is the most serious type of learning difficulty. It may be so severe as to show itself in the results of the psychometric examination.

Elsewhere [25] I have reported a case of a boy who at the age of four had been examined by a highly competent psychologist who was very experienced with children. At that time the boy's I.Q. was 50. At the age of twelve, after a long period of analysis, he had an I.Q. of 110, and his accomplishments later on showed that his real I.Q. must have been over 140.

I do not know whether serious reading disabilities fall in this group or not. Some reading disabilities may be due to strephosymbolia or to the other causes I have already mentioned, but certainly these causes do not explain the really severe cases. Blanchard's studies [26]

[25] Gerald H. J. Pearson, "A Case of Compulsion Neurosis in an Eleven Year Old Boy," *American Journal of Orthopsychiatry*, 10, 1940.

[26] Studies by Phyllis Blanchard include:

"Psychogenic Factors in Some Cases of Reading Disability," *American Journal of Orthopsychiatry*, 5, 1935.

"Reading Disabilities in Relation to Difficulties of Personality and Emotional Development," *Mental Hygiene*, 20, 1936.

"Emotional Factors in a Disability for Reading and Writing Words," *Readings in Mental Hygiene*, New York, Henry Holt, 1936.

"Psychoanalytic Contributions to the Problem of Reading Disabilities," *The Psychoanalytic Study of the Child*, Vol. II, New York, International Universities Press, 1946.

"The Case of Tommy Nolan," *Psychiatric Interviews with Children*, New York, Commonwealth Fund, 1946.

seem to indicate that they are cases of difficulties in digesting and assimilating learning material. In my cases this inability to digest was always associated with a disturbance of the ability to take in and to give out, because of severe intrapsychic conflicts which resemble the conflicts in Wegrocki's case of inability to learn mathematics which is described in the previous chapter.

Case 13. A ten-year-old boy was referred by a psychologist to whom the patient had been taken for a psychometric examination.

The report of his psychometric examination was as follows:[27]

I spent nearly three hours with the child, found him very cooperative and pleasant in manner, but also very distinctly *slow* in reaction and infantile in many of his behavior patterns. I have purposely underlined a word in the preceding sentence in order to emphasize a point which I consider to be of vast importance. It would not be quite appropriate to use such descriptive terms as "dull" or "apathetic," or others which commonly are used in depicting the reaction patterns of mental deficiency. In other words, in spite of the implications of the quantitative psychometric data presented below, most of the qualitative features of the boy's behavior were not those conventionally found among definitely subnormal children.

The psychometric results were as follows:

Stanford-Binet Scale (1916)
Mental Age 7–6
I.Q. 76

Kohs Block Designs Test
Mental Age 10–1
I.Q. 102

Witmer Form Board
Witmer Cylinder
Paterson Form Board
Dearborn Form Board
} Two trials on each
Estimated Mental Age 7–9 to 8–0
Estimated I.Q. 78 to 81

Detroit Reading Test
Grade Score, Test I 2.3
Grade Score, Test II 2.6 (approximate middle, second grade)

[27] I am indebted to Dr. George Carl for this report.

I can best describe this boy's departure from ordinary reaction patterns, on all of the tests, by explaining what happened on the Kohs test, which was given first. Almost at the beginning he seemed to become confused, and was unable to do one of the very simple exercises. Then he did one, somewhat more difficult, without much trouble,—and another immediately following. Again he bogged down badly; and again I felt certain that he had reached his limit of performance. But, as in the former instance, he once more "caught on" and did several more items with facility. This erratic kind of performance was evidenced in other tests as well. Penalties were severe, particularly on Stanford-Binet, as a result. I was constantly under the impression that the boy's intellectual appraisal of the various test situations was normally good, but that the strikingly infantile nature of his emotional response kept him from getting across the line which separates failure from success in scoring the test performances. Actually he did not pass a single item in Year IX on Stanford-Binet, though I am morally certain that he really understood most of the questions quite well.

I have a strong feeling that the lad has been babied a good bit, and has not been given a good chance to develop as much self-resource as he could have. I noticed that as I prepared to take the boy with me to the examining room his mother gave him last minute instructions about doing everything I asked him to do, and otherwise evidenced some concern as to how he might act. *As you doubtless have found out already,* he is very much of a "sissy" in many ways,—dislikes vigorous sports, likes to play with younger children. Many of the speech mannerisms are distinctly on the infantile side.

I am by no means certain that his case is not one of conventional subnormality, but, as mentioned above, there are enough departures from the conventional configuration to make me feel that the difficulties may be attributable to delayedness in development, and dysfunction, rather than to basic lack of intellectual capacity. For one thing, the gross physical and motor organization is of the kind often encountered in cases of subnormal *function,*—in contrast with a condition of subnormal capacity. While, I believe, I tend to bend over backwards in regard to imputing any kind of subnormality to endocrine influences, I should not be surprised to learn that, in this child's case, some factors of that kind are partly responsible for the condition. And almost certainly there are penalizing influences on the side of the affect patterns.

This is particularly a case in which I cannot have strong convictions without the benefit of more data than those secured in the present limited examination.

The patient was a large, rather obese boy who suffered occasionally from headaches and frequently looked depressed, although he always denied feeling that way. He preferred to play with girls rather than with boys but seemed most contented when in the house with his mother. He was docile and tried always to avoid any change. For months on end he always placed his chair in the exact position in the playroom where it had been the first day he saw me, sat in the chair, and showed no desire to play with any toys. He did play with his cap and with his hands, and from time to time he reported a number of fantasies associated with his play, which I will report later. He had a compulsion to wash his hands frequently. He showed mild grimacing movements of his mouth of a very infantile nature.

His father had a marked harelip and a speech defect. He was a successful businessman who seemed more interested in his occupation and his hobbies than he was in his son or his family. His mother was a rather stolid person who originally had babied the patient but seemed fonder of the patient's twin sisters, who were born when the patient was seven, than of the patient. When the patient was six, the mother had a second son, who lived only one month.

The patient was born with a mild inguinal hernia, which corrected itself. He was breast-fed for eight months and then weaned to a cup. At fifteen months he fed himself. There was no fingersucking. He walked at fifteen months and talked at two years; hence his rate of development was not so slow as his I.Q. seemed to indicate. Between the ages of one and three, he, with his parents, had lived with the paternal grandparents, who babied the patient and preferred to dress him as a girl. At four he had a tonsillectomy and in the same year he was pushed by another boy, hit his head on the sidewalk, and suffered a mild concussion. It appeared that his headaches, which had the character of migraine, developed some time after he had been hit again by a boy, when he was eight.

He entered school at the age of five and completed the first grade successfully. He had to repeat the second grade. During this second year in the second grade he was tutored. At the time of examination he was in the third grade but was failing. The reason for his failure lay in his apparent inability to learn the school work and in his methods of thinking, which are well illustrated in the report of the psychological examination and by the following reports from his teacher, who kept notes on his replies to various questions:

Teacher: In what way are a baseball and an orange alike, and how are they different?

Patient: An orange is round and a baseball is square and when you throw 'em they're very soft. What did you say?

Teacher: How are they alike and how are they different?

Patient: An orange is much different from a football.

Teacher: A baseball.

Patient: An orange is round and a baseball isn't.

Teacher: What would you do if you found on the streets of a city a three-year-old baby that was lost from its parents?

Patient: Well, I would take it home to my own home and keep it till she died.

Teacher: Can you give two reasons why most people would rather have an automobile than a bicycle?

Patient: If children's too little to ride in an automobile the car might go down the road and the children might scream for their mothers. You can't have both.

Teacher: How are a book and a teacher and a newspaper alike?

Patient: A newspaper is some kind of paper you can tear easy and a book is heavy paper like drawing and a teacher is made out of skin.

While making a bead chain, the patient very excitedly commented, "I don't have enough blocks to go around. Let me tie the teacher. Put a necklace around her. I'm afraid it's going to choke her. Better not tie it." (Silly giggle.)

Teacher: What should you do if another boy hits you without meaning to?

Patient: The other boy would probably say, "I'm sorry I won't do it again."

Teacher: What should you do?

Patient: I don't know. What *should* I do?

Teacher: What clothing do people need?

Patient: Hats, money, shoes, underwear, corsets, stockings.

Teacher: Can you think of anything else?

Patient: Some more clothes. Jewelry [repeated many times], hair, sweaters, coats, stockings, valuable things, wool stockings, fur coats, tablecloth.

Teacher: What food do we need?

Patient: Cookies, water, towels, water, bathtub, shower, eyes, and nose, mouth, all their body.

Teacher: Can you think of anything else that people need?

Patient: Some people need doctors and have to go to a hospital. Some people have broken arms—don't have anything to wear.

Teacher: What do people need to live in?

Patient: House, land, grass, driveway, garage, door, back door, two front doors, radiator, porch, pictures, living-room furniture.

After the teacher and the class had talked about basic needs for several days the patient was asked if he could think about the things that had been discussed and tell what he thought people needed most. His list was: "Money, clothes, pants, underwear, stockings. Shelter—houses, beds. Meat, ice cream, dishes. Toilet." (Repeated many times.)

Teacher: Do you know where clothes come from?

Patient: Yes, wool. Sheep sometimes.

Teacher: What else do you know about clothes?

Patient: Well—sheep, wool—farms. My milk comes from the cow. My sweater is made of sheep. My pants and socks and shoes are made of sheep. Hair. Other clothes—other little woolen dresses—Mommie's dresses. Fur coats.

Teacher: Do they all come from sheep?

Patient: No. Little Bo-Peep lost her sheep. I don't know.

Teacher: How do you think we can find out?

Patient: Ask somebody at a farm. Any barn that has sheep or animals. They might tell you.

Teacher: How do you think we could find out if we couldn't go to a farm?

Patient: You might go to a stranger and ask them. Maybe you wouldn't know their house or they wouldn't have a telephone.

Teacher: Where does meat come from?

Patient: The store? It grows in the ground. All meat comes from animals. Lamb chops come from goats.

Teacher: Can you tell me the names of some vegetables?

Patient: Potatoes, mashed potatoes, string beans, lemonade in hot weather, orangeade.

Teacher: Are you thinking of vegetables?

Patient: Green beans, peas.

Teacher: What meats can you think of?

Patient: Hamburger, steak, roast beef, tenderloin, cold water, oranges, onions, cabbage, lettuce, tomatoes, bread, orange juice, tomato juice, milk, toast, jellies, eggs, bacon, cookies, crackers, cheese, beets.

The position in which he kept his chair in the playroom, his refusal to play with toys, his preference for playing with his hands and his cap, his dislike of active play, and his preference for staying in the house with his mother had the same basis as his handwashing compulsion, that is, a dislike of getting dirty. This was based on his fear of masturbation. He told me he was afraid to move out of his chair lest he step on a snake whose blood would gush out. Also, the snake might bite his nose and eyebrows. If his hands became dirty, his father would become ill, his mother would go away, or a burglar would enter the house and kill his father, his mother, and a boy. These masturbation fantasies therefore consisted of a fear of castration if he hated his father, his mother, and his dead brother. It seemed that he felt responsible for the brother's death. Certainly his maternal protective behavior to his twin sisters and his constant and insistent denial of any dislike of them, no matter how much they infringed on his rights, seemed to be a reaction formation against his feared hatred of them.

He persistently refused to use his left hand for any real purpose. He told me that his right hand was a man and his left hand a woman. One man dispossesses another of the woman and then both are married to her, but the men have to live in separate houses.

He told me he played mostly with girls because he would like to be the third-grade teacher, a woman, and because he would like to be a girl, for girls' clothes were so pretty. At the same time he told me that though he was afraid of boys because they fought, he would like to be a boy.

He felt responsible for an appendectomy which a girl friend of his had suffered several years before, because he had hit her in the stomach. As I have already mentioned, his fantasies seemed to indicate his idea that he had caused his brother's death. Usually he did not like to mention the dead brother, but he often prayed for him, although the family were not Catholic.

The games he played with his hands were as follows:

1. A baby was playing behind a fence. It got out but came back and its parents fed it. Then it went to bed, got up, and a whirlwind destroyed the house, the parents, and their baby.

2. The playroom (where his interviews with me took place) was my apartment, but when I was asleep there, a tramp came, took my bed away, and ate me up in order to become strong.

3. There was a bad boy whose mother kept him in and whose father punished him. Although the boy did not like the punishment, the patient felt it was entirely just. (On another occasion when I knew he had been punished shortly before, he told me he was quite happy about the whole incident.) The boy's name was Billy. (This was the name of the patient's dead brother and of the family dog, who had been sent away because the twin sisters became ill from eating the dog's hair. The patient was fond of the dog but expressed no sorrow when the dog was sent away.)

4. There was a big boy whose mother was killed in a storm. The boy hurt his hand and had to go to a hospital. The mother was killed, and the boy and his father lived happily ever after.

5. A tramp came after me and bored a hole into my room and through me. He also bored a hole through the patient. This game occurred at the time he was telling me that he was fonder of a girl friend than he was of his mother.

6. His hands were a baby, and he was the mother singing the baby to sleep.

7. A father was in the hospital and the mother went out and left the boy. She returned, bringing a cake, but went out again. The boy did not touch the cake. The mother, father, and boy went to the grandmother's. While they were away a burglar destroyed the house and when the family returned the burglar killed them. The mother still lived, so the burglar shot her in the stomach.

8. A father and mother had no children. They went out to dinner. The mother fainted on her return because she was going to have a baby. The baby, fully dressed, was cut out of the mother's leg. The baby was a girl who was very ill and would die.

9. A father kicked a mother and baby out. The mother kicked out

the father and the baby. The mother and baby went off to dinner and left the father. The mother broke her back and died. Everybody died.

10. A boy went out to play and fell in the river. He came home, was spanked and put to bed without supper. Then he was neglected for the twins. The boy and his mother got mumps and measles and went to the hospital.

This boy had a severe obsessional neurosis which was the result of his attempt to solve his fear of his hatred of his father and mother. He feared his hatred because he believed it had resulted in his brother's death and would result in his own castration and death. He tried to solve this problem by attempting to be both a boy and a girl, with a preference for being the latter as a masochistic defense against his sadism, and by a regression to the anal-sadistic stage of development. He found that this regression was no solution, and he was forced to erect further defenses of reaction formations of docility, obedience, lack of movement, and refusal to make any change, and of isolation, undoing, and diminishing his capacity to learn. He restricted his intake of knowledge because it meant cannibalistic incorporation, for which he would be killed.

None of these mechanisms, however, explain his confused thinking and the alternations of knowing at one time and being ignorant at another, excellent examples of which can be seen in the reports of the teacher and the psychologist. The type of thinking shown here is very like that seen in dreams, whose bizarreness is the result of the fact that the primary processes of the unconscious [28] are freed

[28] In his study of dreams Freud found that the methods of thinking in the unconscious differed remarkably from those used in conscious thinking. In the unconscious, contradictory thoughts can exist side by side without interfering one with the other, or they can be condensed into a single apparently unified idea. Dissimilarities can be made into similarities and vice versa. The affect suitable to a particular idea can be detached readily from that idea and displaced to another idea, for which it is unsuitable. This patient's productions give excellent examples of the type of thinking which goes on in the unconscious and which is technically called thinking according to the primary process. It is an entirely different method of thinking than occurs in logical conscious thought. The latter method is known technically as thinking according to the secondary process. In the next chapter I will discuss fully the whole question of the primary and secondary processes, but I am defining them here in order that the reader will better understand at this point these technical terms.

temporarily during sleep from the logical secondary processes of the ego and of consciousness. His thinking was controlled by these primary processes and so he often appeared unable to think according to the usual logical secondary processes. This made it difficult for him to associate, catalogue, and assimilate any knowledge that he learned.

His regression not only involved his psychosexual life but was a real regression in ego functions also. I believe the real distinction between a disorder of learning due to deflection of attention from the data to be learned to the attempt to solve a serious intrapsychic conflict, and this type of case lies in the fact that in the former the secondary processes of ego activity remain in command, while in the latter the regression causes the primary processes of psychic activity to predominate. Their effect is to disorder the ability to catalogue, associate, and make logical the knowledge which is learned. In these cases the real problem is the accentuation of the primary processes due to regression. These disorders are basically severe obsessional neuroses.

The severe regression from the secondary processes of thinking to the predominance of the primary processes forms an important difference between this group of cases and another group of cases of learning disorders, cases which show a disorder of the relation to reality.

DIMINISHED CAPACITY TO LEARN BECAUSE OF A DISTURBANCE IN THE RELATION TO REALITY

Case 14. A college student was referred because he showed a beginning paranoid schizophrenia. He had a very high I.Q., although his scholastic achievement in high school had been mediocre and he had flunked his freshman year in one college and was barely passing in a second. His family thought that this was due to his indulgence in too much social life and admonished him from time to time to do more studying. When the apparently full social life of this patient was studied carefully, it was found to be an expression of a fantasy of megalomania. Really he felt quite inadequate in social relationships at his own social, economic, and intellectual level. With these people he felt very inferior. His apparently full social life was spent in a small rural community. Here because he was a college student and the scion of a wealthy family, he was a big frog in a small puddle. He served as the adviser for the townspeople and actually helped many who were in difficulties. This was very gratifying to him because it overcame his feeling of inferiority. He did not seem to realize that he could be of greater help if he achieved graduation from college and from a professional school. He failed in school because he was unable to perceive that his fantasy was not realistic.

This patient's other symptoms indicated that he suffered from paranoid schizophrenia, perhaps actually from a true paranoia. I have seen a number of other patients whose failure to learn seemed the result of disordered ability to digest and assimilate their ingested knowledge, but who gradually developed the characteristic clinical picture of schizophrenia. It is a matter of common knowledge that the intellectual ability of certain very brilliant adolescents seems to burn out by the time they reach adulthood. At this time they begin to show more-or-less marked signs of schizophrenia, often of the ambulant types. Their intellectual ability is very mediocre, and this decrease in intellectual ability seems to retard the progression of the schizophrenic process.

DIMINISHED CAPACITY TO LEARN BECAUSE THE CHILD HAS NEVER LEARNED TO TOLERATE THE ANXIETY PRODUCED BY THE LACK OF GRATIFICATION OF INSTINCTUAL DRIVES

Educators, and particularly progressive educators, in the last few years have become aware of a peculiar phenomenon in certain children. These children on entering school seem to lack any interest in learning. Instead of being interested in acquiring knowledge they seem interested only in the immediate gratification of their desires. Learning to read is boring because it requires effort and interferes with their immediate pleasure. No matter how hard the teacher tries to arouse their interest and hold them to this task by making it pleasurable, the results are slight or nonexistent. In fact, these children will state openly that they do not intend to learn and the teacher cannot make them. These statements sound not defiant or stubborn but simply matter-of-fact.

More peculiar still is the fact that such children come from homes which appear to be the best. The parents are interested in the acquirement of knowledge but do not force their children to follow in their footsteps. They interfere as little as possible with the manifestations of the various stages of psychosexual development. Toilet training is done easily and slowly, there is no interference with fingersucking, masturbation, curiosity, or exhibitionism—in short, it seems as if the children are receiving every opportunity for successful development. But when the upbringing of these children is studied carefully, two misconceptions are found. The child has been permitted always to operate on the pleasure-pain principle. He has been protected as much as is humanly possible from any pain or any interference with the immediate gratification of his desires. The parents are not only extremely permissive toward his gratification but actually almost turn themselves inside out to see that he is gratified. They do not wish him to experience any pain or anxiety. These children therefore have not learned to tolerate any anxiety, particularly that which arises when the immediate gratification of an instinctual desire is prevented by reality. As Fliess [29] states, this is one of the typical and most frequent misapplications of Freud's findings. It reverses the whole parent-child relationship, for here the adult identifies with the aggressor, who in this case is the child, instead of vice versa.

As a consequence, the development of the ego defenses of repression, reaction formation, change of aim, and sublimation, i.e., the development of the organization of the ego, is greatly retarded. Sexual curiosity is not changed into curiosity about the nonsexual aspect of the world, but remains sexual curiosity and is gratified directly. Such children have at their disposal no energy to learn, and their desire to learn cannot be stimulated, even by making the subject to be learned as interesting as possible. They will begin to learn only when they are subjected to the slow educational process of being compelled to postpone immediate gratification of instinctual drives and

[29] Robert Fliess, "The Metapsychology of the Analyst," *Psychoanalytic Quarterly,* 11, 1942.

to begin to tolerate the anxiety which necessarily must arise during this educational procedure.

CONCLUSIONS

From the study of clinical cases which show a diminished capacity to learn, it seems possible at this time to conclude that a diminished capacity to learn results from disorders of the functions of the ego and is caused by influences which affect those ego functions. These may be classified as follows:

1. Organic defects and the effect of physical defects and illnesses.
2. Improper and unpleasant conditioning experiences during the process of learning.
3. Current disturbances in object relationships.
4. Emotional reactions such as apprehension of dangers to the child's security, feelings of shame, guilt and embarrassment, feelings of horror and fear, engrossment in instinctual desires, and the focusing of attention on daydreams. These produce a deflection of attention from the subject to be learned.

These first four groups of causes are well known to educators at the present time. In these types the capacity to learn is diminished indirectly.

5. The involvement of the learning process itself in the neurotic conflict. In these cases the diminished capacity to learn may result from an inhibition of the use of learning, from disturbances in the ability to ingest the data to be learned, or from disturbances in the ability to digest and assimilate the learned material. In these cases the capacity to learn is diminished directly by its involvement in the neurotic conflict.
6. Disturbances in the relation to reality.
7. The fact that the child has not learned to replace the pleasure-pain principle by the reality principle and so has never been compelled by reality to tolerate anxiety.

CHAPTER III

The Primary and Secondary Processes

The researches of educational and experimental psychologists have established definite technics and mechanisms by which learning is facilitated. These consist of methods of focusing the attention of the special senses on the material to bc learned and of increasing the use of the memory. The former necessitates arousing the child's interest in the material so that he will voluntarily focus his attention on it, and selecting material containing focal points which are not too complex at any given time and are connected with somewhat similar material already learned by the child, and with the child's life experiences. The ability to remember is increased if the child can use more than one special sense—for instance, vision and hearing instead of vision or hearing alone—to take in the material. It is increased also if the child can reproduce what he is learning by some motor activity—writing or drawing what he is seeing and hearing. The combinations open up the association pathways between the various cortical sensory and motor areas, and later on when a stimulus comes into any one of the cortical areas it finds a facilitated pathway through these opened associational tracks, so that it spreads readily to stimulate the other cortical areas. It is increased also by repetition—the so-called rote memory. Memory is a function which takes place in both the conscious and unconscious parts of the mind. Recall of remembered material through the focusing of the conscious attention may be a voluntary act, or the particular material in the unconscious part of the mind may become energized through some associative stimuli and begin to force itself on the conscious attention.

These processes—the use of the special senses, the voluntary focusing of the attention, and the use of memory—are functions of the ego, largely the conscious ego. In general it may be said that the studies of psychologists have been directed to understanding functions of the ego and the connections between these ego functions and the finer anatomy and physiology of the cerebral cortex and its afferent and efferent connections.

Psychologists have also studied, intensively and extensively, the ways in which the activities of these functions of the ego may be increased and decreased by manipulations from the environment which utilize the basic needs and drives universal in all animal life. These experiments in conditioning methods have shown that learning takes place more quickly and more thoroughly when it occurs in situations favorable to the gratification of such basic needs as hunger, and takes place more slowly and less thoroughly when it is attempted in situations unfavorable to the gratification of these desires or in situations where the individual experiences pain. If the individual is placed in a situation where he is not certain whether the next step in learning will result in a pleasurable or a painful feeling or in an equal combination of both, the ego functions of learning cease to operate, and even what has been learned previously seems to become lost. These studies on the conditioned cortical and subcortical reflexes prove that the pleasure-pain principle—a phenomenon found universally in all animal life—is an important factor in the learning process.

Educational psychologists, on the basis of all these studies, have developed methods by which children are helped to learn their academic subjects, and in general these methods operate very effectively. Psychoanalytic researches have added little to the data about these processes found by psychologists. They make up what Hartmann [1] has called the nonconflictual part of the ego, in which he includes intelligence, perceptual and motor equipment, and special gifts. He calls these nonconflictual because they are inherited as part of the constitutional structure and do not arise as the result of the conflict between the instincts and the external world, as the rest of

[1] Heinz Hartmann, "Psychoanalysis and Developmental Psychology," *The Psychoanalytic Study of the Child,* Vol. V, New York, International Universities Press, 1950.

the ego does. In analyzing any intrapsychic conflict it is necessary to pay attention to the influence of these factors and their development on the timing, intensity, and mode of expression of the conflict. They may even furnish some of the energy of the ego because, as Freud says, perhaps not all ego energy comes from the instincts. As I have shown in the previous chapter, they may become involved in ego conflicts themselves and their functions accentuated or hampered by other ego conflicts. This is seen constantly in connection with memory—which is part of the constitutional inheritance of the individual but is affected deeply by the defenses, such as repression, against the instinct representations and their collateral associations.

Many of the basic discoveries of psychoanalysis, such as the discovery of the existence of the unconscious, and of the defense mechanisms, particularly repression, were made through researches into disturbances of memory, especially the amnesia for the first six or seven years of life found regularly in all people. As a consequence, the psychoanalytic literature contains the results of many studies on memory and its disturbances, which Lewy and Rapaport [2] have summarized.

In order to understand their summary better it is important to remember that Freud [3] noted that perception and memory involve two different psychic systems. The perceptive system receives impressions but retains no permanent trace of them. The memory system retains the permanent impressions from the first system. Lewy and Rapaport say that normal logical thinking goes on in the conscious perceptive system of the mind, is not controlled by the primary process, and prevents the free discharge of instinctual energy for which the primary process strives. The conscious perceptive system operates with small quantities of mental energy, using a vast treasure of stored-up memories, in the service of purposive ideas whose aim is to achieve gratification by changing and dominating the outside world through planned activity. In the dreaming state the process

[2] Ernst Lewy and David Rapaport, "The Psychoanalytic Concept of Memory and Its Relation to Recent Memory Theories," *Psychoanalytic Quarterly,* 13, 1944.

[3] Sigmund Freud, "A Note upon the Mystic Writing Pad," *International Journal of Psychoanalysis,* 21, 1940.

of excitation proceeds in a different direction from that of normal waking activity. Instead of proceeding from the memory images to the motility systems, it follows the regressive path to the original perceptive and sensory images and so becomes subject to the primary process of the unconscious.

The memory apparatus operates as follows: The driving force which puts the apparatus in action is an instinctual striving which appears in the unconscious part of the ego as a wish. This wish strives for free discharge and because it is unconscious, is controlled by the primary process. In this state the energized wish attaches itself to various available memory traces suitable to the expression of the wish. In technical language it cathects them. If the wish in the unconscious system is energized strongly, it and the attached memory traces, particularly those memories which concern objects toward which the aim of the instinct is directed, are able to make connections with the verbal traces in the preconscious system. Then if the wish is acceptable to the ego and the superego the attached memories are able to make their appearance in consciousness, i.e., in the conscious perceptive system. There both the wish and the attached memories are controlled by the secondary process, which operates under the guidance of directive purposive ideas. Through the synthetic function of the ego the cathexis of the striving is transferred to purposeful, selected memory traces, and the result of this selection appears in the form of logical, realistic thinking. Thus the selected memory traces become conscious only if the wish is energized strongly, i.e., hypercathected, which directs the attention to them, and if the underlying striving is acceptable to the ego and the superego. Otherwise they remain unconscious. If the supply of energy is weak and the wish occurs in conditions characterized by repression, i.e., in conditions where it is not acceptable to the ego or the superego, the underlying striving discharges its cathexis freely in a dream or a neurotic symptom.

Schmideberg,[4] in discussing amnesia, says "not remembering" occurs because of immature development of the memory function, for the purpose of mental economy, and because of disturbing uncon-

[4] Melitta Schmideberg, "Infant Memories and Constructions," *Psychoanalytic Quarterly,* 19, 1950.

scious factors. She adds the important concept that affective factors increase the ability to remember. This increase may be due to guilt over an initial attempt to forget certain persons or things. In this case, in the unconscious, forgetting may be the same as killing while remembering is the same as keeping alive. Increased ability to remember may be due to fear of being accused wrongly or to the desire to amass evidence against others. Recollection as the end product of the memory apparatus involves the revival of past impressions, a cathexis which determines their clarity, intensity, and quality, and an expression of the ego's attitude to the memory; the discrimination between present-day reality, fantasy, and actual memory; the association and discrimination of impressions; and the communication of these memories in words, dreams, behavior, and play.

It has long been well known that there are only a few conscious memories of the years of early childhood—before the age of seven—and that these few often concern apparently unimportant occurrences. These have been studied through psychoanalysis and have been found to serve as a cover for a series of important memories which are kept unconscious because of their unpleasant emotional content. Consequently they are referred to as cover or screen memories. Kennedy [5] in discussing these points out that the usual memories of this period of childhood are hearsay memories, the memory of a few isolated facts, and apparently clear and vivid memories which have actually undergone definite distortion. The last-mentioned type are clear and colorful in intensity, contain insignificant, isolated details, and make use of condensation, i.e., frequently repeated everyday occurrences are remembered as single incidents. The patient described in her paper remembered the food in a particular episode as pleasant, although in the actual scene, which Kennedy had witnessed a number of years before, food had left the patient unsatisfied and unhappy. In this example the memories showed only minor changes in content, but there was a reversal in affect due to hallucinatory wish fulfillment. The same patient had other cover memories whose content was due not to hallucinatory wish fulfillment but to ego development, and other memories in which the

[5] Hanna Engl Kennedy, "Cover Memories in Formation," *The Psychoanalytic Study of the Child,* Vol. V, New York, International Universities Press, 1950.

affect had been displaced to a different content. Kennedy quotes Freud's classification of cover memories into three types based on the temporal relation between the cover memory and the memory it covers: 1. Retroactive or regressive cover memories, in which the content belongs to the first years of childhood while the thoughts connected with the content belong to a later period of life. 2. Encroaching or interposing cover memories. In these the cover memory is a memory of an incident which occurred later than the memory which it covers. 3. Contemporaneous or contiguous cover memories, in which the screened memory and the cover memory are connected through content and occurred at about the same time.

The ability to remember consciously, and the ability of the conscious ego to use the memory accurately, becomes disturbed if the memory is cathected in the unconscious by wishes which the conscious ego or the superego regard as undesirable, if it is associated with unpleasant, painful emotional reactions, or if the perception at the time when the memory occurred produced unpleasant feelings.

It can be seen from this discussion of memory that the main contributions of psychoanalysis to the knowledge of the way in which learning occurs lie in a better understanding of the unconscious parts of the ego and of the effect on both the conscious and unconscious functions of the ego exerted by the instincts and by the superego, i.e., in the study of the conflictual part of the ego. In earlier chapters I have reported facts which have been learned from the study of children whose ability to learn is disordered. It is a customary and well-validated method in medicine to learn about the normal functions of an organ through the study of the symptoms and pathology which occur when the organ is diseased. Particularly, a great deal of our knowledge of the normal functioning of the brain has been gained from the study of brain lesions—a procedure stemming from the brilliant work of Hughlings Jackson. In the same way, one can find out a great deal about the normal learning process from the study of the cases which show disorders in the ability to learn.

If we refer to the previous chapter we find that the most serious disorders of learning occur in connection with what I have designated as disorders in the digestion and assimilation of the material to be learned. In this type of learning difficulty, the problem seems to be that a regression in the psychosexual development has occurred and the regression has not only affected the direction and manifestations of the libidinal impulses but has also involved the development of the ego. In these cases—as is apparent from the examples I have given—logical thinking, logical associations, and the recall of memories in a logical order have disappeared and have been replaced by associations and recalled memories which do not seem to have any logical connections or in which the logical connections are not readily understood. The logical thought processes characteristic of the mature ego, which have been designated by Freud as secondary processes, have ceased to exist and have been replaced by the thought processes characteristic of the unconscious—thought processes such as appear in dreams—which Freud [6] designated as primary processes. In discussing the psychology of the dream processes Freud pointed out that the act of becoming conscious depends on the attention. If the attention is needed for other aims and is therefore directed away from a train of thought, the train of thought does not become conscious. If a train of thought leads to an idea which cannot withstand the criticism of the ego, the attention is withdrawn from it. These trains of thought remain in the preconscious part of the mind and may either disappear spontaneously by diffusing energy through all the association paths, throwing all the chains of thought into excitation (which subsides because the need for discharge has been transformed into dormant cathexis), or they may continue because unconscious wishes and ideas transfer their energy to them and draw them into the unconscious. In this case the train of thought has abandoned preconscious cathexis and has been cathected by unconscious wishes. A similar result occurs if, from the beginning, the preconscious train of thought is connected with an unconscious wish and therefore has to be repressed with it, or if an unconscious wish becomes active and of its own accord seeks transference to psychic residues not cathected by the preconscious. An unconscious idea as such is quite incapable of entering into the preconscious and can exert an influence there only by establishing touch with a harmless idea already belonging to the precon-

[6] Sigmund Freud, *The Interpretation of Dreams,* New York, The Macmillan Co., 1913.

scious, to which it transfers its intensity and by which it allows itself to be screened. This transference may leave the idea from the preconscious unaltered, although the latter will thus acquire an unmerited intensity, or it may force on it some modification derived from the content of the transferred idea. The choice as to which particular ideas in the preconscious will be energized by the unconscious wishes does not fall upon such conscious or preconscious ideas as have themselves attracted attention in the preconscious. The unconscious prefers to entangle with its connections, impressions or ideas in the preconscious which have remained uninvolved because indifferent or those which have had attention immediately withdrawn from them.

The trains of thought which have given up their preconscious cathexis lead to dream formation. Dreams arise from an unconscious wish, some desire left over from waking life that has developed enough energy during sleep to make an impression on the conscious part of the ego. Between the manifest dream material and the latent dream thoughts lies the dream work. A study of the dream work affords an excellent example of the way in which unconscious material—either originally unconscious or repressed into the unconscious—forces itself on the ego, becomes preconscious, and undergoes the modifications of dream distortion. Each element of the content is overdetermined, i.e., it appears several times over in dream thoughts. If many thoughts are condensed in one element of the dream content, then in the conscious thinking a single element leads back to a number of thoughts in the unconscious. Each dream element must be traced back to its source separately, without regard to coherence. In dreams, such complicated intellectual processes as arguments for and against, apparent acts of judgment in the dream content, attempts at coherence, jokes and comparisons, and the like are dream material and not the representation of intellectual activity in the dream. The nature of the dream thoughts is indicated by the apparent thinking in dreams, but not the relation of the dream thoughts one to another. The dream uses entirely different mechanisms to portray ideas than are used in conscious thinking. To indicate a logical connection, the dream uses simultaneousness. For causal connection it may use a sequence or may change one image into another; "either-or" may represent "and" and "and" may represent "either-or." An alternative may be represented by the division of the dream into two equal parts. Uniformity may be substituted for antithesis. Unity may be represented by similarity and agreement. An inversion in a dream may assert the opposite, may present the conclusion at the beginning, or may indicate that the dream deals with the past. In dreams there is a transvaluation of emphasis. Transient and hazy elements are direct derivations from the central dream thought.

It can be seen that the methods of thinking in the dream are entirely different from those used in ordinary conscious logical thinking. Conscious thinking itself is of two kinds. One is the conscious direction of the attention to the solution of a definite problem. This conscious direction of the attention eliminates associations which are not pertinent logically. The other is the process of free association. In psychoanalysis, the patient is directed to lie down, relax, and report every thought that enters his mind. His lying down limits his perception of stimuli from the external world. His relaxation enables energy to flood his mind instead of being used in purposeful action. Free association is based on the principle that as the energy from the instincts flows upward through the central nervous system, the unconscious wishes form representations in the mind. The attention is directed to these representations. Neither apparently logical nor apparently illogical associations are excluded. In this way the wishes and impulses from the unconscious are able to appear in consciousness.

In order to understand the relation of these various methods of thinking it is necessary to postulate that there are three different systems in the mind. First, there is the conscious perceptive system, influenced by the perception of the external world, in which the thinking is logical and conscious. The second system, the preconscious, is nonconscious, as its name implies. In this system, the preconscious thought takes any given perception material and tries to create order in it, to construct relations, and to subject it to the requirements of intelligible coherence. As an example, errors which make nonsense on the printed page often are not seen or apprehended in reading. The activity in the preconscious system is controlled by the secondary process. Its function is to complete the work of experimental thought, and therefore it maintains the greater part of the energy to be used for cathexis in a state of rest, i.e., dormant. Its activity will not allow a memory to force its way back to perception, as in dreams, but after the work of experimental thought is concluded, the inhibition of rest is removed and the excitation is led, by a detour, to voluntary mobility for the purpose of changing the outer world so as to permit a real perception of a gratifying object. It can only cathect an idea when it can inhibit any pain connected with it.

This system, like the conscious perceptive system, is of later development than the third—the unconscious system. Here, thinking is governed by a series of transformations which are not recognizable as ordinary psychic processes. These are:

1. Condensation. The intensity of the entire train of thought is condensed into a single unit. When two thoughts, even if they are logically contradictory, have any point of contact at all they are condensed into a unity. This apparent unity may represent a number of totally dissimilar thoughts.

2. Displacement of accent. Every thought has an attached affect, but the amount of affect may be greater with one thought than with another. In the unconscious, the affect frequently is detached from the thought; it may be transferred to another thought, which it accents far above its real value; it may be changed into its opposite; or it may seem to disappear entirely.

3. Distortion. It is evident that when two diverse and perhaps contradictory thoughts have been condensed into a unity, or when the accent has been removed from a thought which really is important and has been attached to another thought, which really is unimportant, the end result will be that the thinking, as we understand conscious logical thinking, will be very distorted.

4. Formation of intermediary ideas or compromises. This is the result of the free transference of intensities and of condensation. In consciousness, this is unheard of, because there the selection and retention of the right conceptual material is most important.

5. The loose connection to one another, often as a pair, of ideas which have transferred their intensities to each other.

6. The existence side by side of contradictory ideas.

These methods of thinking, which Freud has called the primary processes, are used to keep cathecting energy mobile and capable of discharge, and the content and real significance of the psychic elements to which these cathexes adhere become matters of secondary importance. The purpose of the primary processes is to aid the discharge of the instinctual energy and so reduce the tension in the mind in accordance with the pleasure-pain principle. The purpose of the secondary processes is to utilize the instinctual energy by directing it through conscious or unconscious judgment into a valid form of activity.

The primary processes of displacement and condensation are basic psychic processes, but they furnish a distinct hindrance to learning. In fact, the process of learning can only take place when defenses against the primary processes of the unconscious have been developed. At first whatever sensory and motor patterns are formed in response to external stimuli come immediately under the control of the primary processes, so that when thought begins to develop it is the type found in the primary processes. That this is so can be seen when regression takes place either in the formation of dreams or in a severe neurotic regression, as in Case 13, reported in Chapter II. If learned material becomes subject to the primary processes it can be used only for instinctual discharge, not for a valid activity. Its real logical connections are broken up and the whole reduced to chaos. As there is constant pressure from the instincts for discharge, which occurs most readily through the primary processes, there is a constant struggle in the mind to maintain the supremacy of the secondary processes. Examples can be observed daily of the presence of this struggle. For the purpose of resistance, a patient may react to an interpretation by directing attention to a nonimportant part of a remembered experience or dream, which becomes vivid, while the more important element is perceived less vividly. The deflection of the attention to the nonimportant part may be due to an attempt to avoid the important part. In this way, the *non*-important part may be used as a defense against recognizing an unacceptable unconscious wish. The nonimportant part also may have an unconscious meaning to the patient—it may express an unconscious desire. In this way, the nonimportant part assumes an illogical importance and serves as a medium for the primary processes.

This also happens in learning. The child, for unconscious reasons, may direct his attention to unimportant details and retain them, while not attending to the important details. If an affect and an idea are ill-matched as regards their nature or intensity, or if a perception from the outside becomes associated with an affect whose nature or intensity it does not match, our conscious judgment about the idea or the perception becomes confused. This confusion may lead to forgetting the idea or the perception, to an inability to understand them, or to a misperception and therefore to the falsification of the learning process. The tendency of the unconscious to utilize all material to express content must interfere with the learning of logical processes which emphasize form rather than content. This may be one of the reasons for the difficulty in learning some parts of grammar, i.e., subordinate clauses, prepositions, and the like.

The change of an idea into a word is brought about by condensation and displacement. The less precise the word is, the closer it is to the activities of the unconscious. The more precise it is, the closer it comes to the activities of the preconscious. The word is the point of junction of a number of ideas; an ambiguous word may replace two words with different meanings, as happens in the *double entendre* so frequent in late latency and early adolescence. In dreams, only what is pictorial is capable of representation; therefore colorless and abstract expressions are exchanged for those that are pictorial and concrete. This is in the interest of condensation and of the censorship, for concrete terms are richer in associations. In any dream it is doubtful whether an element is to be interpreted in the negative or the positive sense, historically (as a memory), symbolically, or as if it meant what it said. This ambiguousness is the result of the antagonism of the ego to the unconscious underlying wish, thought, or feeling—an antagonism which arises because of fear either of the superego or of reality. For similar reasons a person will use ambiguous words or words will acquire an ambiguous meaning for him; accurate learning will therefore be hindered and the giving out of learned information will be affected. Just as inversion occurs in dreams, so is the ego perception of the external world influenced by the desire for it to be the other way around. It is evident, then, that the use of the primary processes interferes with education. One cannot see the woods for the trees or one cannot see the trees for the woods. To overcome these difficulties, the secondary processes must take supremacy over the primary processes. This occurs through the organization of the ego, which is brought about in a number of ways. I will mention all these ways and will stress one or two to which not enough attention has been directed in the literature.

CHAPTER IV

The Organization of the Ego

The organization of the ego and the supremacy of the secondary processes has usually been achieved long before the child enters kindergarten, and therefore educators do not require teaching methods which deal directly with this change. However, it is important for them to understand what is meant by the organization of the ego. The early organization of the ego takes place in the first two years of life.

In the young baby, an instinctual impulse when aroused would tend to innervate the motor system. But to a large extent this is impossible, because of the motor system's relative lack of development, and the impulse, continuing to strive toward dissipation, is forced to flow into the relatively better developed sensory system. (A similar situation occurs in the adult during sleep, as Freud pointed out in his investigation of dreams.) The instinctual impulse passing outward stimulates the sensory centers, which can only respond by their appropriate engrams—visual perceptions of light, dark, color; auditory perceptions of sounds; gustatory perceptions of flavors; olfactory perceptions of odors; and so on—if such responses can be so designated. At the same time, impressions from the external world stimulate the sensory receptors and cause stimuli to flow inward to the sensory centers, bringing perceptions of the lightness and darkness, the color, the spatial relations, and so on, of real external objects. The definiteness and specificity of these are very different from the lack of organization of the perceptions from the instinctual stimuli. To these are joined also the memory images of previous sensory impressions. The impressions made by these two groups of stimuli must be combined. External and internal must be made into one. This is done, so to speak, in the outer layer of the id, which because it is forced to make this attempt to organize, becomes the beginning of the ego. Therefore combination is an early important law of psychic activity of the ego. This combination, although it has the character of unifying divergent perceptions, is not exactly the same as the primary process of condensation. Condensation also condenses several divergent ideas into one, but it does this for the purpose of discharging instinctual energy.

Let me illustrate. A very small child sees his father in a top hat, which impresses him because it is unusual. If he has an erotic instinctual impulse toward his father, he perceives the hat as a desirable object which can satisfy his erotic wishes. It becomes his father's penis or his breast—because the small child cannot distinguish yet between male and female—which will gratify him orally, like the toy hats filled with candies which are sold on St. Patrick's Day. If he has a hostile attitude to his father at this time, he regards the top hat as a hostile object which he would like to damage—as might happen later when he is in the latency period and would delight in throwing a snowball or perhaps a brick at it—or he may be frightened by this hostile impulse and feel that he must respect and revere the top hat lest it injure him. Thus there are combined the vague perceptions caused by the instinctual impulses energizing the sensory centers, the feelings engendered by those instinctual impulses, and the sensory stimuli aroused by the sight of his father's hat. It is essential in order that the child may understand the external world and adapt himself to it that this combination of his instinctual drives and his sensory perceptions take place. But the process of combination produces distortions of reality. His father's top hat remains the same in reality, but to the child, depending on his instinctual impulses toward it (that is, toward his father), it comes to symbolize—to represent to him—desire, repulsion, or terror, and under each condition its actual appearance becomes changed from what it really is. Also, the perception of the hat separated from his father will arouse the same emotional reactions as he feels at that time toward his father.

Combination comes into being as the result of the first contacts of the id with the sensory perceptions of the external world and is a process by which this contact is made. It would appear, therefore, as one of the first manifestations of the ego, or of that beginning barrier between the id and the external world which later will become the ego. Although this process is not present as a basic law of human psychic activity, as are the primary processes, it appears very early and therefore can be considered an early secondary process in the ego's functions of integrating the external world and the id.

Corresponding to the primary process of displacement there is a displacement of intensity which seems to arise in a similar way at the same time as combination does. If the sensory excitation is very strong, it will overwhelm and reverse the direction of the instinctual excitation and vice versa. This will interfere with the process of combination and so in order to make it effective, it must be possible to displace the intensity of energy from one source to the other. This need produces a facilitated process which becomes one of the early secondary processes of the ego.

It seems to me that the first step in the development of the capacity to learn is the replacement of the supremacy of the primary processes by the secondary processes as a result of combination. How this comes about I do not know, but I suspect that the gradually increasing importance of the impact of sensory impressions on the young baby and the constant repetition of their real existence interferes with the pleasure component of the primary processes. More and more frequently the activity of the primary processes brings pain, and more and more frequently the secondary process of combination brings pleasure, and therefore the latter becomes superimposed on the former. At that point the learning process can really begin. It is common knowledge that when a baby receives only the minimum of sensory stimulation, the development of his intellectual capacity—really his capacity to think logically—is hampered seriously and his thinking as he grows older tends to be under the dominance of the primary processes.

Spitz [1] traces the organization of the ego through the first year

[1] René A. Spitz, "The Relevancy of Direct Infant Observation," *The Psychoanalytic Study of the Child,* Vol. V, New York, International Universities Press, 1950.

or so as follows: In the first month there is no consciousness, conscious perception, or memory traces. The behavior is an uncoordinated diffuse discharge phenomenon with an overflow of reactions and their counterpart of quiescence. There is a high threshold for incoming stimuli, which may form the prototype for a later organization of conflict, for part of the ego, and for repressive processes.

In the first two months learning takes place by means of conditioned reflexes. In the second month appear the first signs of conscious perception and memory traces. By the third month there are definite memory traces, so that now the psyche has an unconscious, a preconscious, and a conscious part. The learning process moves from conditioned reflexes to the human pattern in which cathexes are shifted into memory traces. There is the beginning of object relations with animate, but not with inanimate, objects. These three months are the primary narcissistic stage.

The environment is experienced not by virtue of its object qualities but by virtue of the needs of the infant. In the first two months the emotional organization varies from excitation to quiescence. In the third month there are manifestations of pleasure and displeasure. At three months the first rudiment of the reality principle, i.e., the ability to tolerate postponement of immediate gratification, is established. Under the action of reality, energy can be directed from narcissistic perceptions to the perception of the environment. This results in the laying down of memory traces, which means the psyche will be divided topographically.

The smiling response proves that the ego development begins in the third month. During the first year, twoness rules the development of every new behavior and activity. Learning is acquired by adding to a perception one characteristic of the real object in nature and simultaneously dropping one characteristic which, originally an emotional reaction or a wish, had been perceived at the same time as the original real object was perceived and so had been thought to be really part of the object. In the second three months these subjective elements, which are limited to the narcissistic stage, are dispensed with, one after another. From six to nine months, perception becomes truly objective. Identification and gesture occur in the fourth month. Identification can only take place on the basis of libidinal object relations after the narcissistic cathexes have been liberated for that purpose. At from nine to twelve months, the libidinal object relations become possible because love is now possible. The first rudiments of the ego are the inception of the reality principle, the topographical division of the psyche, the development of the capacity to manipulate cathexis, and the transition from conditioned response to human learning.

Fenichel[2] states that the newborn has no clear consciousness, but just an undifferentiated sensitivity to pain and pleasure and to the increase and decrease of tension. The functions of the ego and of consciousness are not developed, nor are perception, motility, and the ability to bind tension by countercathexis. The flooding of the organism with stimuli at birth, when an adequate defense apparatus is not present, provides the model for all later anxiety. This flooding is unpleasant and evokes the first mental tendency, a tendency to get rid of the state of tension. When the outside world succeeds in helping the infant to cope with these stimuli, he falls asleep. New stimuli, such as hunger, thirst, and cold, awaken him. The first traces of consciousness differentiate not between the ego and the nonego, but between perceptions of greater or less tension. There is a striving for discharge and relaxation which is the direct expression of the constancy principle, which is the oldest psychic mechanism. If every need could immediately be taken care of, a conception of reality would never develop. This first stage, in which there is no object representation, is that of primary narcissism. At this stage the longing for complete relaxation and the longing for objects produces a contradiction of basic importance in human life. The longing for objects which can bring discharge and relaxation is a detour on the way to the goal of getting rid of objects, i.e., of stimuli. Hate is older than love, but in reality the first object relations are neither hate nor love but the undifferentiated forerunner of both. The origin of the ego and of the sense of reality are two aspects of one developmental step. In the development of the sense of reality, the concept of one's own body plays a special role because of the perception of inner tensions and the awareness that an object exists to quiet them. Per-

[2] Otto Fenichel, *The Psychoanalytic Theory of Neurosis,* New York, W. W. Norton & Company, 1945.

ception and one's love reaction are very close together, for one perceives by changing one's body through the influence of the perceived object. Many perceptions start as kinesthetic feelings, and the primitive erotic perceptions are bound up with motor reactions ready for discharge. Perception itself is an activity—for as long as intensive stimuli flood the organism, the organism experiences perception passively. Perceptions take place rhythmically under the influence of centrifugal (motor) throbs of cathexis—the first attempt at mastering the external world. The primitive attempt at mastery of intense stimuli occurs by imitation of what is perceived. Apparently perceiving and changing one's own body according to what is perceived were originally one and the same thing. This primitive imitation of that which is perceived is a kind of identification, the awareness of which brings perception. After the systems of perception and memory have been differentiated, the organism can protect itself from too many stimuli by shutting off the function of perception through fainting, traumatic neurosis, or the return of the ego into the id in sleep; these are the models for all future defense mechanisms and can be used against internal as well as external pains. Repression is the specific blocking of the perception of particular instinctual demands.

Hunger repeatedly disturbs the peacefulness of sleep, and this compels a recognition of the outside world. Swallowing is the first reality. Originally, recognizing reality means to judge whether something helps to give satisfaction or whether it raises tensions; in other words, swallowing or spitting out is the basis for all perception. In the unconscious all sense organs are conceived as mouthlike and primary identification is putting into the mouth. In this there is no distinction between instinctual behavior and ego behavior. The first oral love, the first motor reaction to external stimuli, and the first perception are the same thing. It is interesting to note that imitation of the world by oral incorporation is the basis for magic.

Perception in infants differs from that in adults. Objects are not sharply distinguished from each other; the first images are large in extent and consist of wholes, not of parts put together; the more primitive senses, especially kinesthetic and depth sensations, prevail; the perceptions from different sense organs and the perception of motility overlap. The world is perceived by the instincts as a possible source of satisfaction or as a possible threat. Thus instinctual wishes and fears falsify reality. The pleasure principle is incompatible with correct judgment. The latter is based on consideration and postponement, and the time and energy saved by postponement are used in its functioning.

Self-esteem is raised if an unpleasant stimulus is gotten rid of. Every token of love from a more powerful adult has the effect of a supply of milk to the child, because it increases his self-esteem. The small child loses his self-esteem when he loses love and attains it when he regains love. This makes children educable. They need supplies of affection so much that they are ready to renounce other satisfactions if rewards of affection are promised or if withdrawal of affection is threatened. For this reason if reading or any other learning, particularly of an academic subject, raises tensions of great severity because the subject is associated in the unconscious with proscribed instinctual urges or with instinctual urges which are very strong, or if an excessive degree of inhibition is present because of fear, the subject will have to be rejected and a learning difficulty will arise.

The stage of primary narcissism with omnipotence is followed by a period of passive-receptive mastery, in which difficulties are overcome by influencing powerful external objects to give what is needed. Motility and active mastery develop through the gradual substitution of actions for mere discharge reactions. This is done by interposing a time period between stimulus and reaction, which implies the ability to tolerate certain tensions and to bind primitive reaction impulses by countercathexis. The prerequisite for action is the mastery of the bodily apparatus and the development of judgment. Learning to walk, to be clean, and to speak are the main steps in the development of the mastery of physical motor functions. Judgment is composed of the anticipation of the future in imagination, by testing reality in an active manner and in small doses to determine what might happen to one passively and in unknown doses.

Hendrick [3] divides the primary functions of the ego into the execu-

[3] Ives Hendrick, "Instincts and the Ego during Infancy," *Psychoanalytic Quarterly,* 11, 1942.

tant functions, whose role is effective performance, and the defense mechanisms, whose role is the avoidance of anxiety. Some measure of self-determination is found only in isolated components of the total structure, for instance, ocular fixation, feeding, the rudiments of language, and the control of the elementary responses of the hands, arms, and legs, such as reaching and crawling. Although these functions may be highly efficient in themselves they are not integrated into complex units. In their development they follow basic principles. First, when the essential physiological apparatus has matured, there is a stereotyped behavior pattern. This is followed by the appearance of reflex function and the manifestation of cortical inhibition. Following this, the child attempts to adapt the motor function to the situation through a stage of constant practice which is like the repetition compulsion. This repetitive phase terminates when skillful use, loss of stereotypy, and ability to adapt to the situation are acquired. These stages are restored regressively when a conflict, anxiety, or ego defect necessitates neurotic adaptation. The return of the stereotyped pattern is seen in monotonous play, in childhood psychoses, and as part of the acquisition of the learning skills. Although the partial functions yield work pleasure, there is a primary pleasure in effective integrated performance because the organism strives to experience a type of pleasure whose source is independent of the libidinal aims.

THE ROLE OF THE DEVELOPMENT OF THE MOTOR SYSTEM IN THE ORGANIZATION OF THE EGO

There is another condition that aids in the establishment of the supremacy of the secondary processes and in the organization of the ego. The reflex arc is the basic mechanism in the functioning of the central nervous system. An impulse, whether arising as a result of a stimulus from the outside world impinging on a sensory receptor or originating in an internal instinctual drive, strives toward discharge through the motor portion of the reflex arc and until such discharge takes place, produces tension. As soon as motor discharge has occurred the tension ceases. If motor discharge does not occur, the impulse passes through the central nervous system and it produces thoughts, which may be conscious or unconscious. These are in themselves a method of reducing tension but not as effective a method as motor discharge.

Freud [4] has pointed out that dreams occur because during sleep the access to motility is hindered and instinctual stimuli, combined with whatever sensory stimuli may be present, tend to flow away from the motor apparatus toward the perceptive apparatus and hence produce what appear to be perceptions from the external world. These perceptions are under the control of the primary processes. The less possibility there is for the motor discharge of tension, the greater will be the control by the primary processes. In the young baby, whose motor system still is very defective even at the end of the first year although his sensory nervous system has been well developed even at birth, the primary processes are in complete control. The greater the opportunity the baby has to learn to use his motor system, and the quicker he develops some voluntary control of his motility, the shorter will be the period of the ascendancy of the primary processes.

Hendrick [5] states that the aim of the instinct to master is an alteration of the external situation. This instinct is manifested by manipulation, locomotion, comprehension, and reasoning, which are ways of adjusting the environment to the self. The simplest manifestations are the use of the sense organs, the use of the peripheral muscular apparatus, and the rational association of ideas. He quotes McGraw, who showed that the development of each of a series of useful motor abilities is as follows: first there is a reflex pattern shown by stereotypy, next a period of inhibition of this reflex, then the reappearance of the pattern as a cortically controlled function, and lastly modification of this function by use and practice. The need to practice partial function until proficient is the first objective evidence of the instinct to master.

Hoffer [6] says that the knowledge of the self results from our visual,

[4] Sigmund Freud, *The Interpretation of Dreams,* New York, The Macmillan Co., 1913.

[5] Ives Hendrick, "Instincts and the Ego during Infancy," *Psychoanalytic Quarterly,* 11, 1942.

[6] Willie Hoffer, "The Development of the Body Ego," *The Psychoanalytic Study of the Child,* Vol. V, New York, International Universities Press, 1950.

auditory, and olfactory interest in the world. The inner perception of the external world is developed through the pleasure-pain series. An experience of pleasure and of the self emerges when external stimulation or increased inner demands are relieved, so that a restoration of the previous condition results. This relief is in two stages. First, an attempt is made to relieve the increased tension by a negative hallucination, which is an inner psychical act. A negative hallucination is a temporary abolition of internal or external stimuli and is not due to the abolition of the mental representation of stimuli which occurs in repression. It is one of the earliest and most primitive of mental processes. In later life it is related to the pathological state of derealization. Second, there is the physical act of discharge, which is the organism's attempt to rid itself of surplus stimulation or inner demands. Perceptions through vision and through touching—particularly the latter, which elicits two sensations of the same kind at the same time if the child touches part of his own body—lead to the distinction between the self and the nonself and are the processes which produce the spread of the feeling of the self over the infant's body.

Up to ten weeks there is motor excitation, i.e., searching for the breast, and attempts to relieve the excitation by mouth activities, which are due to hunger and are influenced by former feeding experiences. At sixteen weeks there is genuine perception with activity. The infant sees his hand, focuses on it, and with his eyes follows the hand movements to his mouth. He perceives also the motor contact of his hands with objects which are within his reach. At this age memory begins to function, and the child, by the meticulous choice of what he wishes to introduce into his mouth, begins to show the function of reality testing. The administration of the breast or bottle in demand feeding as a substitute for fingersucking may stimulate the formation of object relationships at the expense of body-ego formation. When the mouth ego is established, satiation will be followed by two needs, for sucking and for sleep. Here the second follows the first.

Two sensations, oral and tactile, are aroused simultaneously through fingersucking. As a result, the hand becomes closely allied to the mouth for the purpose of relieving tension. After the twelfth week it is put into the mouth intentionally to relieve oral tension. This is the first achievement of the primitive ego.

Gesell[7] says that the hand-to-mouth response is anticipated in utero because the fetus usually assumes a position in which the hand is close to the mouth. Until the second quarter of the first year, sucking depends entirely on touch. Later, it is initiated by the sight of the breast and bottle. At the twelfth week the infant's hand helps in the feeding process. From this time on the hand-to-mouth responses are rhythmic and intensive but the duration is more important than the intensity. The sixteen-week-old baby plays with his fingers, touching himself and being touched simultaneously. Sometimes there is competition between feeding-sucking and finger-sucking. If the child introduces its fingers at the time the nipple is in the mouth it may be because he did not experience the expected or accustomed oral stimulation in the feeding act itself. At first the hands are used with the mouth to discharge tension. Later, under the influence of eyes, they are transformed into tools to control the external world.

Hoffer says that in the oral-sadistic phase, i.e., in the second part of the first year, the self-destructive drives are directed outside the body or are handled within the body by an increase in motor activity. The pain barrier permanently protects the infant from turning the destructive instinct against the self. The increase of primary narcissism does the same thing. The infant does not hurt himself because he likes himself so much. The result therefore is more libidinization of the body. If these steps toward deflection of self-destruction fail, then self-biting, refusal of food, and starvation occur.

Restrictions of the development of the use of motility, imposed by the parents, by motor disabilities, or by prolonged illnesses, will hinder the development of the supremacy of the secondary processes. Of course this applies particularly to such restrictions occurring in the first years of life. All teachers know that learning is aided by the use of several parts of the body at one time. The ability to remember is increased if the child says, writes, and looks at the material to be memorized. However, teachers do not so well realize that topics which concern the body ego are learned more easily than those that

[7] Arnold Gesell, *The First Five Years of Life,* New York, Harper and Brothers, 1940.

do not concern it. A teacher [8] told me that she found that her class of retarded children learned to read better if the reading material concerned parts of the body. Kubie [9] points out the close connection between language and the ego representations of parts of the body. He says that no new reflex can be conditioned in satiated animals—all processes of learning depend upon the existence of a state of craving. The child's world begins with his body, and the force which instigates the child to expand knowledge is the presence of bodily desires. Each new fact of experience enters into the psychic life by relating itself to those already present. Therefore each new fact perceived by the child, and all new knowledge, must have special points of reference to bodily things. As each new aspect of the outside world is perceived, it comes to have a special relation to parts of the body.

Waelder [10] believes that the ability to learn mathematics is based on the ability to deal with abstractions. Women are more interested than men in the total use of the body for love. Therefore, they do not have as much incentive for dealing with abstractions as men do. Mathematical abstractions have to do with narcissism—the playing with and counting of the fingers and toes. The libidinal trend is away from object relations and toward narcissistic relations. Sublimation of this narcissism (if this is a sublimation) onto abstract numbers allows one to use mathematics. The use of mathematics does not result from the drive to look, as in reading, but is a mental movement in three dimensions.

Motor actions which result in discharge of tension are perceived in the perceptual apparatus before the action takes place. If the tension from an ungratified instinctual desire can be relieved by the movement of my hand, I first perceive the movement of my hand in my perceptual apparatus, and this perception is followed by the actual hand movement. (I may be aware of this perception consciously, but more commonly the perception occurs only in my unconscious.) It has usually been concluded that the perception of

[8] Personal communication by Mrs. Eli Marcovitz.

[9] Lawrence Kubie, "Bodily Symbolization and the Development of Language," *Psychoanalytic Quarterly*, 3, 1934.

[10] Personal communication by Dr. Robert Waelder.

the movement pattern is a learned process. Certain random or reflex movements result accidentally in the discharge of tension, and as a result the pattern of these random movements becomes perceived the next time that discharge of tension is necessary. Following this perception of the movement pattern the action takes place. However, recent observation of babies [11] may indicate that the perception of the movement pattern is present first, that the pattern itself is not the result of a learned process but is inherited, and that the infant comes to perceive the pattern before the actual movement has ever been accomplished. Whichever is the fact, if motor activity is restricted too much or for too long, the tendency to regression is increased and learning ability is decreased. Educators, however, should remember that the human being has a constant tendency to regression, particularly during the years of childhood.

During the prelatent period the ability to learn is increased by those measures that help the establishment of the supremacy of the secondary processes. The education of the child during this period will be directed, ideally, to a very gradual lessening of opportunities for the immediate discharge of instinctual tension and for the gratification of the child's needs. During the latency period the teacher has to understand that the child's ability to learn is helped by a certain amount of opportunity for the free motor discharge of instinctual tension and for the gratification of the child's desires. It is well known that a child tends to become restless when the opportunity for the discharge of instinctual tension in free play is restricted.

[11] Gerald H. J. Pearson, "A Clinical Note on Ego Development," *Bulletin of the Philadelphia Association for Psychoanalysis*, 2, 1952.

CHAPTER V

Factors That Hinder the Organization of the Ego

THE ORGANIZATION of the ego is hindered by a number of factors. It has been well established by psychoanalytic researches that the constant presence of too much unsatisfied instinctual tension produces such strong feelings of unpleasure that the child seeks only for opportunities for discharge and is unable to develop any other methods by which the gratification of the instinct can be directed and controlled. A baby who suffers from constant starvation does not pay much attention to his surroundings, and does not learn to use his hands and eyes and ears. He does not develop at the same rate and to the same degree as a child who is well fed. He is overwhelmed by his sufferings and therefore beginnings of organization in the ego will be slight or nonexistent. Balint [1] states that the early state of the ego shows something like object love which is revealed in clinging needs and extreme rage if interrupted, and he gives clinical and theoretical material to prove that unless the newborn infant is able to have object love, he will die. Peto [2] states that poor object relations due to the mother's behavior even in the first few days cause feeding problems which cease when the mother's problem is reduced. Spitz [3] studied the clinical pictures of six important infantile illnesses—marasmus, anaclitic depression, extreme motor restlessness, copro-

[1] Michael Balint, "Early Developmental States of the Ego: Primary Object Love," *International Journal of Psychoanalysis,* 30, 1949.

[2] Endre Peto, "Infant and Mother," *International Journal of Psychoanalysis,* 30, 1949.

[3] René A. Spitz, "Psychiatric Therapy in Infancy," *American Journal of Orthopsychiatry,* 20, 1950.

phagia, eczema, and three-months colic. In marasmus there is an arrest of psychic development, with regression leading to mental impairment and death. In anaclitic depression there is depression with weeping, unappeasable screaming at the approach of strangers, withdrawal, eating disturbances, sleep disturbances, and developmental arrest. In motor restlessness the main activity is rocking in a knee-chest position. In coprophagia the children show rejection of all toys except their own feces, and their general reactions are disturbed to the point of paranoid suspiciousness. In eczema there is reflex irritability which is present at birth, conspicuous retardation in capacity for negative responses in the field of social-perceptive discrimination, and retardation in the field of imitation and learning. This indicates a severe disturbance in the formation of object relationships on the basis of identification. Spitz found that these conditions were caused by emotional starvation from neglect. The effect depended on the length of time the child was neglected, on the time when the neglect occurred, on the degree to which age-adequate stimulation was withheld, and on the amount of maternal hostility to the infant. He states that no infant should be deprived of a love object for more than three months in the second half of the first year. There should be no deprivation of toys. (Up to six months, the preferred toys are rattles; after six months, hollow blocks.) There is a need for locomotion and for auditory and visual stimuli.

Although Hoffer [4] says that the ego as a contour is inherited and its differentiation from the id is phylogenetically outlined, he points out that there are three sources of traumata which interfere with ego development. First, if there is an increase of excitation which is so great that the negative hallucination used to deal with it will work only for a short time, there will be a loss of the oral sucking activity and of appetite. This means that there will be a withdrawal of cathexis which will be followed by a turning inward of the oral aggression and by attempts at ego control through biting the fingers with the gums; failure of these attempts will lead to cessation of self-control, expressed in crying accompanied by convulsive activity. Second, a trauma may result if there is an inadequacy of the self. And third, it

[4] Willie Hoffer, "Mouth, Hand and Ego Integration," *The Psychoanalytic Study of the Child*, Vols. III–IV, New York, International Universities Press, 1949.

may occur if there is a failure of the mother, i.e., a failure of the non-self. I believe there is a fourth source of trauma—restrictions on the use of the motor apparatus, whether these restrictions are due to prolonged and severe illnesses, to the circumstances of housing, or to parental prohibitions.

In older children the clinical pictures of lack of ego organization are well illustrated by the work of Kanner,[5] Redl,[6] and Beres and Obers.[7] Kanner in his discussion of early infantile autism describes the results of the lack of ego organization very well. He states that these children show a pensive physiognomy and either are mute or have a kind of language which does not communicate. They retain their intelligence. They have a skillful relation to objects but show a profound withdrawal from contact with people. They have an obsessive desire for the preservation of sameness—the status quo must be maintained at all costs, as if they desire to live in a static world. Sometimes the child will modify existing conditions, but if anyone else does so the child becomes very unhappy and furious. The autistic child differs from the obsessional in that he forces other persons to be more obsessive than himself. He becomes greatly disturbed at the sight of anything broken or incomplete. This applies to people as well as objects and there is no sympathy or solicitude for a person with a scar, for instance. For him the whole must be preserved in its entirety. Memory of previous situations is phenomenal. Kanner believes that a repetition compulsion, not an obsessive compulsion, is the cause of the behavior of these children and that its dominance is the result of early traumata and the inability of the ego to develop newer methods of synthesis. The dominance of the repetition compulsion results in difficulties in learning.

Redl believes that a lack of organization in the ego shows itself by an inability to cope with frustration and with instinctual uprushes. This results in impulsiveness. Such children may remain reasonable

[5] Leo Kanner, "Conception of Wholes and Parts in Early Infantile Autism," *American Journal of Psychiatry,* 108, 1951.

[6] Fritz Redl, "Concept of Ego Disturbances and Ego Support," *American Journal of Orthopsychiatry,* 21, 1951.

[7] David Beres and Samuel J. Obers, "Effects of Extreme Deprivation in Infancy on Psychic Structure in Adolescence," *The Psychoanalytic Study of the Child,* Vol. V, New York, International Universities Press, 1950.

under the impact of an unexpected change because there is an apperception of the inherent structure of situations and things and because there is a low level of ego content and a high melting point in the group. If the regime is severe they show no hostile impulses, but if the regime is permissive they have no control over themselves and recklessness or anxiety develops.

Beres and Obers define three character types seen in adolescents which are the result of extreme deprivation in infancy. The first of these is the infantile character. In this type the ego and the superego develop inadequately and function on infantile and archaic levels without intrapsychic conflict. Such adolescents adhere to the pleasure principle rather than the reality principle, are unable to tolerate frustration, and demand immediate instinctual gratification. There is no evidence of a feeling of guilt, but anxiety appears in the presence of an objective danger. Their ability to sublimate is limited, and their school work is poor. The second type is the neurotic character. Such persons show evidence of severe conflict in their behavior although they may be unaware that they have a conflict. Finally, there is the schizoid personality. The authors state that extreme deprivation in infancy causes intellectual retardation.

Severe physiological or emotional deprivations in early infancy result in an inability to make combinations and to form an organized ego. The more severe these deprivations are, the greater are the resulting defects in the development of the ego. These defects result in a failure of the secondary processes to achieve supremacy over the primary processes and therefore in an inability to learn.

THE STRUGGLE BETWEEN THE PRIMARY AND SECONDARY PROCESSES IN CHILDHOOD

Children of all ages from time to time show the presence of the primary processes. As a matter of fact philological studies indicate that language itself has developed through a stage where the primary processes still have great ascendancy. Freud [8] in reviewing a paper by the philologist Karl Abel points out that the strange tendency of the

[8] Sigmund Freud, "The Antithetical Sense of Primal Words," *Collected Papers,* Vol. IV, London, Hogarth Press and the Institute of Psycho-Analysis, 1934.

dream work to disregard negation and to express contradictions by identical means of representation tallies with Abel's examples of a peculiarity in the oldest languages known to us. In these languages there is no word *no,* and many words, such as the Latin *sacer,* which means both *holy* and *accursed,* have exactly opposite meanings, not differentiated by spelling or sound. Other words are combinations, for instance, *old-young* or *far-near,* and the sense of these is determined either by an added part of the word or by explanatory accompanying pictures. In other cases the word may be sounded forward or backward although the meaning remains the same. This kind of behavior with words, which apparently was general among prehistoric and early historic peoples, is found very frequently in children long after they have learned to talk well. It is particularly characteristic of the child in the early latency period and in early adolescence. As a form of humor, called by adults "silliness," children will make plays on words by reversing them, *god* and *dog,* for instance, and by using the same word to express opposite meanings. Particularly between the ages of six and eight,[9] nonsense rhymes have a great appeal. Such rhymes, usually self-composed, are chanted over and over singly or by groups. Children at this age delight in listening to nonsense rhymes, such as those composed by Edward Lear. Often important information is turned into nonsense for this purpose. Children at this age also normally show, in their playful speech, condensations such as appear in dreams. For example, one intelligent boy of six jokingly said, "I am going to eat the radiator." Any teacher of a class of early adolescents realizes he has to be very careful what words he uses because his pupils delight in snickering at the least double meaning they can perceive.

Children generally, but particularly at the times I have mentioned, are in the throes of a conflict to preserve the organization of their ego against the driving forces of the instincts. At frequent intervals they have to relieve the tension generated by this conflict. The instinct is allowed to find discharge in a playful manner, and at this time all learned material suddenly becomes subject to the primary processes. The child talks "nonsense" or acts in a "silly" fashion.

[9] Arnold Gesell and Frances L. Ilg, *The Child from Five to Ten,* New York, Harper and Brothers, 1946.

This relief of tension through instinct discharge by the use of the primary processes is necessary for the child. If it occurs at the proper time and place, it may be permitted, though not encouraged, by the adult educator. The educator should see that it is not used at improper times, such as during classroom activity; if an individual child or several children persist in using it in such situations there is need to study the child and the situation to discover if too much pressure has been placed on the functions of the organized ego and too little opportunity supplied for the adequate and realistic gratification of instinct.

It seems probable that the chanting of words denoting excretory activities is a step between the supremacy of the primal processes for the sheer discharge of instinct and of the secondary processes of the organized ego and is really an attempt to combine both processes.

The development of the use of metaphors and similes in speech also is an example of the gradual overcoming of the supremacy of the primary processes and their replacement by the secondary processes of the organized ego. At three or four if the child wishes to demonstrate his courage and strength, he plays he *is* a lion. He combines his ideas about courage and strength with his ideas about a lion, and then condenses his combined ideas about the lion with his image of himself. He becomes a lion, and so not only demonstrates his courage and strength (both of which attributes he realizes he woefully lacks in reality) but gives expression in play to his destructive, devouring, and murderous impulses. There is no question that he *becomes* the lion, for if his lionlike play becomes too marked he will suddenly become frightened and will stop the play instantly. Here a definite condensation has taken place between his ideas of certain traits, his knowledge of a lion, and his internal perception of himself.

As he gets older, say six or seven, he is more inclined to state under similar circumstances, "I am a lion," but he does not behave as if he were one. He is using a metaphor. Metaphor is defined as a figure of speech in which the name, action, or descriptive term characteristic of one object is applied to another to suggest a likeness between them. In general the displacement is from the physical to the psychical. He does not believe he is a lion, as he formerly did, but he makes the condensation through his speech.

Later on instead of saying he is a lion he will say that he is *as* brave *as* a lion. Here the employment of the simile, a figure of speech using the conjunctions *like, as,* or *so,* shows that condensation has been replaced by a judgment and comparison. The primary process of condensation has come under the supremacy of the secondary processes of the organized ego.

In poetry the primary processes of condensation and displacement still remain in the ascendancy, and metaphors are much more commonly used than similes. In fact, in the writings of some modern poets it would appear that the primary processes are completely in the ascendant, for their writings do not make "sense" to the understanding of the ordinary organized ego.

Ella Freeman Sharpe [10] has written an important study of metaphor. She states that metaphor can enter into language or into the arts only when the bodily orifices become controlled. Then only can the angers, pleasures, and desires of the infantile life find metaphorical expression and the material express itself in terms of the immaterial. The child while he acquires control over the anal and the urethral sphincter is acquiring speech. After control has been achieved, he no longer can discharge feeling tension physically, but he can discharge it through speech, and this activity is substituted for the physical activity of other body openings, whose use is now restricted. Words themselves become substitutes for bodily substances.

Sharpe states that words are derived from two sources. Some arise as imitation of natural sounds—onomatopoeia. This is sense perception without thought, and the words so formed become the expression of feeling without thought. The others arise from the roots of speech, the organized crystallized sounds, about five hundred in number, which emerged in primitive civilizations and include all essential names needed for expressing relationships involving man and man, man and the environment, and man's self-preservative and procreational powers. These roots are the expression of ideas without feelings, and from them ideational language evolved. Affective language is a direct expression of feeling. In infancy the psychical discharge of feeling is accompanied by a bodily one. Later the physical discharge is replaced by a metaphor. For example, the patient who

[10] Ella Freeman Sharpe, "Psychophysical Problems Revealed in Language—An Examination of Metaphor," *International Journal of Psychoanalysis,* 21, 1940.

says, "I am all vaporing about my lamentable condition," would have expressed this feeling in infancy by a long flow of urine, by the passing of flatus, or by bleating. The patient who says, "I am bleating about my lamentable condition. I have wandered off the point and cannot find it again," would in infancy have cried because he had lost the nipple and could not find it to suck on. Sharpe notes that the metaphors in cases of depression depict a child lying wet, cold, and helpless in bed. She believes many metaphors originate in the physical experiences of early life.

Psychoanalytic research has proved that the development of language results from the ability of the child to learn to control his excretory organs. Lipin [11] mentions that the day a small boy mastered the technic of urinating in a standing position he suddenly burst forth with many new words and phrases, adding notably to a vocabulary that had been limited to relatively few, simple, disconnected words.

Psychoanalytic research also has shown that words themselves represent the products of excretion, as Spring [12] has illustrated well.

In this chapter I often have referred to the struggle of the primary processes to retain their original supremacy. Neither the primary nor the secondary processes have any energy in themselves. They are simply methods of using energy. Actually, the primary processes and the secondary processes are not struggling for supremacy. It is the instinctual energy that is striving for discharge. Up to a certain point this striving could be accomplished more readily through the methods of the primary processes, which facilitate discharge only, than through the methods of the secondary processes, which lead to purposeful action in the environment. The instinctual strivings desire no knowledge of the external world but desire only discharge, and the process of combination is possible only because the perceptions from the external world may furnish an avenue for the discharge of instinctual energy.

[11] Theodore Lipin, "A Note on the Learning of Voluntary Urinary Control," *Bulletin of the Philadelphia Association for Psychoanalysis,* 2, 1952.

[12] William Spring, "Words and Masses," *Psychoanalytic Quarterly,* 4, 1935.

CHAPTER VI

Development of the Relation with the External World I: The Faculty of Attention

UNDISCHARGED instinct produces a painful psychical tension and shortly after the process of combination has developed there ensues a tendency on the part of the immature ego to repudiate this tension as part of itself and to project it onto the external world. Soon the ego comes to use the mechanism of projection as a way of dealing with impulses, desires, and feelings which are unpleasant to it for some reason. Projection is a useful mechanism because it invests external objects with interest and so makes them important, but when it is used to deny that the person can have impulses, feelings, and desires which are unacceptable to the ego, it causes a difficulty in the perception of what is internal and what is external.

Weiss [1] points out that when one induces an obsessional neurotic to give up his isolations and his magical acts of undoing, one exposes him to the danger of not being able to distinguish psychic reality. His secondary defenses are against hallucinations and delusions which have a frightening content. He suffers from an intermixing of the internal and the external worlds. In agoraphobia, parts of the mind are represented by external localities. Feelings about the weather and the time of year are often projected mental states. There may be projection of the subject's impulses, attitudes, and character

[1] Edoardo Weiss, "Psychic Defense and the Technic of Its Analysis," *International Journal of Psychoanalysis,* 23, 1942.

traits onto other people: women in men's dreams or men in women's dreams may represent projected parts of the dreamer's own personality. This phenomenon of projection, an outgrowth of the process of combination, is also a definite component in the learning process and is important in the learning of academic subjects.

Four steps are necessary for learning. First, there has to be the projection of instinctual libidinal impulses onto the subject matter to be learned. These invest the subject matter with interest and arouse the individual's desire to make them part of himself. Only a small part of this interest results from the way in which the teacher presents the subject matter—although this is very important. The major part of the interest is determined by whether the subject matter presents a possible way for the discharge of instinctual energy for the particular individual at that particular time. Second, the ego has to be in agreement with the projected libidinal impulses. It has to be able to come to terms with them; otherwise it will defend itself against the projected instinctual impulses and refuse to be interested in making the subject matter part of itself. The third step will be the introjection of the matter to be learned along with the projected instinctual impulses. In this way the matter to be learned becomes part of the psychic reality of the individual. Fourth, there has to be a secondary differentiation of the projected instinctual impulses from the matter that has been learned, so that the latter becomes an acquisition and is differentiated from the impulses, which themselves may have components which are frightening to the ego.

If the child is exposed to a severe traumatic condition—if the learning of the subject matter is associated with pain or danger—the functions of learning may be blocked by a concentration of all of the child's mental energy on one task, the mastery of overwhelming excitation. The excitation already at hand must be mastered before new stimuli can be accepted, and the ability to combine is blocked because the blocking of the perceptive and apperceptive avenues prevents the influx of further painful excitation. This is seen clearly from the study of traumatic neuroses. In these conditions there is a regression in the ego because its more organized functions can no longer master the overwhelming impact of the trauma. This results in a general loss of differentiation of the specific qualities of the higher ego functions, and the person has to use more primitive and unspecific measures for the mastery of the trauma. These regressions serve other purposes. Such patients regress to childhood reactions because as children they were helped by omnipotent adults. Also they regress to a passive-receptive oral type of mastery and demonstrate an attitude of helplessness and passive dependence after their failure to succeed actively. This is more common in persons who were always inclined to this type of mastery.

In learning, therefore, not only is it necessary that the individual be able to use the mechanism of combination and to invest the subject matter with interest but there must be no frightening or painful experiences occurring at the same time. The impulses from the external world and from the sensations within the body alter the equilibrium of the tensions in the id and make the id sensitive to the external world as well as to its own tensions. The sensitivity of the id to something outside itself is the first phase in the development of the ego—the medium between the tensions of the id and the environment. From this time forward, the perceptions of the external world become more and more important to the individual, as they have to be in order to satisfy the need for self-preservation. In fact, in the ordinary person the demands of the external world assume an unjustifiable importance. Psychoanalytic research has demonstrated that too much importance has been given to the external world in the general conscious thinking of mankind, and too little to the demands of the id itself. This is true of the ordinary "well-adjusted" person, but more true of the neurotic, whose basic difficulty frequently, though not always, has been the excessive demands made on him by his childhood environment and the relative lack of importance which his environment has given his instinctual needs. The fear of external retaliation by castration and loss of love, the use of the defense mechanism of projection (by which id demands are viewed by the neurotic as external to himself), of the defense mechanism of introjection (by which he attempts to make some object in the environment part of himself), of the defense mechanism of repression (whereby he makes the external world all-important and his own internal needs of no importance) all indicate that the process of development tends to emphasize the importance of the perceptual system and hence of the learning process. This is a necessity because the sexual impulses can receive complete biological gratification only by the reproduction of the species—a process that can be accomplished only by finding a sexual object in the external world. Therefore to the development of the ego through the increased sensitivity of the id to the impact of the external world is added the emerging from the id of a real desire to seek a *modus operandi* for the real gratification of the sexual instinct instead of simply a discharge of tension.

From these two sources arises the desire to direct the attention to the external world and hence the desire to learn. Therefore anything that interferes with the need to perceive the external world will interfere with the learning process.

I am saying simply that the old adage, Experience is the best teacher, is true. Unfortunately this saying is usually invoked to point out that an unpleasant experience, like that of Benjamin Franklin and his whistle, teaches the individual not to repeat it, and it is forgotten that the saying applies more truly to learning through pleasant experiences, for once the individual has had a pleasant experience he desires to repeat it. It is interesting how many of the homely maxims and sayings of our daily speech place the emphasis on prohibitions. This is another strong indication that the basic concepts in education are opposed to the direct, and often to the indirect, gratification of the instinctual drives. This is desirable because the aim of education is to increase the degree of civilization and culture, a state diametrically opposed to the free gratification of instinct.

From time to time it may be important for the individual to learn not to do something, because it is dangerous or nonuseful, but in each instance in which he learns not to do something, his ability to penetrate into the environment is hampered and his ability to learn is limited. Conversely, the more pleasant his experiences, the more he will want to penetrate into the external world and the more need he will have to perceive it. As the small child begins to perceive the external world he finds much in it that is unpleasant and even painful. As he begins to perceive his own feelings, which indicate his instinctual desires, he finds that they too may be unpleasant in themselves, either because of his relative helplessness to gratify them or because of the unwillingness of the external world to do so. Basically the human being desires only pleasure or the avoidance of pain or discomfort. This adherence to the pleasure-pain principle is more apparent in the young prelatent child than it is in the child of the latency period, the adolescent, or the adult, for during these other periods the supremacy of the pleasure-pain principle becomes more and more subordinated to that of the reality principle. (I will discuss the importance to education of these two principles in a separate chapter later.) The young child desires not to undergo any unpleasant or painful inner or outer experience and to avoid repeating such an experience if it does occur. As I mentioned before, he finds that his connection with stark reality is often unpleasant. Either it furnishes him with no pleasant gratification or it is directly painful. This knowledge comes to him through his daily experiences and is recognized as soon as he is able to distinguish even slightly between himself and the rest of the world, i.e., as soon as he has developed a thin layer of ego. He can avoid the unpleasant outer world by shutting his avenues of sensory intake against it. The young baby who sees something that arouses unpleasant feelings in him promptly shuts his eyes or turns his head away. If he touches something that hurts him he pulls his hand away. The unpleasant experience leaves a trace in his memory, and the next time he is in a situation that he remembers as painful he goes through the motions of avoiding the perception of it. He remembers also the experiences which are pleasant and strives, as well as he can, to repeat them.

However, unpleasant feelings arise also from another source. He has inner needs which, if unsatisfied, give him unpleasant feelings. He tries to avoid the perception of these unpleasant feelings, but he cannot shut them out as he can the perception of unpleasant external experiences. In order to reduce the unpleasant feelings he tried to remember some former set of circumstances when these unpleasant feelings were removed by the gratification of his needs. If he is uncomfortable because of hunger he begins to remember a former time when the disagreeable feeling of hunger disappeared because he was fed. He then tries to relive that experience by putting his finger in his mouth and sucking it or simply by making sucking motions with his mouth. As Freud says, he substitutes hallucinatory wish fulfillment for the real gratification. In other words, he substitutes a perception of a pleasant memory or combination of pleasant memories for the perception of the unpleasant feeling, hoping by doing so to reduce his discomfort. This fantasy therefore interferes with his need to perceive the temporarily unpleasant external and internal world. If the fantasy actually reduces his feeling of discomfort, even though the reduction may be only temporary, during this temporary period his learning ability is reduced. During the process of development the more the external world consists of pleasurable situations and of experiences through which the child's inner needs are gratified, the more his need to perceive the external world and so to learn is increased. The more the external world consists of unpleasant and painful situations or of experiences that are perceived as painful because they do not gratify the child's inner needs, the more his need to perceive the external world and therefore his ability to learn are decreased and the more he will console himself with the hallucinatory wish gratification of fantasy. (I hope no reader ceases to read this book at this point. He then may go away with the idea that only if the child is shielded from all unpleasant external situations and has his every desire gratified immediately will he develop into a mature adult. This is one of the major misconceptions of the findings of psychoanalytic research, and already the attempts to apply this misconception to the rearing of children have wrought incalculable harm to the development of many children. Throughout the whole of this book I will from time to time emphasize the importance for the educator of not misapplying the fact that the ability to learn develops more effectively when it is helped by pleasurably toned experiences.)

The small child because of his weakness, his incapacities (particularly his motor incapabilities), and the absence or incomplete development of skills finds the external world full of unpleasant and even painful experiences. He therefore frequently resorts to fantasy. As he becomes more capable the need for recourse to fantasy decreases, although all human beings throughout life fall back from time to time on the gratification of fantasies, in the form either of conscious daydreams or of true unconscious fantasies.

During the time the fantasy predominates, the individual's relation to reality is altered and his need to perceive and deal with the real world is reduced. This disturbed relation to reality resulting from the use of fantasy is a universal human phenomenon, occurring everywhere to a greater or less degree. Many people have a firm belief in immortality and the superiority of the hereafter over this present life. Yet in spite of this belief, when they become ill they call a doctor and insist strongly that he help them get well. Certain people have a fanatical belief that the present social and economic philosophies practiced in the Soviet Union are greatly superior to those of the rest of the world, but they do not attempt or even dream of going to live in the Soviet Union.[2] Both of these groups base their beliefs on their fantasies more than they do on reality; therefore their relation to reality is disturbed. This type of disturbance of the relation to reality must be distinguished from the disorders of the reality-testing function of the ego which occur in the psychoses and the neuroses. In these conditions there are true disorders of the ego function of reality testing. In the substitution of fantasy for an unpleasant reality there is no disorder of this function. In fact, in the examples I have cited the function of reality testing operates very efficiently. There is simply a disturbance of the relation of the ego to reality and a tendency to depend more on the fantasy than on reality.

It is necessary therefore to encourage the perceptive intake of the child by making the stimuli presented to him pleasurable and interesting. At best, stimuli from the external world are not as pleasurable as those that arise from fantasies, and therefore there is a constant tendency to look inward rather than outward. This tendency operates to hinder the establishment of the supremacy of the secondary processes of the organized ego and has to be combated vigorously by the educator, who must accentuate the pleasure value of the external world.

The same tendency is constantly being aided by the tensions produced by unsatisfied instinctual needs and wishes. These interfere at all times with the mechanism of combination even though they may aid it through the mechanism of projection, provided a certain degree of gratification results. When there is too much tension be-

[2] I am indebted to Dr. Robert Waelder for these illustrations.

cause there is too little of the necessary gratification of the instinctual desires, or when the ego finds itself unable to deal with the instinctual impulses, it may employ the defense mechanism of regression instead of taking recourse to fantasy. This is set in action by instincts which, blocked from direct satisfaction, seek a substitute. The person fixed on the anal level advances with reluctance to the phallic phase and will always be prepared to relinquish the phallic phase if there is the slightest disappointment or threat. If there is no strong fixation at a particular level, intense and sudden disappointments and dangers will produce regression. There are three types of regression. First, there may be regression from the later stages of psychosexual development to more infantile ones; second, there may be regression from object relationships to primary narcissism. If this deep type of regression occurs, it is a resumption of the very oldest type of defense, i.e., the blocking of the ego; third, there may be regression in the ego from the supremacy of the secondary processes to that of the primary processes. In regression the ego is very passive. The ego that is apt to resort to regression is strong in one respect, weak in another. Its critical function and the need for preparatory thinking must have developed especially early in the phase when thinking functions were magically oriented. The need for the defensive ego to start functioning early causes it to continue to use archaic and immature methods. The ego must have been strong enough to enforce its protests against instincts at an early date but remained too weak to fight out this conflict by means of more mature mechanisms. In contrast, people inclined to introverted daydreaming who later develop conversion symptoms show a relative inhibition of intellectual functions. Weiss quotes Fenichel as saying that behind all the active types of mastery of external and internal stimuli there remains a readiness to fall back to passive-receptive types of mastery. This passive-receptive type of mastery is inherent in education which is not a leading out but a putting in. A child cannot concentrate too long on the passive-receptive learning of skills. After a brief period he becomes active in order to overcome the tendency to regression. Learning of skills, therefore, becomes a passive-receptive impulse and so is united with oral, anal, and phallic passive-receptive tendencies. If there has been, or is, anxiety about these, learning becomes anxiety-ridden and often impossible.

Libidinal regressions and regressions in object relationships usually occur without any regression in the developmental structure of the ego, so that the secondary processes of the organized ego maintain their supremacy to some extent. In a small number of cases there is added to the libidinal regression a regression from the secondary processes to the primary processes. In this the organization of the ego suffers a breakdown and the primary processes become ascendant. When this happens the ability to associate and assimilate learned material ceases because the material cannot be organized logically. This occurs only when there is a very severe pathological condition. In a relatively few instances the development of the organization of the ego seems to have taken place only partially and its supremacy is maintained only by extreme effort. Either there is no supremacy and the primary processes appear alternately with logical thinking or a very slight difficulty causes the primary processes to be in the ascendancy for shorter or longer periods. Children with such "weak" egos learn only very slowly or are incapable of learning. Such conditions can be seen clinically in the psychoses of early childhood.

If the very young child is exposed constantly to unpleasant and painful experiences, or if he suffers from too much tension because there is lack of reasonable and suitable gratification of his instinctual desires, he will be forced to substitute fantasy for the perception of reality to an undesirably high degree and consequently his ability to learn will be hampered. Every teacher knows that if a hyperactive child in grammar school is forced to sit still for too long a time he will begin to fantasy and so will not learn. Also he knows that if he presents the subject being taught in an uninteresting (i.e., unpleasurable) way, his pupils will lapse into daydreaming and will not learn. If the child's recourse to fantasy does not succeed he may begin to use regression.

THE USE OF ATTENTION IN THE LEARNING PROCESS

The attention must be directed to the external world if that world is to be perceived and learned. I have already discussed the mechanisms by which the attention originally becomes directed to perceptions of the external world. Out of this develops an important function of the ego—to direct attention to a particular situation or stimulus in order to master it. If the ego is confronted with an external situation which it invests with great importance, the attention is directed toward it and deflected from the multitude of other external situations existing at the same time which the ego does not then invest with importance. The frontiersman fleeing from the Indians constantly noted the presence or absence of bird songs as an indication of the approach of an enemy, but paid little attention to the differences between the songs of various species of birds. The ornithologist traversing the same forests also notices the presence or absence of the songs of birds, but his attention is directed to the specific song of a particular species. In the first instance, the presence or absence of bird songs is invested with importance and the attention is directed to that. In the second, the song of a particular bird is invested with importance and the attention is directed to that.

In logical thinking the attention is directed to the next logical thought, which is invested with importance, and is deflected from the numerous nonlogical associations which are always present but which under these circumstances are not invested with importance. In the free-association technic of psychoanalysis exactly the opposite is required. All associations, no matter how apparently illogical, are invested with equal importance and the attention is directed to them.

The ego also directs its attention to the instinct representations arising from the id. At one time a particular instinct representation may be invested with importance and attention is paid to it and deflected from all others.

The deflection of attention calls into play many other psychic mechanisms of defense to assist the ego function of centering attention. The process of centering attention is usually unconscious although occasionally its presence as a conscious effort may be perceived.

In childhood, particularly during prelatency, the defensive functions of the ego are relatively weak in the presence of instinct representations and therefore the ability to center attention is not as great as in later years. The child is distractible. His attention is easily distracted from one instinct representation, from one stream of thought, from one external situation, to another. Children of the latency period, adolescents, and adults are less distractible. The degree of distractibility depends on the relative strength of the instinct presentations and the defensive functions of the ego. When instinctual drives for whatever reasons become unusually strong the individual becomes distractible. When one instinctual drive for whatever reason becomes unusually strong, the individual becomes indistractible; his attention is centered upon the particular drive. When no particular train of thought or external situation is invested with importance, the individual appears to be distractible. His attention is readily distracted from one situation to another and he seems to have no particular *interest* at that time. When a particular train of thought or external situation is invested with great importance, that is, when the person is deeply interested in it, he cannot be distracted from it. As I write this, the radio is playing and there are many pleasant sights surrounding me, but my attention is not distracted by them. Many adults and adolescents and a number of children in the latency period can work well and with interest on a particular intellectual problem while the radio plays. Their accomplishments would be no greater if it were silent. Such people are not distracted by the sound of the radio.

The usual procedure in Western culture of starting the formal education of a child at about the age of six is based on an unconscious recognition by educators that the child before this time is too preoccupied to do school work—that is, he has his attention too centered on the intrapsychic conflicts occurring in the edipus situation to be able to center it at the same time on the process of acquiring academic knowledge.

I am still not certain whether or not such phenomena as reading readiness really are the results of maturation, of myelinization of the cortical association tracts. More careful investigation may show that they result from the lessening of the child's intrapsychic conflict after the solution of the edipus conflict and the consequent beginning of the latency period.

Educators tell me that it is common for a child who has been quite successful in scholastic achievement during his grammar-school life to begin to develop difficulties in learning about the seventh grade. These difficulties continue for about a year or longer and then disappear. The increase of sexual desires at puberty reinstates the intrapsychic conflicts of the edipus period and the child's attention becomes centered on these conflicts and therefore directed away from the subjects to be learned.

Usually it is considered that the distractibility of a particular child is due to either the strength of instinct representations or to the developmental weakness of the ego's function in centering attention. This is probably a correct assumption on which to proceed, but it is possible that certain people are congenitally predisposed to distractibility. Further studies on this specific point will be required before this possibility can be eliminated. Centering of attention on the academic subjects to be learned and the inhibition of deflection of the attention to other internal or external situations is necessary for a successful learning process. In order for the attention to be centered on the subject to be learned, the impulses from the external world must arouse pleasurable feelings in the child and he must anticipate gratification for his instinctual desires. These instinctual desires affect the activity of the preconscious system and consequently the faculty of attention. Freud observed that the preconscious system can cathect an idea only when it can inhibit any pain flowing from it. Some disorders of attention therefore may come from the fact that certain trains of thought are associated closely with feared and disliked ideas, and one reason for the shortness of a child's attention span may be the presence of many fears. I believe clinical experience bears this out. Children may direct little real attention to scholastic ideas or their attention may be withdrawn from them because they have the unconscious desire to remain a baby or not to grow up. Thus scholastic learning may become entangled with unconscious wishes. Because of this entanglement the learning is never accomplished, or if it is, the learned ideas are repressed. Conscious worries also may attract the person's attention and therefore prevent his centering his attention on the subject to be learned.

Intrapsychic conflicts, whether perceived consciously as worries, feelings of guilt, shame, and embarrassment, or daydreams; or occurring in the unconscious portions of the ego, attract the attention to themselves and deflect it to a greater or less extent from all other external or intrapsychic constellations. These disturbances may be classified into several groups:

1. Engrossing conscious apprehensions of dangers to the child's security.
2. Engrossing conscious feelings of guilt, shame, and embarrassment resulting from fear of real detection and punishment or of superego disapproval.
3. Engrossing conscious feelings of horror and fear.
4. Engrossing conscious involvement with instinctual desires.
5. Focusing of attention on daydreams.

In the learning process the ego has to endeavor to keep the attention focused on the perceptions of the external world which it desires to take in. At the same time, it has to attend to the stresses within the id and to the emotional representations of these stresses in itself. A relatively small degree of id stress is necessary if the ego is to direct attention to the perceptions of the external world. An abundance of tensions in the id and of the emotional representations in the ego of the stresses in the id are always present. The satisfactory direction of the attention to the perceptions of the external world that are to be learned, presupposes a degree of strength in the organization of the ego, particularly of the function of integration. This function can be overwhelmed if the stresses of the id, of the emotions, or of the intrapsychic conflicts become too great. If the function is too weak, it may be overwhelmed by ordinary stresses and conflicts. In either case the learning process is hampered or may disappear.

It is essential for the learning process that the attention of the ego be directed to the external world by the pleasure-pain principle. The main activity of the id is the unceasing attempt to discharge tension by any means possible, without regard to the desirability of such discharge, to the effects on the individual of such blind discharge, to the possibilities of obtaining gratification of specific instincts through such discharge, or even to the real possibility of such discharge taking place. The id cannot take these possibilities into consideration because it has no organization. Its increasing attempt to discharge tension must be put under the control of some organization, and this organization must become capable of perceiving the external world, so that the discharge of tension may occur where and when it will result in real relief and real gratification, to the benefit of the individual. (When one uses the term "individual" one is no longer thinking of the unorganized id but of some degree of ego organization.) Through this organized direction of perception to the external world the individual learns, and this learning takes place most effectively when it results in the gratification of the pleasure principle. This presupposes a relation with reality not disturbed too much by recourse to fantasy. Fantasy itself occurs in the ego and therefore has some degree of organization, but it is governed more by the need of the unorganized id to discharge tension than it is by the need to gratify specific instincts. Therefore it is not only a means of satisfying the pleasure principle in a hallucinatory way but also a way of clinging to the unorganized activities of the id. Learning is an ego function and cannot take place unless the ego becomes differentiated from the id.

So far, I have tried to show that the requisites for the development of the ego and for the establishment of the supremacy of the secondary processes over the primary processes through combination, and hence, for the development of the willingness to learn, are adequacy of the gratification of the instinctual needs in early infancy, a maximum amount of pleasurable stimuli from the external world, and a maximum opportunity for the baby to use his motor system. If any one of these three situations is not present, the development of the child's ego and consequently of his ability to learn then or in later life can be impaired grievously. Similar principles apply in the education of the older child.

CHAPTER VII

Development of the Relation with the External World II: The Mechanisms of Incorporation and Identification

As SOON as the process of combination and the direction of the attention to the perception of the external world has begun, the thin layer of ego which has developed on the surface of the id starts to serve as an intermediary between the id and the external world. The synthetic function of the ego has begun. The direction of the attention to the perception of the external world confronts the individual with new problems, and the solution he develops for these problems increases the functions of his ego and teaches us a great deal about the learning process. He begins to perceive that the source of his gratifications, his comforts, and his pleasures is not himself but his mother, and he keeps his attention riveted on her in order to assure himself that his needs will be gratified. Whenever he has a feeling of discomfort he turns to her in the hope of having this feeling relieved. However, this knowledge forces on him the realization that he is unable to gratify himself and that if his mother is not within the range of his perceptive system she may have disappeared and then he will not be able to gratify his desires and relieve his discomforts. This realization marks the beginning of his object relationships, which form an increasingly important part of all his future life. He needs the object in order to obtain gratification for his instincts and he is afraid that he may lose the object and be unable to obtain gratification. As there are many times, even if their duration is short, when he suffers feelings of discomfort, such as hunger, before his mother comes to relieve him, he begins to dread these feelings of discomfort. They seem to him very powerful because he cannot do anything about them, and as they seem beyond his control, he begins to dread that he may lose his mother and so suffer inordinately. He finds that fantasy may relieve this dread and discomfort temporarily. In the fantasy he dreams that his mother is with him or he is with her all the time. The fantasy is increased by the fact that it is only because he knows he is a separate being from her that he suffers dread and discomfort. He feels that if he were his mother and he and his mother were not separate entities, he would never again be frightened or uncomfortable. In order to be his mother he would have to be like her, so he begins to imitate her. Every mother is overjoyed when the baby begins to recognize her, i.e., when he smiles because she smiles, frowns because she frowns, and so on. These responses mean not that the baby recognizes her—he has long since done so—but that he is now trying to be her by imitating her. During this period of development the main organ through which he obtains gratification, and with which he is able to approach the outer world, is his mouth. Satisfactions are found, pleasures are obtained, objects are investigated, things are felt to belong to him, by putting them in his mouth. His fantasy, therefore, by which he believes he would be able to possess his mother and always be with her and thus to relieve himself of feelings of dread and discomfort, is that of taking her completely into his mouth and swallowing her. The process that is formed during this fantasy is known technically as *incorporation*. The oral basis of the psychic process of incorporation is well recognized in common phraseology—one country "swallows" another, i.e. possesses it, a person has a "hunger" or "thirst" for knowledge, "devours" his books, "devours" another with a look, and so on —and is met with frequently in folklore and in religious rituals. The purpose of the process is to obtain possession of the external object by devouring it. The child wishes to possess his mother by devouring her. If he devours her, he and she will be one person. At the same time he believes that if he is like her, he and she will be one person. So if he incorporates her into himself he will be exactly like her and never again will he suffer dread of losing her or discomfort from his unsatisfied desires.

The process of learning is based on the process of oral incorporation in which the desire to take in has been displaced from the mouth to other avenues of sensory intake. This can be seen readily in clinical examples. In one patient the desire to eat and smoke excessively occurred at times when she was forced to inhibit her intellectual hunger. Strachey [1] says that oral desires stand out not only in the function of expressing words but also in the taking in of words by hearing and reading, both of which unconsciously mean eating.

There is a close resemblance between the process of learning and the process of digestion. In learning, sensations are taken in through the sensory organs and carried to the receptor cortex. The various receptor cortices, through the facilitated pathways of the association tracts, cause an association of sensations. These associated sensations, through facilitated pathways, form concepts which again are associated through facilitated pathways. These concepts are translated into visual and auditory ideation, which in turn is translated into words, either verbal or written, and so can be given out through speech. Liss [2] says that the purpose of the learning process is to supply an adequate system of gratification as substitutes for elementary biological functions and products. He tabulates the various processes as shown on page 134, overleaf.

Another step in the learning process therefore is the incorporation of the external world and the object to be learned into the individual through the devouring action of the special senses. This action has been displaced from its original organ—the mouth. It has been well established clinically that severe disturbances of eating in infancy result in disturbances of the capacity to incorporate and therefore, in later life, to learn. The displacement of the process of incorporation from the mouth to the other avenues of sensory intake so that learning can take place is interfered with if there is a state of un-

[1] James Strachey, "Some Unconscious Factors in Reading," *International Journal of Psychoanalysis,* 11, 1930.

[2] Edward Liss, "Emotional and Biological Factors Involved in Learning Processes," *American Journal of Orthopsychiatry,* 7, 1937.

Biological	*Psychic*	*Cultural*
intake via gastrointestinal tract	intake via 5 senses	intake via 5 senses
↓	↓	and
oral	oral anal } zones genital	symbol equivalents—arts and sciences
↓	↓	↓
metabolism	psychodynamic process	psychodynamic process
↓	↓	↓
excretion	output via 5 senses	output via 5 senses and symbol equivalents—arts and sciences
↓	↓	
anal genital	oral anal } zones genital	

satisfied hunger, for only when there is some degree of certainty that hunger will be satiated and the need to suck satisfied can the displacement take place. The need to incorporate cannot be displaced if its original function of reducing the discomfort of hunger cannot be accomplished, for it is only when experience has shown that the need to incorporate is not satisfied entirely by oral intake that the displacement to other organs occurs. It is a well-known fact that children in school do not learn so well if they are hungry. This results not only because their attention is deflected from the perceptions of the external world to the painfulness of the hungry feeling, but also because under the influence of the discomfort, a regressive displacement of the need to incorporate from the avenues of sensory intake to the mouth takes place.

It seems probable that teachers unconsciously recognize the basic relationship and the eventual antithesis between eating and learning and that this recognition causes them to forbid children to eat in the classroom. Practically, I am not sure this attitude is the most advantageous one. There are certain children with so much oral need that they can both eat and learn well at the same time. Neither learning nor eating alone can satisfy this need, and if eating is forbidden, there is so much unsatisfied desire that the regression I mentioned earlier takes place, and they do not learn so well. Also, eating has an important connection with object relationships, which form an important part of the learning process. I will discuss this shortly. There are a number of interesting clinical connections between eating and learning by reading. Fenichel [3] says that reading while eating distracts the attention from the oral-erotic excitement and that food addiction is the basis for reading addiction. A person with no capacity for waiting craves books obsessively to reassure him, as morphine in the pocket reassures the drug addict, money in the pocket reassures some other people, and food in the stomach, still others. A reading phobia is the repression of a craving for reading.

Incorporation combined with imitation is the psychic process that leads to the psychic result of identification. As the child grows a little older, the process of incorporation is extended to include all the avenues of sensory intake. He combines all of the sensations he receives from his mother through his eyes, ears, and mouth, and through his senses of taste and smell, of touch, of equilibrium, of position, and of movement, into one whole in his mind, which becomes the memory of his mother. He can now recall this memory and perceive it when he is away from her, and at these times he strives to behave as he remembers she did, until eventually he finds himself automatically behaving like his mother. He has incorporated her and as a result has identified himself with her. To describe the same process another way, he has studied her, memorized her, and so learned her, and because he has learned her she exists as part of himself. He does this in order to relieve his fears that his inner needs will be ungratified and that he then may suffer pain and discomfort. The processes of incorporation and identification and of studying and learning end in the child's acquiring of new skills to help him gratify his inner needs through the external world. The more he studies and investigates the external world and the more he

[3] Otto Fenichel, *The Psychoanalytic Theory of Neurosis,* New York, W. W. Norton & Company, 1945.

learns skills in dealing with it, the better he will be able to lead a comfortable life and the less he will suffer dreads and anxieties.

The process of learning consists of directing the attention to the external world, discovering that such direction of attention leads to the recognition of new sources of gratification and also of new fears and anxieties, being impelled to do something about these fears and anxieties, bringing into action the mechanisms of incorporation and identification, and through these acquiring new skills to obtain better means of gratifying the instincts. The process of incorporation takes place in the ego, and through the end result of identification, the ego's capacity to mediate between the external world and the id is enlarged and increased. The learning process therefore results not only in an accumulation of new perceptions (facts) but also in the growth of the organization of the ego and in an increase of the ability of the ego to use that organization (skills) to function better in the world. This is the explanation of the old saying, Knowledge is power.

The desire to incorporate expresses itself, after displacement takes place, as curiosity. Curiosity, the desire to know by seeing, hearing, touching, or any other avenue of sensory intake, is an important basis of learning. Its pleasure value is a displacement onto the sensory organs of the pleasure and utility value of the desire to take in by the mouth during the oral-intaking phase of psychosexual development.

Fenichel states that primitive perception combines an activity of the perceptual organs which is inseparably connected with motility and the incorporation of the perceived which results in changing the ego to resemble what has been perceived. The child wants to look at the object in order to feel along with it. Later on the desire to perceive is joined with sadism, and perception has a different significance. The person may look at something in order to destroy it, may look at it in order to be reassured that it has not been destroyed yet, may use looking as a substitute for destroying, or may incorporate the object through the eye, like the lover who looks at his sweetheart when about to leave her. The interests of the very young child are centered about his own body and the bodies of other people, and because of this the original desire to know—the original curiosity—always is directed to sexual facts. Freud [4] says that the period of infantile sexual investigation begins in the third year. This curiosity is not awakened spontaneously but is aroused through impressions of important experiences such as the birth of a sibling or the fear that another child may be born. This fear develops from some fantasy the child has at this time. Invariably the child's investigations end in failure, and the first attempt at intellectual independence produces feelings of a profoundly depressive nature. Also, the child's early curiosity leads him to observe factual realities which to him are revolting, such as the sight of the female genitals for the boy or the sight of the male genitals for the girl. As a result, an inhibition of curiosity will develop, its completeness depending on the degree of the child's reaction. Similarly, certain observations, such as the sight of the size of the father's body and genitals as compared with the little boy's own or the observation that the mother has breasts or pubic hair, both of which the little girl lacks, arouse very strong erotic or hostile desires in the child and because he feels unable to deal with these desires he tries instead to inhibit his curiosity. If the early sexually and physically directed curiosity receives disapproval or punishment, the child, in order to avoid the feeling of displeasure, will inhibit his curiosity so that only a small portion can be used. The extent of the inhibition will depend on the severity of the disapproval or punishment. It is such situations that cause all children to inhibit, to some extent, the pristine curiosity of early childhood by the time they reach the age at which they begin academic studies in school. Only the very occasional person retains even the greater part of his early childhood curiosity.

However, these inhibitions also divert the curiosity from its original concentration on physical and sexual phenomena only to all the phenomena of the world, both internal and external. It is sublimated. If it is well sublimated the person develops a real interest in research. Instead, in some cases the curiosity will be displaced and the child constantly will ask questions, often of a useless nature. If the curiosity is repressed there will be a blocking of all intellectual

[4] Sigmund Freud, *Leonardo da Vinci,* New York, Random House, 1947.

interest. Fenichel[5] believes that a high percentage of feeble-mindedness is the result of such repression. The ego may be induced to keep its intellect permanently in abeyance by repression of sexual curiosity for the reasons already mentioned or because of intense unconscious scoptophilia, because sexual curiosity is related to sadism and consequently stupidity may represent obedience to or rebellion against the parents, because stupidity from the inhibition of curiosity may enable the child to gain access to scenes which would be kept secret from less stupid children, or because the function of thinking has been sexualized and its inhibition has the meaning of castration or the avoidance of castration. Freud[6] says that if the curiosity is fixed by infantile impressions, the later adult will investigate with the same passionate devotion another would give to love. In such a person, where curiosity seems to be the primary interest, the sexual life will be stunted. If the period of sexual investigation comes to an end through too severe sexual repression, the early association with sexual interest may affect the investigatory impulse in three ways: the desire to investigate shares the fate of the sexuality, the curiosity becomes inhibited, and the intelligence is narrowed for life. If the intellectual development is strong enough to withstand the sexual repression, after the disappearance of the infantile sexual investigation it offers its support to the old associations in order to elude repression, and returns as compulsive reasoning. It is distorted and not free, but is forceful enough to sexualize even thought itself and to endow intellectual operations with the pleasure and anxiety of actual sexual processes. Investigation often becomes the exclusive sexual activity and the feeling of settling problems and explaining things in the mind is put in place of sexual gratification. The indeterminate character of infantile investigation remains, reasoning never ends, and the desired feeling of solution never comes. In the most rare and most perfect type of reaction, inhibition of thought and compulsive reasoning are escaped. The severe sexual repression does not place the feeling of pleasure in the unconscious, but the libido withdraws from the fate of repression by being sublimated from the

[5] Otto Fenichel, *The Psychoanalytic Theory of Neurosis,* New York, W. W. Norton & Company, 1945.

[6] Sigmund Freud, *Leonardo da Vinci,* New York, Random House, 1947.

outset into curiosity and so reinforces the investigatory impulse, which puts itself in the service of intellectual interest. It pays homage to sexual repression by avoiding all occupation with sexual themes. Freud believed Leonardo's sexual life was an example of the last type, for he had a powerful investigatory impulse but his sexual life was stunted, being restricted to ideal homosexuality.

The psychic faculty of curiosity is closely related to the psychic mechanism of incorporation. I do not know whether it arises as the result of the transformation of part of hunger and the need to ingest food into a psychic faculty or whether its development follows the course of the transformation of part of the physical need to eat into the psychic mechanism of incorporation. In either case it is an ego function, as incorporation is, and is affected by the same vicissitudes which affect the mechanism of incorporation. I have mentioned the great importance of curiosity for the learning process and how the latter is injured if the gratification of curiosity has to be renounced directly. Curiosity can also be injured indirectly, if adverse influences affect the mechanism of incorporation. Incorporation is the psychic counterpart of the infant's desires, the desire to be fed because hungry, to suck, to get pleasure from putting articles in the mouth, to possess by holding in the mouth or swallowing, and so on. If these physical needs and their oral means of gratification have been either stimulated excessively or inhibited by fear or pain, the ability to incorporate psychically will be affected adversely. Curiosity is an oral character trait and may be marked by all the voracity of the original oral appetite. Reading as a substitute for eating is an oral-sadistic incorporation of alien objects. The linking of the ideational fields of looking and eating may be due to the child's having seen a younger sibling nursed. Reading may be correlated with intense inquisitiveness—a spasmlike, voracious looking which is a substitute for gluttony. Such oral uses of the ego represent a regression of visual perceptions to incorporation aims that were once connected with perceptions in general. As the result of the process of incorporation a part of the external world is, through its stimuli, taken into the mind of the child and becomes a part of himself. He selects this part of the external world either because he likes it—it gives him pleasure—or because someone whom he loves loves him better (a pleasure which he desires) if he selects it. It may be difficult for another person to understand that he selects a particular portion of the external world to incorporate because he likes it, for that portion may be disliked by the other person. Undoubtedly just as there are specific forms of metabolic hunger—one person liking proteins, another carbohydrates, because of specific and individual physical needs—just as, to state it colloquially, One man's meat is another man's poison, so there are specific and individual forms of curiosity hunger, which we call interests. Like the specific forms of hunger in the individual which are caused by his constitutional metabolic characteristics, there are specific, probably constitutional needs of an individual which require gratification from definite groups of external stimuli and which differ from person to person. A famous musician [7] told me that he wished that tests could be devised whereby the interests (psychic hungers based on constitutional instinctual needs) of every child could be determined at an early age so that his education could be directed mainly to the development of skills which would gratify those needs. This would be a solution to some of the difficulties surrounding the teaching of music to children. The stimuli from the external world cannot be incorporated unless they are of a nature that will gratify the child's inner needs. He has to be interested in them and they have to be interesting to him. Educators for a long time have known that a child will not learn—cannot learn, would be a better way to put it—if he is not interested in the subject matter, and the more the subject matter can be made interesting the better he will learn. However, there is so much in the subject matter which is not interesting—does not gratify the instinctual needs of the child—but has to be learned anyway, that it is impossible to depend entirely or even largely on the child's hungers. It seems a pity to try to interest a child in dramatics if his need for exhibitionism is not very great, or if his basic instinctual needs are gratified better by some form of peeping than by exhibiting. To him the exhibitionism needful for dramatics is lacking and therefore dramatics are boring, while the same instinctual impulse could be gratified pleasurably by scientific research, which to him would never be boring. To

[7] I am indebted to Mr. George Biemel, formerly of the Philadelphia Orchestra, for this suggestion.

a child with a stronger drive toward exhibitionism, however, such research would be boring beyond words. It seems to me essential that the teacher understand that one child may have a specific group of hungers and another an entirely different group. If the teacher himself has the same group of hungers as the first child but a different group from the second, he may find it difficult to understand why the second child is so uninterested and rejects all his efforts to make the subject matter interesting—to the irritation and annoyance of both teacher and child. You cannot force candy on a child who is not hungry for it and if you try you will only make the child annoyed. It is desirable for a teacher to recognize and appreciate the specific hungers of the child and therefore endeavor to present the data to be learned in a manner by which the specific hunger can be satisfied. If the child has a strong exhibitionistic drive the material should be presented through the medium of dramatics; if the child's drive is to peep, it should be presented through the medium of scientific research. The ability to do this depends on the degree of intuition possessed by the teacher. There are no tests by which the specific hungers of any one child can be determined, and every psychoanalyst recognizes that the tests for aptitudes, vocational guidance, and the like which have been evolved by the educational psychologists are of little value in this connection because they do not take into consideration that the replies to the test have been filtered through the complicated defense systems of the ego and therefore provide little real information as to the basic needs of the child.

The small child who is on a self-demand schedule may be hungry on a particular day only for proteins and eat nothing but meat. On another day his hunger will be not for proteins but for carbohydrates. However, throughout the year he will eat a properly balanced diet. Yet the parent knows that to become an adult and a civilized person the child must learn to eat according to cultural customs and will have to acquire a taste for foods that do not interest him. Similarly, the good teacher knows that the child has to learn and to acquire a taste for learning many things in which he has no inner interest. How do these acquired tastes and interests come about?

THE USE OF THE MECHANISM OF IDENTIFICATION IN THE LEARNING PROCESS

As I have mentioned, the process of incorporation ends in a change in the ego—the incorporated material becoming part of the individual himself. In this way he becomes like the object in the external world which he has incorporated. To speak technically, he has identified himself with the object. The need of the child to identify with the adult is a most important mechanism in the ability to learn, to acquire ego skills, particularly the ego skills of an academic nature. The child envies the power, self-sufficiency and apparent freedom from fear of the adult and desires to be like him so as not to be tormented with feelings of fear, inadequacy, and incapability. The adult is also the source of pleasure because he gratifies the instinctual desires of the child. When the source of pleasure is absent the child becomes apprehensive lest he suffer pain and discomfort, for then he may feel his instinctual desires but will be unable to gratify them. The child believes that if he could himself become the source of pleasure, the adult, then he would no longer be apprehensive when the adult was not present, for he would never be exposed to feelings of pain and discomfort. In short, the child wishes to be the adult in order to avoid his feelings of anxiety and dread. Consciously and unconsciously from the time he becomes aware that his ego is separate from his environment he attempts to identify with the adult.

Identification is one of the most important psychic mechanisms by which the ego acquires skills and so strengthens its ability to deal with the pressures of the instinctual desires and the dangers of the external world. Freud [8] states that it is the earliest expression of an emotional tie with an object, and he differentiates it from object choice. Object choice concerns what one would like to have. Identification concerns what one would like to be. Identification is ambivalent and is derived from the cannibalistic incorporation of the first oral phase of psychosexual development. There are a number

[8] Sigmund Freud, *Group Psychology and the Analysis of the Ego,* London, International Psychoanalytic Press, 1922.

of types of identification. The first is identification through love. This is seen in the efforts of the young baby of either sex to be like his mother in order to possess her. It can be observed first as attempts at simple imitation and later as his tendency to react to and do things in her way. This is not a studied conscious imitation but takes place constantly and automatically through the process of incorporation without the child being aware of what is happening. The identification through the desire to possess because of love enables the child to learn his language and his daily routines and actions, and to accept all the early cultural instruction, of which toilet training and its offshoots of cleanliness, neatness, and the like form the most important part at this time. In the average family the process is encouraged by the praise given to the child by his parents for each new step he takes in activity. It is only as the child gets older and the parents begin to notice that the child is presenting to them not only those of their actions which they like but also the things which they dislike to observe in themselves, that they complain about the child's identification with themselves.

The identification with the mother is aided by a second reason for identification. Balint [9] and Emich [10] in discussing it at length have pointed out how this type also contributes to the learning process. To the infant the world is unknown and because it is unknown it is very frightening, for the child's experiences have taught him that both internal and external stimuli cause organic tensions and demand unexpected requirements from him which are very unpleasant. If the situation is one that the child can know and if he has the capacity to assimilate it, the unknown will be converted into the known and the fear and tension will be relieved. If the child is unable to know the new situation easily he may attempt to know it through imitation, the principle being, "If I act like him, I won't be surprised and hurt by him," or, "If I eat him, I will never be hurt." In this he attempts to know by acting out the likeness of the situation. Identification is knowing, so neurotic individuals overuse this

[9] Alice Balint, "Defense Mechanisms," *International Journal of Psychoanalysis*, 24, 1943.

[10] Minna Emich, "The Need to Know as Related to Identification and Acting Out," *International Journal of Psychoanalysis*, 25, 1944.

mechanism in various ways. In order to feel safe, a neurotic person may say, "I must know everything about everyone and everything, or I do not know anything about anyone or anything." In this way dangers can be minimized.

The ability to displace the idea of one thing to another, for example by identifying any thick mass with feces, or any liquid with urine, helps the child to find substitutes for the primitive sources of pleasure that have to be given up under the pressure of education. Through this identification between an unknown and a known the child attempts to avoid unpleasantness and obtain pleasure while increasing his knowledge of the external world. He can transform the strange and frightening world into one familiar and enjoyable. An airplane is a new means of transportation. If one has to travel on it one experiences apprehension lest one be killed. This apprehension is removed by identifying the safety belt, the chair, the fine food, the magazines, the hostess, and the use of oxygen, in the unconscious, with a return to the mother's arms. Starting and stopping are the most difficult parts of the flight because they enforce the change from fantasy to reality, and consequently the apprehension returns.

Except for direct gratification, identificatory thinking is the only way that we can approach the dangers and discomforts of the external world. This is important in the field of education, for the relation between the ego and the external world is the main problem dealt with by all educational methods. Balint says that there are two types of thinking, objective and identificatory. In identificatory thought all explanations have to be in terms of the self. The basis of early identifications is not the resemblance of the object to the ego but the fact that the object may serve as a means of gratification to the child's instincts. The essence of the small child's play lies in his *becoming* a dog or a train rather than just playing with toys. The identification of his ego with an object is the basis for his identification of one object with another. The child can only become fond of something unknown if he can succeed, by the help of his instincts, in identifying it with something known. In this connection Roheim [11]

[11] Geza Roheim, *Social Anthropology,* New York, International Universities Press, 1950.

points out that the mind of the primitive tends to identify different objects by noting resemblances, not differences. Eissler [12] states that in order to learn, a person must recognize a situation as familiar, as having occurred before. He found that in the delinquent the capacity for learning was stunted because if learning is to occur the situation must be familiar, and the delinquent refuses to recognize anything but the new.

Identification differs from loving. Loving forces a person to recognize that the object and the ego are different. Identification is an attempt to deny the separation between the ego and the external world by incorporating the latter in the ego. In this way a painful, disturbing state of affairs is transformed into a pleasurable one. Identification with the parents takes place because the child loves them for bringing him pleasure and because they are the powerful representatives of the frustrating external world. The climax of the edipus period is succeeded by educability. This means the desire to do things because the child wants to, not because the parents have ordered him to. This willingness is an attempt to preserve self-esteem in the face of a superior power. Sometimes this attempt becomes a violent protest. His narcissism seems incapable of tolerating any command, and the result may be negativism—if the child is told to do the opposite, he will do what is required.

Educability results in a splitting of the ego, one part of which remains the vehicle for the original instinctual wishes, while the other becomes the vehicle for the wishes incorporated through identification, that is, becomes the superego. At this time the most self-willed children may become the most conscientious. From the point of view of the part of the ego which is allied with the instincts, the child is in mortal danger because of education, for the coming into life of the superego is a sentence of death on the instincts' primitive life. With the splitting of the ego the child does not deny a misdemeanor, but denies that *he* did it. He tries to regard the part of his mind which is disagreeable because of the threats of education as alien and outside of himself. He is not the guilty person, someone else is and this some-

[12] K. R. Eissler, "Ego Psychological Implications of the Psychoanalytic Treatment of Delinquents," *The Psychoanalytic Study of the Child,* Vol. V, New York, International Universities Press, 1950.

one else is given a name and becomes a permanent guest. This is an attempt by projection to rid himself of the disturbing part of his ego, that portion which is allied with his instincts and which has become disagreeable to him as a result of his identification with the behavior of his environment. Later, with the development of the sense of reality, repression eliminates from consciousness the knowledge of those affects and wishes which have been projected.

Identification is always in the interest of narcissism. Through identification the child yields to external forces by means of mimicry. Love and understanding are the two factors which bring about a relation with reality. Through education the child learns to replace identification by understanding. His understanding is increased when he learns that adults can admit mistakes and that his parents and other adults are neither omnipotent nor infallible. After understanding has developed, reason and love for other people help the child to try to influence the external world in the direction of his wishes.

Another type of identification combines elements from the two types already mentioned—identification by love and identification to overcome fear. About the age of three the small boy begins to have a different kind of object relation. Instead of wanting to possess his love object—his mother—by being like her, he desires to possess her for his own gratification and pleasure. He no longer identifies with her, but desires her as an object. At this time he becomes involved in competitive feelings with his loved, feared, and envied father, who does possess the mother as a love object. He desires now to possess the father's position and attributes, and begins to identify with him in order to do so and at the same time, to dethrone his father. This type of identification occurs as the result of his mixed feelings of hate, fear, and love toward his father and is brought about by the presence of the sexual triangle. It is an identification not through love but through ambivalence. This type of identification also played a part, as I have shown, in the earlier identification with the mother, for this was partly an attempt to overcome the frustrations of his primitive needs by doing things in his mother's way, rather than in ways of which she disapproved. It developed from envy of the power of the mother, who could frustrate him. This type of identification through ambivalence with the father during the edipus situation is not useful in learning academic skills. The same is true of the type known as identification with the aggressor,[13] in which the identification gives the child a sense of power and makes him therefore feel equal to a threatening authority. If this type of identification is continued for a long time, the child really begins to join forces with the hostile power and has to surrender a large part of his own interests.

Identification is one of the most important mechanisms in the process of learning. Among primitive peoples and in cultures where the child readily can observe and understand the fact that the adult's particular activity is directed specifically to a known goal, it remains the most important factor in the need to learn ego skills. The small boy in a primitive culture observes his father making a net, taking the net to the water, using it in the water to catch fish, bringing the fish home to make part of the family meal. Through his desire to identify with his father he tries to make a net and go through the various observed phases of fishing, until by repeated efforts he becomes an accomplished fisherman, perhaps superior to his father. The small boy in the highly skilled Western culture observes that his father goes to his office, but what he does there he knows only from hearsay, out of which the boy weaves his own fantasy ideas, which may have little basis in reality. When he starts school he is presented with the fact that he is expected to learn to read, to make mathematical calculations, and to do other things which his own observation cannot show to be an essential part of his father's business life; others may assert that they are, but he has learned that frequently hearsay cannot be believed. Therefore he does not understand that the requirement to learn academic subjects will fill a part of his need to identify with his father. The learning of academic skills in Western culture does not take place through the universal need of the child to identify with the father. Instead other motives have to be utilized.

In Western culture the teacher stands as the link between the child's wish to identify with the parent of the same sex and the use of this desire as a motive for learning academic skills. As I mentioned earlier, if the child loves the teacher he wants to please him. The best way he

[13] Anna Freud, *The Ego and the Mechanisms of Defense,* New York, International Universities Press, 1946.

knows to please the teacher is to do what he asks, that is, to be like him. Because he loves the teacher and wants the teacher to love him he identifies himself with the teacher as he formerly did with his parents. In making this identification he learns the academic skills which he observes the teacher knows. Of course all of the dynamics in this process go on unconsciously and no one realizes they are there, but the end result is noticed.

As one watches children through their years of growth, one is impressed by the fact that the motive of learning in order to be rewarded by the teacher's love is very important and powerful and continues not only through grade school but also often into senior high school and college. The educator has the expectation that somewhere in the process of development the child will acquire the desire to learn for the sake of learning. This is not one of the basic hungers and needs, so the fulfillment of the educator's expectation does not occur as the result of a maturational process but comes about in another way. In the process of identification, characteristics and attributes of the teacher as well as the teacher's academic abilities, are incorporated to become an integral part of the child's ego. He identifies himself with the teacher because he loves him and expects love in return if he learns and if he behaves like the teacher. His ego therefore tries to make itself like the loved and admired teacher. He swallows the teacher whole, so to speak, in order to identify with him. If, to the child, the teacher seems to be interested in learning, he too must become interested in learning in order to be like the teacher and so be loved by him. The interest in learning is also incorporated into the ego and when enough of these identifications have been made the child becomes interested in learning to please the incorporated ideal of being interested in learning. When he has accomplished any part of this task successfully the child feels a glow of pride. This is an expression of love from the part of the ego which represents the incorporated teacher, to the part of the ego which represents the child. If he fails in any part of this task the child feels very humiliated because the second part of his ego cannot come up to the first part's demands. The successive incorporations of several admired and loved teachers gradually form a particular part of the ego, the ego ideal, which is partly conscious and partly unconscious. Eventually, perhaps toward the middle or end of high school, or perhaps in college, the individual begins to desire to learn for the sake of learning. Through his identifications with various teachers he has developed an ego ideal of the desirability of learning. He wants this ego ideal to be pleased with him and to love him and so he strives to fulfill its demands. At this point he cares less and less whether he loves the teacher or the teacher loves him. He learns in order to please his ego ideal—which remains with him the rest of his life and goes with him wherever he goes.

At about the same time, he begins to perceive unconsciously that all of his learning of academic subjects, however remote they have seemed formerly, is directed toward an identification with and an attempt to surpass his father. The child in primitive culture arrives at this goal fairly directly, the child in Western culture only by the detour of identification with the teacher.

As identification with the teacher takes place because the child loves the teacher, any emotional reaction of a different nature, such as hate, anger, or fear, will interfere with the identification and therefore with the learning process. No one desires to imitate someone whom he hates, unless such imitation would enable him to attain some desired libidinal goal, as when the boy identifies with the hated, feared, yet loved father in order to possess the libidinally desired mother. There is no such libidinal prize to be anticipated in the identification with the teacher, so that the learning of academic skills takes place solely by identification with the loved object. This identification is made in the expectation of libidinal rewards. The reward which is most gratifying to the child is that of love from the adult, whether this be the parent or a professional educator. When the child loves the teacher he will do anything to please him, even to learning the most uninteresting subject, but he anticipates a real expression of love from the teacher in return. As long as he gets it he will continue to learn. If he dislikes the teacher, for whatever reason, if the rewards of the teacher's love do not gratify him sufficiently, or if the teacher dislikes him, he will refuse to learn even a subject that is somewhat interesting in itself.

At the present time, educators have, in their theories, a great tendency to discount the validity or the usefulness of this mechanism as a part of learning, although they unconsciously are using it all the time. The more progressive schools are discarding marks, promotions, merit badges, and the like, all of which are recognized by the child not as a sign of his achievement, but as a sure indication of the teacher's love. The child who toward the end of the term becomes worried lest he not be promoted to the next grade basically is not worried about this, but is afraid that his teacher and his parents will not reward him with love if he is not promoted.

There is another mechanism which also operates in the learning process. The child of school age wishes to be able to do everything his peers do. If he observes that they are learning to read, their motives being as obscure to him as they are to them, he also wishes to learn to read. Competitive envy is a real intrapsychic motive in learning academic and other ego skills and exists in the child even though the adult, parent, or teacher, particularly when the latter is on the staff of a very progressive school, deliberately tries to make all learning situations noncompetitive.

CHAPTER VIII

Psychoanalytic Concepts Concerning the Higher Mental Functions

UP TO THIS point I have tried to show that the organized ego has two sides. One is directed to the external world through the perceptive system. The other is directed toward the id. The ego has to learn to synthesize the perceptions from the external world with the needs for gratification of the instincts. It is the combination of the impinging of stimuli from the external world and, more important, the constant needs of the instincts for discharge, which supplies the energy for the use of the perceptive system in relation to the external world. When this combination begins to be established the constant needs for discharge appear in the ego as needs for the gratification of the instincts. The ego has to learn methods by which such gratification can be obtained satisfactorily in relation to the external world and the realities of time, place, and so on. This means that the ego has to develop an elaborate and complicated system of mechanisms of defense—by which the instinctual drives can be controlled and redirected until a really satisfactory method of gratification, and therefore of discharge, can be obtained. As Liss has pointed out, all cultural activities are transmuted biological functions and products through which the psyche offsets the loss of the pleasure values of the biological function—which has been restricted through cultural and reality prohibitions—first by the displacement of the pleasure value from the biological function to the cultural one, and second by the evolution of the latter as a substitute and recompense for the loss of the former. The purpose of the learning process is to supply adequate systems of gratification as substitutes for elementary biological functions and products. The successful resolution of the edipus situation and of sibling relationships contributes profoundly to this end.

French [1] discusses the process of learning as part of the ego functions of defense and synthesis. The central function of the ego during childhood is learning, that is, satisfying the need to adapt the child's instinctual needs to external reality. This takes place in two stages. He states that in early childhood the child cannot escape painful impressions and therefore resorts to the desperate defense of denying painful fact by fantasying or by acting out protective fantasies in play and in talk. In later childhood the value of defense by fantasy is lost because the reality-testing faculty is stronger and the ego's need for synthesis makes it impossible for opposites to exist side by side. Also, his greater freedom of physical movement and his increased powers of psychic activity enable the child to evade dangerous and painful external situations. As a result, he develops the defense mechanism of the restriction of ego activities. This is a real renunciation and loss of interest in the abandoned object, not a neurotic inhibition, which would be a substitute for forbidden instinctual wishes.

The child sees and is told many things which for the time he can master only in imagination. He is introduced to the adult world, which can be grasped only by his imagination because it has little reality for him. The discrepancy between the abilities of the child and those of the adult is so great that identification can be achieved only by small steps. Urged on by the need to be like his parents, the child copies what he can and fills in the rest with fantasy. The urge to emulate his parents becomes an incentive for the continuous learning process. Unless the urge to identify with the father can find an outlet in fantasy and in play, the energy of the boy's phallic sexuality must be concentrated upon envious competition with the father and upon the fear of the inevitable consequences of such hopeless competition. French states that if one defense mechanism relieves tension at one point, it must be combined with another to counteract the tension increased at another point—for instance, repression must be supplemented by a substitute gratification, such

[1] Thomas M. French, "Defense and Synthesis in the Function of the Ego," *Psychoanalytic Quarterly*, 7, 1938.

as sublimation or symptom formation; reaction formation must be supplemented by projection and rationalization. The denial in fantasy by word or act must be reinforced by a real token. The need to supplement fantasy with reality, to give fantasy actuality by living it out through some real object, is a cruder example of the synthesis that must play an important role in the establishment of the reality principle. The reality principle requires renunciation of immediate pleasure and the endurance of pain for the sake of future pleasure, which can be present only in fantasy. The capacity to be at least temporarily satisfied by fantasy seems to be important in learning to wait, i.e., in learning to withstand the pressure of immediate needs. The pressure for immediate satisfaction becomes a drive for the realization of one's fantasy. In this synthesis fantasy is modified into purposes. There are all possible gradations between ambitious daydreams and driving ambitions.

The restriction of the ego—learning to accept one's limitations—is a normal step in ego development. There are two ways of dealing with obstacles in the way of wish fulfillment. The person can struggle to overcome the obstacle, or he can accept the ego limitations and adapt to them. Normally one either chooses between these two or combines them. Substitution of vicarious for direct gratification is a normal ego adjustment to objects. The devotion of parents to children is a vicarious gratification of their own narcissism.

In another paper [2] French goes on to say that the ego's practical task is to adapt the instinctual drives and the tensions they arouse to the realities of the external world and to reunite conflicting needs. In this conflict the intellectual task is to examine the reality situation. This is spurred by the desire to solve the conflict between the instinctual drives and reality and the conflict between the opposed instinctual drives in the mind. Too intense a conflict impairs the ego's capacity for intellectual grasp; popularly stated, a person "loses his head" in a crisis. As a result of his clinical observations in psychoanalysis French [3] concludes that each step in learning involves the

[2] Thomas M. French, "Some Psychoanalytic Applications of the Psychological Field Concept," *Psychoanalytic Quarterly,* 11, 1942.

[3] Thomas M. French, "A Clinical Study of Learning in the Course of a Psychoanalytic Treatment," *Psychoanalytic Quarterly,* 5, 1936; Thomas M. French, "Reality and the Unconscious," *Psychoanalytic Quarterly,* 6, 1937.

substitution of a new for an old method of gratification. The incentive for using scientific methods must be derived from insight into the fact that the old method is inadequate. This realization initiates a series of experiments which, at first, are not likely to be successful. If sufficient energy can be withdrawn into real life, the residue of energy attached to childhood conflicts can be projected, or treated as a foreign body, without belonging to or being in vital relationship with the ego. This is well illustrated in the type of dream where the dreamer is observed as if he were someone else.

There is in everyone a constant tendency to revert to the wishes and emotional patterns of childhood and to irrational modes of thinking. If regression is so easy and attractive, what are the incentives that can induce one to follow the path of normal development? Regression fulfills the pleasure principle but takes no account of the reality principle, by which present pain must be endured for the sake of an assured future pleasure. This hope of future satisfaction is very weak when pitted against immediate satisfaction. How is one able to renounce immediate pleasures and even endure pain in the hope of pleasure in the future? The ability to do this is found in the nature of the unconscious. The unconscious is compelled to yield to wish-fulfilling tendencies and also to the compulsion to relive painful experiences. The reality principle is not a modified form of the pleasure principle but a fortunate synthesis of the pleasure principle and the repetition compulsion. The psyche wishing to obtain pleasure is compelled to come to terms with the memory of its mistakes and their unhappy consequences, and it makes a virtue of necessity when it accepts a minimum of renunciation for the sake of future pleasure, in lieu of a merciless and futile compulsion to repeat its previous suffering. It is because of the struggle between the unconscious urge for pleasure and the repetition of the unhappy consequences of these wishes that there arises the urge to accept the reality principle.

Intense psychic conflicts interfere with this step because the acceptance of reality requires the ability to learn. Acute conflicts not only make this new learning impossible but also destroy discriminations which have been learned previously. If an individual or animal is pushed to take a step in learning which is beyond his capacity, the learning attempts are replaced by reactions of frustration or by stereotyped reactions. The reality principle involves a modification of the pleasure-pain principle to take account of future pleasure and pains, and a transformation of the repetition compulsion into learning by taking account of the differential aspects of reality. Too great conflicts absorb the psyche in the pain of the conflict and in vain attempts to wish it away—in attempts to deal with it by renunciation or by disastrous repetitions of previous traumatic experiences—and leave no free energy to be devoted to considering the differential criteria of reality. Such results are easily observed in neurotic and psychotic persons. Learning is only possible when there is enough free energy at hand to use in paying attention to those less obtrusive aspects of reality which make it possible to distinguish between the painful experiences of the past and the favorable aspects of the present. It is not the most painful elements in reality which the neurotic ignores but those emotionally indifferent aspects which are valuable solely as differential criteria to help one find new possibilities of gratification and to avoid past mistakes.

As a test of these conclusions, French compares the solution of a patient's conflict as revealed in a nightmare with a hypothetical rational solution of the same conflict. The dream was precipitated by the analyst's discussions, which the patient felt as a frustration. He felt angry, and reacted to the situation with a dream expressing a wish to get rid of his rival for his mother's love and a feminine and masochistic wish to be attacked by the analyst (the father). The dream thus takes no account of present reality—the analyst will not hate the patient even if he is angry—but acts as if the patient were in the presence of his loved, hated, and feared father in the early edipus situation. The patient's unconscious has not learned to take account of the difference between his present situation and his childhood relation to his father. The dream is not able to get rid of the painful real elements in the situation. The aggressive wishes are not fulfilled, but end in terror because it is better to have a threatening, punishing father than to lose him entirely and because the patient wants love from the father but is unable to rid himself of the destructive energy that estranges them. His own rage is reflected back on himself. This is an emergency substitute for the tragic realization that if the patient gets rid of his father, he will have him no more. The frustration of the patient's sexual wishes toward the mother is as apparent in the dream as in reality. The dream does not wipe out the traces of the conflict.

Seen as a whole, the dream resembles the reactions of a person in waking life who attempts by a clumsy trial-and-error method to adjust to a reality situation in which he is not well oriented. Disappointed by the analyst, the patient turns for consolation to dreams of his mother. He realizes he cannot have undisturbed possession of her, so he turns his energy to trying to get rid of his rivals, only to discover that in this way he runs the danger of losing his father, whom he still continues to love. Faced with this danger, he recalls that his father will not let him get away with his aggressive impulses and wakens to reassure himself that it is all a bad dream. The dream as a whole has not been able to avoid recognition of the essential real elements of the childhood situations, but their painful affect has been verbalized to some extent in sleep. Freud has pointed out that the hysterical symptom has two parts, an unconscious pleasurable wish and a need for punishment for that wish. The dream similarly has two elements, the wish for sleep playing the same role in dreams as the need for punishment in hysterical symptoms. The wish-fulfilling hallucinations of a dream really justify themselves because they *always* make allusions to reassuring facts and memories of incidents which have actually happened.

The dream deals with the realities of a childhood situation rather than with the present situation. The wish-fulfilling tendencies in the dream are unable to eliminate the unpleasant real elements. The dream solution differs from a hypothetical real solution because the dream recognizes the patient's desire for his mother, his wish to get rid of his father, and his fear of his father's punishment not as a progression from cause to effect, but rather as a series of reactions to a number of unrelated problems. If the patient could gain a view of the unsolved childhood problem as a whole, he would be in a position to learn a lesson from it and to apply that lesson to his relation to reality.

The actual frustration by the analyst intensified the conflict between the patient's sexual and his aggressive impulses and weakened the ability of the ego to synthesize them.

The fundamental difference that distinguishes rational waking behavior from neurotic or dream behavior is that in the latter the ego has an inadequate synthetic capacity, can deal with conflict only in a fragmentary way, and tends to repeat, in a stereotyped manner, reactions to previous traumatic experiences. Rational behavior requires an ego whose synthetic capacity makes it possible to view a situation as a whole and also to pay attention to differential criteria between two situations, so as to learn from past experiences instead of repeating them.

In the case cited, the analysis provided the patient with an attainable goal and so enabled him to use the learning process.

It can be seen from what I have said that the nonconflictual elements in the psychic processes, such as intelligence, memory, and special abilities, are greatly influenced by the conflictual elements, and that the latter play a most important role in the learning process. There is need at this point to consider the relation between intelligence and the higher mental functions, and the relation of these to the learning process in general and to the learning of certain specific skills.

Rapaport [4] states that genetically the thought processes arise out of the need to hallucinate images and ideas of objects to gratify instinctual desires. This stage of hallucinatory wish fulfillment is part of the primary process. All ideas which represent the same drive are equivalent, and condensation and displacement are used to get tension discharge. Under the secondary process, no discharge is attained until an experimental discharge of small amounts of energy proves that tension will be reduced through the discharge of a large amount. Topographically, the thought process may be unconscious under the primary process, or preconscious and conscious under the secondary process. Structurally, thought processes are integral parts of the ego. Biologically, thinking is experimental action which uses small amounts of energy.

Bischler [5] defines the relation between intelligence and the higher

[4] David Rapaport, "On the Psychoanalytic Theory of Thinking," *International Journal of Psychoanalysis,* 31, 1950.

[5] W. Bischler, "Intelligence and the Higher Mental Functions," *Psychoanalytic Quarterly,* 6, 1937.

mental functions. He says that the higher psychic activity is derived from the instinctual desires. The will is a combination of sadomasochistic tendencies and the internalized edipus complex, and is the co-ordinated expression of partial drives arranged in a hierarchy and subjugated to suppressed drives. Intelligence is the capacity to solve new problems by thought, when confronted by a new situation which cannot be solved by instinct or habit. The act of intelligence, a search by groping, takes place in three steps. As a point of departure one first asks oneself a question. Then one searches for a hypothesis which will offer an opportunity for readjustment, and finally one attempts to check and verify the hypothesis.

Intellectual activity is only part of awareness. The function of awareness is to perceive and register inner stimuli. Adaptation is living in sympathy with the environment. The feeling of sympathy to the environment is rooted in sexual trends and uses the mechanisms of identification and introjection. If the adjustment is disturbed by external circumstances one feels oneself unadapted. This feeling is the result of a weakening of the libidinous relations between the ego and the object, or of the intervention of sadistic drives which disturb the equilibrium between the subject and the environment. Intellectual activity is used to restore the state that existed before the interruption, or to create a condition where the feeling of being unadapted disappears. The individual is separated from mystical ties by the awakening of consciousness and thought and so is able to redirect himself.

There are three types of mental activity: intuition, analytic or logical rational thinking, and invention or imagination. Each intellectual act begins with sensations arising either from within or from without. From these sensations arise perceptions which develop into an image. This image, if it is not expressed through motion, changes into an idea.

A simple perception combines the results of the active use of a sensory organ, and of attention and volition, and the pleasure in the use of the organ, and has an affective accent which either is positive or has been reversed to the negative. Perception is a mode of identification, for one perceives only what is interesting. It needs a positive affective trend. Negative feelings are derived from the reversal of the feeling of sympathy when the individual is subjected to the pressure of sadistic impulses. Introjection is the first step in perception and the first consequence of it. One introjects only if there is a positive feeling tone. With each perception there is projection, which leads to invention and imagination.

The word intuition is derived from *intueri,* which means to look attentively, to observe. Intuition is an extended or refined form of perception and is really identification or introjection of a passive type, that is, through a feminine, masochistic attitude. The repressed instinctual tendencies play the main part in intuition. Logical comprehension differs from intuition by being rational: it is based on a preliminary analysis of the situation, followed by a reconstruction.

Kupper [6] adds an important concept regarding the use of the intelligence. He says that the ego's attempt to integrate the instinctual impulses with external reality motivates the development of speech, thought, and intellect. In the intellectual person the conflict between the instinctual desires and the external world is solved by repressing the instinctual drive and displacing it into speech, thought, and intellect so that they become instinctual satisfactions in themselves. When the repressed affect threatens to break through, there is a regressive attempt to find instinctual satisfaction and security by reverting to omnipotent fantasies at a narcissistic level which existed before the repression occurred. One patient who thought much about the control of nature and about unity with God was defending himself against a pre-edipal nonverbal attachment to his mother.

Individuals who usually think abstractly and theoretically use thinking to avoid action, usually of a violent nature. The perception that their unconscious desires are very violent may cause them to regress to animistic thinking with emphasis upon omnipotence in speech and thought. Within recent years there has been increased search for absolute truths. This is a regressive phenomenon aimed at keeping in check the unconscious desires in the human being for cruelty, violence, and destruction which have been stimulated in the last quarter century by their outbreak from repression in many parts of the world. It is well known that in certain pathological conditions

[6] Herbert I. Kupper, "Psychodynamics of the Intellectual," *International Journal of Psychoanalysis,* 31, 1950.

there is an attempt to master emotional conflicts by striving to solve abstract philosophical problems.

Ferenczi [7] describes certain people who if they want to think must interrupt a particular movement in which they happen to be engaged, and can continue it only after the completion of the intellectual act. They show the same lack of movement as appears in the statue "The Thinker," which represents the idea that our prehuman ancestor could not begin to think unless he stopped using his muscles. Such people suffer from severe intrapsychic inhibitions. Every independent effort at thought must first overcome strong ego defenses by employing the energy saved by the suspension of co-ordinated motor movements. This is not a simple displacement of muscular energy into psychic energy, for during thinking such persons only suspend voluntary co-ordinated movements, not the motor innervation. While they think, the tonus of their resting musculature is increased. They have to concentrate their attention wholly upon the organ of thought and therefore cannot carry on simultaneously a coordinate movement which also requires attention. This condition may be observed in persons who suffer from a severe obsessional neurosis or from schizophrenia if the dynamics of their neurosis is a fear to act lest they do harm. Such patients tend to think more than the average person does. In such persons the neurosis may produce a failure of the process of making an action automatic, and so they cannot learn well and do well automatic actions like skating, swimming, driving a car, or riding a bicycle. In some children hyperactivity is an attempt not to think. These children know that they cannot discuss their problems when they are active and use their activity as a way of avoiding thinking about and discussing their problems. Every attempt I made to get one boy to discuss his feelings resulted in his immediate flight into activity, usually of a hostile nature. The content of this activity often furnished a clue to his thinking, as happens regularly in the psychic defense of acting out. Similarly, a certain number of constitutionally hyperactive people are not good scholars or thinkers. They leap before they look. The tendency in pro-

[7] Sandor Ferenczi, "Thinking and Muscle Innervation," *Further Contributions to the Theory and Technique of Psychoanalysis,* London, Hogarth Press and the Institute of Psycho-Analysis, 1926.

gressive schools to use activity as a method of learning may interfere with the learning and intellectual development of such children.

In contrast to the first group, Ferenczi describes people who are incapable of carrying out complicated thought processes while at rest but can do so if they are engaged at the same time in active muscular movements. Such persons have a rapid flow of ideas and very active fantasies. They must distract their attention from their thought processes in order to retard their overwhelming rush, and they squander muscular energy to restrain their fantasies and to enable themselves to think logically.

The regular parallelism of motor innervation with the psychic acts of thinking and attention speaks for the essential similarity of these processes. Freud says thought is an experimenting through the use of small masses of excitation, and locates the function of attention at the motor end of the psychic apparatus.

Fenichel summarizes all the psychoanalytic concepts of thinking. He says the ability to recognize, love, and fear reality develops before speech. Words allow for more precise communication and also for making more precise the anticipation by trial actions. The anticipation of action becomes thinking proper and finally consolidates consciousness. The undifferentiated predecessor of thinking has all the characteristics of the primitive ego. It has a wide scope of concepts, similarities are taken as identities, parts are taken as wholes, and concepts are based on common motor reactions. Every single thought before formulation has gone through this wordless state. The acquisition of the faculty of speech is the decisive step in the formation of the ego because the tying up of words and ideas makes thinking possible. A shift from emotional fantasy to sober reality takes place which serves the purpose of combating anxiety. Distortion of this is seen in the flight of the compulsive character from all emotion to the shadowy world of words and concepts. The lofty intellectual interests of puberty master the instinct excitement of that period. The achievement of speech turns omnipotence of thought into omnipotence of words. The child's earliest speech is a charm directed to forcing the external world and fate to do things that have been conjured in words. Certain words retain magical power, e.g., obscene words, oaths, solemn formulae, and poetry. Muscular actions accompany thinking. By thinking the ego tames two archaic reactions, the drive to discharge tensions and the tendency to hallucinatory wish fulfillments. In fatigue, sleep, intoxication, or psychosis, every thought is more similar to dream thinking than to logic.

Prelogical thinking is relatively unorganized, tolerates and condenses contradictions, is ruled by emotions, is full of wishful and fearful misconceptions, is directed only to striving for discharge, and is carried out through pictorial, concrete images, not through words. This preconscious, pictorial thinking is a magical type because the object, the idea of the object, the picture or model of the object, and parts of the object are all equated. Similarities are not distinguished from identities, ego and nonego are not separated. What happens to the object may by identification be experienced as happening to the ego, and what happens to the ego causes the same thing to happen to the object. Children behave as if they believe that if they cannot see they cannot be seen. The prelogical emotional thinking uses symbolism. This means that a conscious idea may be used as a symbol for an unconscious, objectionable idea. The use of symbols is a falling back into earlier, primary stages of thinking. In dreams the symbol appears in two aspects, as a tool of the dream censorship and as the visualizing of abstract thought. Archaic symbolism is a part of prelogical thinking and is not the same as the use of the mechanism of distortion, which represents a repressed idea by a conscious symbol. In prelogical thinking the penis and the snake are the *same thing*. The sight of a snake produces emotions about the penis. In distortion the idea of the penis is disguised by being *represented* as a snake.

Concepts are formed in prelogical thinking by a method based on the feeling that comprehension of the world radiates from instinctual demands and that the stimuli that produce the same reactions are identical. Early ideas are not sums built out of distinct elements, but wholes comprehended in undifferentiated ways and united by the emotional responses they have provoked. Prelogical thinking remains as a substitute for unpleasant reality. In the older child and adult there are two types of thinking, which prepare for dealing with reality in two different ways. One is used as an anticipation of what is probable, the other as a substitute for reality, an anticipation of what is desirable. Fantasies are of these two types. There is creative daydreaming which prepares for future action and there is fantasy which is a refuge for wishes which cannot be fulfilled. Logical thinking presupposes a strong ego which is capable of postponements, tolerant of tensions, rich in countercathexis, and ready to judge reality according to experience. If the ego is weak, tired, asleep, without confidence in its ability, or desirous of the receptive type of mastery, then pictorial thinking becomes more attractive than objective intelligence. A tired person prefers movies to Shakespeare and illustrated magazines to difficult reading. Dissatisfied persons without any possibility of influencing their situation ask for pictures and comic strips rather than for difficult intellectual pursuits.

Anna Freud [8] states that inhibitions in thinking or reckoning result not because there is an attempt to avoid dealing mentally with certain ideas or numbers but because they are associated with past sexual activity against which the ego has defended itself. The associative connection between the use of words and the instinctual drives is well illustrated by difficulties in hearing and speaking. The inability to hear or understand words can occur at different levels. In some cases the words are not heard. One patient who developed this habit did so to avoid being bothered by her mother's scolding and nagging, to appear dumb so as not to be ridiculed by her brother, and to try to appear as if she did not take in anything so that people would not think she was greedy. The taking in by the mouth was displaced onto taking in by the ears. The words may be heard and understood but reproduced in a fashion that alters the sense. One patient did this to get me angry, so I would attack him, and to make a fool of me, if my garbled statements were repeated to someone else. This was an expression of both his sadism and his masochism. The words may be heard and understood but not remembered. One patient did this because he wanted to be talked to. This was a displacement from the desire to be breast-fed, i.e., to be given medicine, food, attention, and the like, to taking in by the ears. The difficulty in remembering was used as a method to obtain instinct gratification. These last two types are more pathological than the cases in which the words are not heard. The words may be heard but have no mean-

[8] Anna Freud, *The Ego and the Mechanisms of Defense,* New York, International Universities Press, 1946.

ing. The perception is intact but there is lack of cathexis of the words. This is the most pathological type. Fliess[9] says the use of language is connected with the physiological processes of the opening of the urethral and anal sphincters. Basically all speech shows mixed types of urethral-erotic, anal-erotic and oral-erotic regressive impulses. He quotes Abraham, who said that the desire to be gratified by sucking may be changed to the need to give by way of the mouth. Such patients cannot work out the problems connected with their other activities, particularly urination, any more than they can control their need to talk. While the libido is discharged orally, the erotogenicity is urethral, so that the speech discharges both sexual and aggressive impulses. In this way verbalization undoes repression. It forms derivatives of repressed unconscious ideas, communicates these derivatives to the object, and expresses affective experiences in the course of free association. The physical act of speaking may precipitate the release of quantities of affect which is connected with repressed ideas.

Greenson[10] says that originally all words had a hallucinatory character and were associated with wish-fulfilling visual images. The change from these visual images to words goes through a succession of stages. The child first learns to distinguish images from reality. Then he learns to distinguish images from thoughts (i.e., the preconscious develops), and finally he learns the capacity for abstract thinking. He points out that obscene words force the listener to imagine concretely and realistically. He cites a case in which the mother tongue was the bearer of unresolved pre-edipal conflicts, as obscene words often are. A new language may have superego qualities. He says that learning a new language is harder for an adult than for a child because the adult has to introject new objects and resists giving up the old. Learning to speak involves the mechanisms of auditory incorporation, of identification, and of changing passivity into activity. It is influenced by the outcome of the conflicts between the mother, breast, and child.

[9] Robert Fliess, "Silence and Verbalization. A Supplement to the Theory of the Analytic Rule," *International Journal of Psychoanalysis,* 30, 1949.

[10] Ralph R. Greenson, "The Mother Tongue and Mother," *International Journal of Psychoanalysis,* 31, 1950.

Buxbaum [11] says that severely neglected children take a long time in learning to speak. Also, she notes that pronunciation and mannerisms of speech often may express unconscious contents.

SUMMARY

As has been shown, psychoanalytic research has contributed a great deal toward a better understanding of the dynamics of the process of thinking and therefore of the learning process. Thinking itself originates in the following way: A sensation arises either from an ungratified instinctual desire or from an external stimulus. In the former case the sensation is unpleasant; in the latter it is invested with a positive interest. The sensation immediately demands discharge through action. If the action is impeded for any reason whatsoever, the sensation is associatively connected with previous memories and becomes a perception. If the motor reaction to the perception again is impeded, thought occurs. Originally in the infant this thought took the form of hallucinatory wish fulfillment and used the mechanics of the primary process. As the child found that hallucinatory wish fulfillment did not lead to gratification, the thought became directed more toward a preparation for later action which would bring the desired gratification of the instinctual desire, and consequently the discharge of its energy. In this way the mechanics of the primary process were placed under the supremacy of the secondary process. Thinking and the use of words began to form substitutes for kinds of physical gratification, and throughout life they remain connected in the unconscious with these physical processes.

The main contributions of psychoanalysis to knowledge about the learning process are embodied in the following observations:

1. Two different processes of thinking exist in the mind, the primary and secondary processes, and these have different aims.
2. The learning process can only take place as the organization of the ego substitutes the supremacy of the secondary process for that of the primary process.

[11] Edith Buxbaum, "The Role of a Second Language in the Formation of Ego and Superego," *Psychoanalytic Quarterly,* 18, 1949.

3. Learning can take place only when objects in the external world are invested with instinctual energy. It is through this investment that the attention is directed to them.

4. When objects are so invested they can be introjected into the mind through the process of incorporation.

5. In our culture the desire to learn academic subjects needs the reinforcement of an identification with the teacher through the pupil's love of the latter.

6. The learning process will be impeded if there have been difficulties and discomforts in the early use of the physical mechanisms out of which the later psychical mechanisms of learning develop.

PART TWO

Ego Psychology and the Education of the Child

CHAPTER IX

Defense Mechanisms of the Ego: Repression, Reaction Formation, and Sublimation

I HAVE discussed in a rather condensed way the complicated subject of the learning process and the contributions that psychoanalytic research has made to our knowledge of the mechanisms by which learning takes place. Learning is a function of the part of the personality known as the ego. The basic function of the ego is to be aware of external reality through the perceptive system, to be aware also of the presence and nature of the instinctual drives, and to synthesize these two opposing forces in such a way that the instinctual desires can be gratified in a realistic manner. In the previous chapters I have discussed mostly the methods by which the ego perceives and deals with the external world—the way in which the individual learns about the external world and the way in which he learns skills to deal with it—although any such discussion would be impossible without some reference to the instinctual life. These methods and technics are a necessary part of the education of a child—perhaps particularly of his education in academic subjects—and should be known, understood, and used by teachers. It is equally important to understand the mechanisms used by the child in learning how to control his instinctual life and to direct it toward adequate, realistic methods of obtaining gratification.

It is not understood what an instinct is. It seems to be a property of living matter and to take the form of an outwardly directed drive. Its energy, or perhaps the instinct itself (because what we call an instinct may be only a form of energy), almost certainly is derived from chemical processes in certain cells or group of cells. Like all metabolic changes the production of the instinct and its associated energy takes place silently, and the individual has somehow to become aware of its presence.

When an instinctual impulse occurs, its presence is felt in the id as an increase of tension. The id cannot tolerate this increase of tension and demands that the instinctual impulse be discharged immediately, in order to restore the tensionless state. As far as the id is concerned, there is no conflict in this process of the increase of tension and the discharge and return to a tensionless state, for the id has no organization and therefore no knowledge as to whether there is any real possibility of instinctual discharge, or whether that discharge is practical in relation to the real external world, to time, to place, to circumstances, to the other people in the environment, or to the customs, mores, and laws by which they govern themselves. These matters, which often render the discharge of the instinct impractical or impossible, are known only to the ego, through the perceptive system and through its connections with the superego. It is necessary that the ego be able to perceive the states of tension in the id. It does so by perceiving the so-called instinct representations—ideas, conscious and unconscious, and feelings, conscious and unconscious. These ideas and feelings appear first in the unconscious portion of the ego. Soon some part of them or all of them break through into consciousness and the individual becomes aware of ideas or feelings that inform him that he has an instinctual drive which seeks expression and gratification. Whereas in the id the instinct is recognized only as a feeling of tension which demands discharge, in the ego the ideas and feelings that represent the feeling of tension in the id indicate a need for some activity which will discharge the instinct and at the same time gratify its aim.

To illustrate: at 4 P.M. a change occurs in the metabolism of many persons in our Western culture. The individual's readily available supplies of protein, carbohydrate, fat, and necessary chemical salts have been used up and new supplies are about to be required. He is not aware that this has occurred, because this action goes on silently. Perhaps in the next quarter or half hour he may consciously notice that he feels irritable, tired, or somewhat faint, or that he is looking at the clock to see what time it is. He is not aware why he feels or acts this way. These conscious feelings and actions represent thoughts in his unconscious ego about food and sensations of hunger. In his id the chemical changes in his body are felt as tension. A quarter or half hour later he will become aware of a feeling of hunger and will begin to wonder when his dinner will be ready. No longer will he look at the clock without knowing why, nor will he be unnecessarily irritable or feel tired or faint. He will consciously know that he is hungry, and it then will be up to him actively to see about satisfying his hunger as soon and as fully as he can in accordance with time, space, opportunity, the demands of other people, and the customs and laws of the social organization.

In order to do this he must have an organization in his ego which will connect his perceptions of the feeling of tension in his id with his perceptions of the external world, with his remembered perceptions of past times when he has been hungry and of the ways in which his hunger was satisfied, and with his perceptions of the customs and manners of his social organization in regard to meals. It can be seen that this complicated organization in the ego is necessary so that he will not try to satisfy his metabolic needs with stones instead of bread, or mistake a genital sexual need for the metabolic need for food.

This brings up another concept about instincts. Each separate instinct, regardless of how it is classified, has a definite, precise aim, arising in the body as a chemical change and appearing in the ego as a need for a specific form of gratification. I will refer to this concept of the aim of an instinct a little later.

At the same time that the metabolic changes in the individual's body are felt as tension in his id and as ideas and feelings of hunger in the unconscious part of his ego, there may be chemical changes occurring in other organs in his body. He may have some genital sexual desires. These also will be felt as tension in his id and will appear in the unconscious part of his ego as ideas and feelings about having intercourse. The aim of these genital sexual desires will be for him to penetrate the vagina of a woman with his penis. Again his ego must perceive this desire and correlate it with the demands of the external world and of his superego. It is difficult to gratify two desires at once; the ego must therefore decide which instinctual drive is more urgent and which gratification is more necessary at this particular time, so that it may be permitted to appear as conscious thoughts and feelings. This selective action of the ego requires a further organization. The individual will need certain mechanisms by which one group of instinct representations can be kept unconscious while another group is permitted to appear in consciousness so that he becomes aware of them and can satisfy them. The instinct representations of the genital sexual desire, which in this instance are kept in the unconscious part of the ego, are being co-ordinated by the ego with the individual's perceptions of the external world and of the demands of the superego. This whole process goes on in the unconscious. At the same time, the instinct representations which are permitted to appear in consciousness, in this case the desire for food, are being further co-ordinated with his conscious perceptions of the external world and of the memories of his training in morals and manners. Further elaborations of these are also going on in the unconscious part of the ego. The end result of all these elaborations and co-ordinations, both conscious and unconscious, appears as his conscious judgment about when and where he will eat.

This process of prohibiting specific instinct representations from appearing in consciousness is called *repression*. Before I discuss more fully repression and its important role in the education of the child, and before I discuss the many other ego mechanisms of defense, it is necessary to mention some further facts about instincts. In the adult, it is possible for either the desire for food or the desire for genital sexual gratification to be gratified directly and in reality if it becomes conscious. This is true also for many other instincts, both those classified by Freud [1] as the erotic instincts and those he grouped together as the death or aggressive instincts. Many of these can be gratified directly and in reality during adult life. There are, however, an equal or greater number of instincts of both main groups for which no real and direct gratification is possible, because such gratification would result in an insolvable conflict with reality, with external and intrapsychic prohibitions, and would end in terrible pain or in catas-

[1] Sigmund Freud, *Beyond the Pleasure Principle,* London, International Psychoanalytic Press, 1922.

trophic dangers or destruction of the individual himself or those people with whom he has a close relationship.

When a man loves a woman he may bite her playfully and gently as he kisses her. At the same time he may be conscious of the thought, and may say to her, that he would like to eat her all up and would feel happy in doing so. This playful behavior is a conscious representation of an instinctual drive—a *real* desire to eat her up. However, if he permitted this desire to be put into action, he not only would suffer the actual punishment of the law for murder and cannibalism, but would lose his love object entirely and would suffer the remorse of his conscience and the loneliness of being bereft of his desired and loved sexual object. So if this instinctual desire, which exists in every human being, should appear in his conscious mind in the form of real, not playful, ideas and feelings of cannibalism, he would be horrified. The fact that it appears as a form of play indicates that the cannibalistic instinctual desire actually exists in his unconscious. From time to time it produces a feeling of tension in the id that calls for discharge and demands gratification by the ego. Such instinctual desires, whose direct gratification would be impossible, still have to be gratified and it becomes a task for the ego to find some method of gratification for them. Hence the ego has to develop another form of organization, another method of defense, by which the aim of the instinct can be changed so that its gratification will be practical and possible. The instinct cannot be held in repression indefinitely because the id cannot tolerate the constant feeling of tension. The problem for the ego is to devise some practical method of gratification. The ego does this in several ways. Some part of the instinct can be gratified—that is, the tension can be relieved—through the discharge of the instinctual energy by means of a conscious or unconscious hallucination. For instance, a situation may be set up in the mind in which the action is gone through in the imagination and thus the energy is discharged. The instinct can be gratified also in dreams, whose purpose often is the discharge of the energy of such ungratifiable instinct drives. Neither of these methods, however, is completely satisfactory. Both put a premium on the discharge of the instinct energy and do not take into consideration that this energy may be put to use in the problem of living if it can be redirected as to aim and, to a lesser degree, as to object.

The ego defenses against instinctual drives whose gratification for certain reasons will bring the ego into danger can be classified dynamically as follows:[2]

- A. No change in the character of the instinct
  - 1. The ego denies the perception of the instinct
    - a. Repression
    - b. Isolation
  - 2. The ego denies the use of motility to the instinct
    - a. Renunciation
- B. The character of the instinct changes
  - 1. There is a change of object
    - a. Displacement
    - b. Identification
    - c. Turning the impulse against the self
  - 2. There is a change of aim
    - a. Sublimation
    - b. Reaction formation
    - c. Desexualization
  - 3. There is a change of subject
    - a. Altruistic surrender[3]

The ego defenses may also be classified according to the time of their appearance in the course of the child's development. Anna Freud,[4] who attempted this method of classification, points out that as yet we do not have enough knowledge of the development and history of these mechanisms to make such a classification with any certainty.

- A. Earliest—before ego and superego are differentiated
  - 1. Regression
  - 2. Reversal into the opposite
  - 3. Turning the impulse against the self

[2] I am indebted to a lecture by Dr. Robert Waelder for this list.

[3] This list does not include all the known mechanisms of defense. Those omitted are undoing, regression, introjection, projection, reversal into opposite, turning from activity to passivity or vice versa, depersonalization, asceticism, and intellectualism.

[4] Anna Freud, *The Ego and the Mechanisms of Defense,* New York, International Universities Press, 1946.

B. When the ego has become differentiated
  1. Early
    a. Projection
    b. Introjection
  2. Later
    a. Repression
C. When the ego and the superego are differentiated
  1. Sublimation

These mechanisms of defense against instincts are developed in order to avoid suffering. The child soon learns that there are certain things he desires to do but must not do, lest his parents disapprove and express their disapproval through ostracism (arousing the child's fear of desertion), through withdrawing their approval (arousing his fear of loss of love), or through real or threatened punishment (arousing his fear of castration). To avoid the unpleasant results of his actions he becomes afraid of his instinctual desires and of their representations, and he develops methods (mechanisms of defense) to keep these representations out of his conscious mind. Later on, as he grows older and has less actual need for his parents, he substitutes his superego for the parents' prohibitions and, fearing the same punishments from his superego as he feared actually or in fantasy from his parents, he continues to defend himself from the conscious knowledge of these instinct representations. The presence of these instinct representations in the unconscious part of the ego is indicated by a feeling of anxiety in the conscious part of the ego when the instinctual desire becomes activated. In childhood this will be the individual's fear of the reaction of his parents to him—objective anxiety. In late childhood, in adolescence, and in adult life this will be a fear of the reaction of the internalized images of his parents—superego anxiety—and also a fear of the real consequences of the action which may result from the direct expression of the instinct—a fear which is founded on his observations and his experiences. I will discuss the subject of the superego in a later chapter.

Six of these defense mechanisms are very important in the process of education and detailed knowledge of them is important in any discussion of the education of the child. These six are identification, projection, regression, repression, reaction formation, and sublimation. I already have described the important role played in the learning process by identification, projection, and regression.

REPRESSION

I discussed earlier how instinct representations, the ideas and feelings which inform the ego of the presence of specific instinctual needs, through the process of combination develop temporal association with perceptions of the external world, so that if I am hungry, I may feel hungry or think of food or of eating or have the memory of some delicious meal I have had at some former time, or I may actually smell or taste some food, substituting a hallucination—a sensory perception which is imagined, not actual—for the feeling of hunger or the thought of food or eating. If I have to keep all these instinct representations in the unconscious because of some of the fears mentioned above, I use the mechanism of repression. I am not aware that I have repressed them, but from this time on, as long as the repression lasts, I am no longer able to become aware of the feeling of hunger or any of the ideas associated with it—no matter how far afield from the feeling of hunger such secondary associated ideas may seem to be. Thus the defense mechanism of repression is the enemy of memory, of the learning process, and of the education of the child. For education, it must be possible to bring memories of former experiences readily from the unconscious part of the ego into the conscious part; any group of previous internal and external perceptions must be easily available to the conscious part of the ego at any given time. These requirements cannot be met when the defense mechanism of repression has been imposed on the instinct representations, and on all of the ideas and feelings connected through association with the ideas and feelings which more directly depict the presence of the ungratified instinct. In brief, the baby is thrown out with the bath water and is not recoverable unless the reason for the repression, and therefore the repression itself, is removed.

Repression [5] is an attempt to avoid danger. It is a preliminary phase

[5] Sigmund Freud, "Repression," *Collected Papers,* Vol. IV, London, Hogarth Press and the Institute of Psycho-Analysis, 1934; Sigmund Freud, *The Problem of Anxiety,* New York, W. W. Norton & Company, 1936.

of condemnation and lies between actual flight and conscious condemnation. If an external stimulus was perceived as unpleasant or frightening, the individual would fly or would consciously try not to perceive the source of the unpleasant or threatening stimulus. If an idea or feeling which the person disliked appeared in consciousness, the impulse would be condemned by conscious judgment. However, neither flight, sensory inhibition, nor condemnation is necessary when repression is used, for repression has the function of rejecting something and keeping it out of consciousness. It cannot occur before the distinction between the conscious and the unconscious has been made. The motive of repression is the avoidance of the pain of punishment. We say that anxiety creates repression. Anxiety originates as the fear of an external danger. The little boy is afraid of his libidinal feelings toward his mother (an internal danger) only because they involve an external danger—castration. In the girl, the main fear is that of loss of love. Repression occurs not because of the tension and pain produced by the lack of gratification of an impulse, but because the necessity of avoiding the pain of punishment is stronger than the pleasure of the gratification would be. It is called into play by two different situations —a dreaded instinctual impulse may be awakened by an external perception, or may arise internally.

Repression emanates from the ego, usually under the command of the superego, as a process of after expulsion. The instinctual drive that is repressed is always an active one which has come into conflict with the ego. Repression falls not only on the instinct but on the representations—i.e., the ideas and feelings directly connected with the repressed instinct—and on all the mental derivatives—the ideas or trains of thought in some way associated with it. Repression must be repeated whenever impulses which are regarded as dangerous, such as hostile impulses (particularly aggressive impulses modeled on those of the edipus situation), pre-edipal impulses with passive aims, and regressive pre-edipal sadistic impulses are energized.

Repression produces amnesias, but it is not entirely or even largely the foe of the learning process. As I have previously pointed out, it keeps the attention of the conscious part of the ego directed to the instinctual demand most urgent at the particular time and thus aids the direction of the attention to the part of the external world which will satisfy the specific instinctual need. In technical language, the part of the external world which will satisfy this need is cathected with the instinctual energy and being so erotized it assumes great temporary importance to the conscious ego. If I go to a delicatessen when I am hungry, I will be greatly interested in all the foods displayed and probably will buy more than I intended. If I go to the store just after I have eaten, I will have no interest in the display, will become bored if I have to stay any length of time, and probably will purchase much less than in the former instance. In the first instance, all other interests are repressed in the service of the specific instinctual need. In the second, my attention is distractible because only the usual repressions are acting. An adequately acting mechanism of repression is essential to the focusing of the attention on a particular situation, and so the child must develop such a mechanism in order to be educable.

All psychoanalysts are familiar with the fact that the most important cause of neurotic symptoms is that repression has become ineffectual. The formerly repressed instinct representations try to return to demand direct gratification of the instinct. Since such direct gratification is inadvisable, impractical, or actually impossible, the demands of the instinct released from repression appear as neurotic symptoms. An adequate degree of repression is necessary for a healthy mind; if a child has never developed a reasonable mechanism of repression he is incapable of learning in school.

In one of the chapters on learning difficulties I described a type of child who seems to lack any interest in learning and to be concerned only about the immediate gratification of his desires. He is bored by learning to read because it requires effort and interferes with his immediate pleasure. Even the teacher who tries to make the task itself pleasurable cannot arouse his interest. As I pointed out, this trait is the result of overpermissive methods used by the parents, who have gone out of their way to protect him from any pain and to see that all his desires are gratified. Children of this type consequently do not learn to tolerate any anxiety, especially the anxiety resulting when reality interferes with the immediate gratification of an instinctual desire. Therefore, the development of the ego defenses of repression, reaction formation, change of aim, and sublimation, i.e., the development of the organization of the ego, is greatly retarded. Instead of being changed into curiosity about the nonsexual aspects of the world, sexual curiosity is gratified directly. Such children lack any energy to learn, and are uninterested in learning even if the subject is made attractive. Not until they have been compelled to postpone immediate gratification of instinctual drives and have begun to tolerate the resulting anxiety will they be able to learn.

Repression, and particularly the necessity for prolonged repression of specific instinct representations, forces the ego to undertake the task of finding methods other than direct expression for the discharge and gratification of the repressed instinct. Without the presence of repression, it is questionable if the defense mechanisms of reaction formation and sublimation could be developed, and the individual would be fighting a constant and losing battle against direct discharge. The defense mechanism of repression is therefore an important aid to the learning process, although it may also be an important interference with it. Like all defense mechanisms it is extremely useful at the suitable time and place but becomes a serious hindrance if used unsuitably, particularly if it has to be used to excess.

REACTION FORMATION

At about the age of two the child derives great pleasure from inflicting pain on other people—usually the most-loved ones—and in having pain inflicted on him by them. In the boy the need to inflict pain predominates slightly; in the girl, the need to suffer pain. (The reasons for this difference are not important in this connection. I am simply stating an observable fact.) This is an expression of a part of the child's erotic instinctual drives, which at this age require direct gratification. If the child of this age were an adult and were to gratify his sexual desires in this way he would be considered a sadistic or masochistic pervert. That this sadomasochistic attitude of the two-year-old is sexual is indicated by the fact that a small degree of sadism and masochism is present during sexual intercourse—the man finding pleasure in inflicting mild pain on his partner, the woman finding pleasure in having mild pain inflicted on her. The large amount of sadomasochism seen in the young child, however, has been reduced considerably in the adult. This reduction in amount has occurred for several reasons. As the individual has matured, the aim of the sexual instinct has been deflected from nongenital sadomasochism to genital penetration or to being penetrated. Sexual energy is now expressed not through the organs which can give sadomasochistic pleasure—teeth, hands, feet, buttocks, for instance—but through the genitals. This deflection does not affect all of the sadomasochistic energy, nor can the remaining part be entirely discharged and gratified through sexual intercourse. Part remains in repression, and because it is in repression, it demands periodical discharge or the individual would suffer from frequent attacks of anxiety. How does the ego accomplish this periodical discharge? The ego could use the defense mechanism of changing one form of expression into its opposite. The sadism could be changed into masochism or vice versa. Still there would remain the same problem of how the changed instinct could be gratified directly, so this method of changing the instinct into its opposite, useful in other instances, here would be inadvisable. Instead the ego can turn the instinct representations—ideas and feelings—in the unscious part of the ego into their opposites. The gloating over being cruel now becomes satisfaction and pride in being kind. The desire to be hurt becomes pride and satisfaction in preventing other people from being hurt. These opposite instinct representations can then be released from repression, permitted to emerge into consciousness and to be expressed in actions. These actions still gratify and discharge the sadomasochistic instinct. This new defense mechanism is known as *reaction formation*. Through it cruelty becomes kindness, jealousy becomes the desire for social justice, selfishness becomes generosity, dirtiness becomes cleanliness, disorderliness becomes orderliness, wastefulness becomes the desire to save, and so on.

Freud [6] says that during the latency period pregenital sexuality awakens the contrary feeling of displeasure. From the end of the fourth year to puberty, reaction formations such as shame, disgust, and morality are formed at the expense of excitations from the erotogenic zones and are barriers erected against the total activity of these instincts. For example, disgust is a reaction formation against

[6] Sigmund Freud, "Character and Anal Erotism," *Collected Papers,* Vol. II, London, Hogarth Press and the Institute of Psycho-Analysis, 1933.

smell. Jones[7] says that in a little girl the common feeling of hatred toward the mother and passionate sexual attachment to the father may manifest itself by a reaction formation of excessive devotion to the mother and increasing antipathy to the father. As a cruel little child grows up, the idea of cruelty may be split off from the ego into the unconscious, and its place may be taken in consciousness by the reaction formation of horror and sensitiveness to pain and suffering. A disobedient child may develop unusual docility. Jones states that reaction formations eventually form quite a number of character traits: for example, the morbid tendency of puritans to be shocked is an excessive reaction formation. Abraham[8] says that shame originates as a reaction formation against scoptophilia and exhibitionism.

Reaction formation as a defense mechanism differs, it should be noted, from the defensive mechanism of reversal of instincts. Instinctual drives have paired forms of expression—sadism and masochism, peeping and exhibitionism. When the defense mechanism of reversal of instinct is used, the preponderance of one form of the pair is decreased while that of the other is accentuated, and the accentuated form is gratified directly and thus discharged. In reaction formation an opposite group of ideas and feelings is substituted and the substituted ideas and feelings are admitted into consciousness and gratified directly, so that the instinct tension is discharged.

Reaction formation is used largely to deal with the so-called pregenital instinct drives and in these instances is often desirable and useful. The extreme jealousy of the small child who wants everything for himself and does not desire to give anything to anyone else—except perhaps his mother—must be controlled in some way as he gets bigger, lest, with increased strength and ability, he become a murderer and a robber. Somewhere early in the latency period his extreme jealousy disappears. Instead of desiring everything for himself he begins to practice an exaggerated form of social justice. He will give up anything he wants provided every one of his contemporaries makes an

[7] Ernest Jones, "Freud's Psychology and Some Instances of the Influence of Dreams on Waking Life," *Papers on Psychoanalysis,* New York, William Wood and Company, 1923.

[8] Karl Abraham, "The Psychosexual Differences between Hysteria and Dementia Praecox," *Selected Papers on Psychoanalysis,* London, Hogarth Press and the Institute of Psycho-Analysis, 1927.

exactly equal sacrifice. He becomes extremely resentful if another child appears to be favored in some way that he is not, and demands that the other child be not so favored or that he himself receive exactly the same favor—regardless of whether or not he wants or needs it. Later, in adolescence and adult life, this reaction formation will become toned down into ideas and feelings of justice and of social, economic, and political equality. The psychoanalysis of adults who seem to have a great drive toward social reform reveals that they have a strongly developed reaction formed against jealousy and envy. They actually are very jealous people and their unconscious jealousy is gratified and discharged through the reaction formation. Their activities are much more desirable and acceptable to their peers and more comfortable to themselves than they would be if they acted as the robbers and murderers they are in their unconscious instinct representations.

However, the defense mechanism of reaction formation can become very hampering if used too often or too exclusively. The small child urinates and defecates whenever and wherever he feels inclined. He does this not only because he does not care to do otherwise but also because his behavior gives him a great deal of pleasure. During the process of his toilet training he has to learn that he can get the same or greater pleasure in more acceptable ways and that he must control the desire to get gratification from whatever of this pleasure still remains in the original form. He learns to defecate and urinate at the proper time and place. In short, he becomes clean.

Case 15. A very beautiful girl in her mid-twenties complained that she had no men friends and felt irritated that she was not married and was not a mother, as so many of her friends were. However, it was impossible for her to get married because men were dirty about their persons. She knew none that bathed three or four times a day, as she did, or perfumed themselves all over and particularly on the seat of their trousers, as she regularly did on the seat of her skirt. She could never sleep in the same bed with a man who did not do these things. The girl did not work, although her parents were in the lower economic group. She avoided doing anything that would make her dirty. She spent most of her day bathing, washing clothes, and so on. She felt very proud of her excessive cleanliness and was unable to understand how other people could tolerate not being as clean as she was. Consciously, she felt and expressed this great need to be clean and acted on it with much energy. The need to be clean was a conscious expression of an instinct representation. In the unconscious part of her ego the instinct representation was different. Unconsciously she had ideas of being very dirty, and she felt that the state of being dirty was a very pleasurable one. These unconscious ideas and feelings were changed from "I wish to be dirty" to "I wish to be *not* dirty" before they were permitted to become conscious. She then acted with energy and pleasure according to the conscious idea (she was concerned constantly with the need to be *not* dirty), but these actions gratified and discharged her desire to be dirty. The instinct was gratified and discharged, but the instinct representations in the conscious part of the ego were changed by the addition of the negative.

There is a long list of character traits—orderliness, conscientiousness, routine ways of working, and the like—which are forms of gratification and discharge of the pregenital instinctual drives. The unconscious part of the ego permits the instinctual drive to develop toward expression and then changes its form into its opposite before it is permitted to emerge into action and perhaps into consciousness as a character trait. The aim and object of the instinct does not change. Many character traits are the result of such reaction formations. However, the statement that character traits result from the pregenital instinctual drives is made so frequently that it tends to give the impression that character traits have no other basis. Character traits are really the acting out of forgotten infantile masturbation fantasies. In these fantasies pregenital instinctual drives play an important role.

A moderate degree of character building occurs when the child has to learn to prevent certain instinct representations from appearing directly in consciousness and to permit them to appear there in the form of their opposites instead. This has long been recognized by traditionally oriented educators, who have placed desirable emphasis on the need for the child to learn to do things disagreeable to himself, i.e., to do things which are the opposite of what he would like to do. The traditionally oriented educators generally have overemphasized this form of character building. The result has been the excessive development of the defense mechanism of reaction formation, with such socially hampering effects as occurred in the case described. On the other hand, the progressively oriented educators have underemphasized the need for reaction formation, with equally deplorable results of an opposite nature.

The defense mechanism of reaction formation is useful in the child's learning how to control and redirect the gratification and discharge of his instinct energy. He will be able to get real pleasure and happiness in his life if he becomes clean, just, and conscientious, provided he does not become so over clean, over just or overconscientious that he spends all his energies in pursuing these reaction formations at all times and under all circumstances. If he uses reaction formations to this extent he discharges all his instinct energy through them and, like the patient I mentioned, has no energy for any other pursuits. He therefore develops poorly, if at all, the more important defense mechanism of *sublimation*.

SUBLIMATION

With the possible exception of repression there is no term that is used more frequently and more incorrectly by nonanalysts, particularly teachers, than sublimation. Its constant misuse by such persons is not entirely the result of their own lack of understanding of the term but is due also, to a large degree, to the fact that psychoanalysts themselves do not understand very well the nature and dynamics of this form of defense against instinct. An instinctual drive which is being gratified and discharged in a manner that is completely acceptable to the superego, to the ego, and to the environment operates very silently because it causes no conflict. It is therefore extremely difficult to study. Under such circumstances neither the patient nor the psychoanalyst desires to pay much attention to the study of such a beneficial form of adaptation.

In the case of the young lady with reaction formations against dirt, the instinct had the aim of obtaining pleasure through her being dirty, and dirtying her loved object, with excreta. Her behavior was simply the direct expression of the instinct, with a "not" interposed in front of the aim. There was therefore no blocking in the discharge of the instinct, and the route through which it was discharged was exactly that of cleanliness–not-cleanliness. Neither the aim, the object, nor the route was changed, simply the connected idea. Any observer would say, "She was too concerned with being dirty and with the dirtiness of other people."

A sublimation is entirely different. The instinct, the desire to be dirty and to dirty, for instance, arises. Its presence causes in the id a feeling of tension and a need for discharge. So far the process is the same for all instincts. The unconscious part of the ego directed toward the id recognizes the tension, and instinct representations appear in it, but these instinct representations are different from those that appear in reaction formations. Instead of appearing as thoughts and feelings about dirtying and being dirtied, they appear as thoughts and feelings about creating something new or making a representation of something which has been thought of or perceived. The instinct is not repressed, but the aim has been changed—or perhaps, to speak more correctly, has been inhibited. This change or inhibition of aim is accompanied by desexualization. The aim of dirtying and being dirtied is a pregenital sexual aim. In a sublimation the sexual factor is withdrawn. The instinct is not repressed, but it continues toward discharge with all its original energy now completely directed to the idea and feeling of creating and representing. As a result, there is an alteration in the ego.

In reaction formation no such alteration takes place. The ego remains the same and demands only that a "not" be introduced into the desire before the desire can appear in consciousness. In sublimation the ego and the aim-inhibited instinct work together. The ego demands no alteration in the instinct representations or in the instinct, nor does it repudiate the instinct. It alters itself to go along with the instinct, its aim-inhibited representations, and sometimes its changed object. Now the aim-inhibited representations can pass readily from the unconscious part of the ego to the conscious part, and the latter, in order to discharge the energy more effectively, develops skills to use the energy. The girl I described might, instead of being constantly occupied with the desire not to be dirty, proceed to show interest in painting or modeling or sculpture. She could engage in these activities until she acquired skills. More skill would be developed if she received instruction, until finally she might produce works of art. If she had inherited the proper degree of cortical structure, i.e., associational pathways and the like, her productions might become highly skilled, to the point where she might earn her living by them or even become a famous artist. The end result would be the contribution of something of value to the real world. (Not all valuable contributions are sublimations.) Hermann [9] states that sublimation is an activity in which the sexual impulse does not succumb to repression but instead is deflected from its real aim and is used to lead to achievements serving a social or higher interest and involving an adaptation to reality. In this way there is progress from the pleasure to the reality principle. The impulse to restore is fundamental in sublimation. Painters often say that their hands are the instruments of something within them. If the sublimation is successful there is conscious ego gratification and enrichment, and a lack of ego gratification indicates a serious disturbance in the sublimatory process. Sublimation will be impossible if guilt and anxiety are overstrong. If the pleasure in a sublimation is accentuated, it can become a compulsion, a counting compulsion, for example. This result is found usually in persons with a high I.Q. If a sublimation is partly attained but never completed, there is no conscious pleasure in the activity but instead a feeling of inferiority and displeasure. According to Hermann the child who does homework because he fears punishment, or because he wishes to placate the teacher in order to get gifts and favors, has not achieved true sublimation. Learning failures have to do with failures of sublimation. There may be complete failure to sublimate, specifically a failure to sublimate peeping, or peeping may be oversublimated, in which case there will be no conscious pleasure in the activity: instead there will be a marked feeling of displeasure by contrast with colleagues and because the person becomes displeasing to the teachers and the parents.

Alpert [10] described the case of a boy whose weak superego and

[9] Paula Hermann, "A Contribution to the Problem of Sublimation and Its Relation to the Processes of Internalization," *International Journal of Psychoanalysis,* 23, 1942.

[10] Augusta Alpert, "Sublimation and Sexualization," *The Psychoanalytic Study of the Child,* Vols. III–IV, New York, International Universities Press, 1949.

weak authority figures made prolonged instinctual gratification easy. This colored all his ego activities and undermined the executive functions of the ego. A quick and easy gratification, patterned on autoerotic practices, was the patient's expectation in all undertakings. The patient's education had been too permissive and his creative powers had been released but not channelized into sublimation. Alpert points out that games are an early landmark in the development of sublimation because they satisfy sexual strivings in a desexualized way. At the same time, through play, the child learns to develop ego skills. The continuance of sexually gratifying games into the latency period constitutes one warning that there is an interference with sublimation. Genital sexual drives cannot be sublimated. Sublimation is a mechanism which operates only with pregenital sexual drives.

Deri [11] defines sublimation as a deflection of the instinct from the original aim and from the original object, or as the gratification of instinct by acceptable social or cultural activity. Sublimation is the result of ego defenses against pregenital impulses. After defenses have been developed against their direct discharge, the fate of these pregenital impulses is as follows: Part are retained as forepleasure during the genital sexual act, part become reaction formations and character traits, and part are diverted from their aims and object into gains through achievement. Only such pregenital impulses as have their source in bodily organs subserving self-preservation can be sublimated. Sublimation begins in the phallic phase when, despite the narcissism, there is greater interest in the object than in the organ. If the pregenital desires are given up because of fear, then the degree of sublimation will be just enough to prevent an outbreak of fear; but if they are given up because genital satisfaction is of greater value, then the degree and stability of the sublimation will be greater. Genital impulses cannot be sublimated, because they subserve solely the purpose of enjoyment. The normal individual, if he cannot find an adequate love object for external reasons, can only repress his sexual desires or regress to masturbation.

Hermann says that art furnishes an interesting example of how difficulties in sublimation occur. If toilet training occurs through too

[11] Frances Deri, "On Sublimation," *Psychoanalytic Quarterly,* 8, 1939.

great restrictions or too great indulgence there will be a fixation at the anal level. As a result, a superego antagonistic to anal and aggressive instinctual impulses will develop, and the ego will have to erect the defenses of reaction formation, ego restriction, and inhibition against these impulses. These defenses will interfere with the beginnings of sublimation. If the impulses at the phallic level are improperly trained by either too great restriction on creativeness or by disappointments about creative wishes, a superego antagonistic to creativity will develop and so the defenses of repression, ego restriction, and inhibition will be necessary. If there is improper training of the partly sublimated impulses by too realistic teaching of art too early and too seriously, the ego skills of mastery to control the impulse will be overdeveloped, or the ego will give up because the skills are too difficult to acquire. If there is a lack of opportunity for art, then the environmental restrictions will result in the impossibility of developing the ego skills of mastery. The instinctual impulses in art at the anal-erotic level takes the form of the erotic pleasures of smearing and the preoccupation with the excretory products, and the aggressive impulses of mastery and the restoration of destroyed objects. Ego restrictions and inhibitions are antagonistic to sublimations partly at the partial-sublimation level and partly at the impulse level. Reaction formation and repression are antagonistic to sublimations mostly at the impulse level.

It is surprising how frequently a person some of whose unnecessary repressions have been removed during a psychoanalysis will begin to develop automatically an interest in some form of endeavor in which he has displayed no previous interest, will work hard to acquire skills, and will produce creditable performances. A woman who had never before been interested in painting had suffered from an unconscious fear that she might soil and wet herself. When this fear became conscious the repression of some of her anal drives was removed; some time later the patient started to attend art school and was highly praised by her instructors for her oil paintings. When, as in this case, a reaction formation is reversed, the patient is confronted with the problem of whether to be uncivilized—dirty, as the first patient I mentioned wanted to be—or whether to repress the desire to be dirty. If repression takes place, further analysis will help a sublimation to occur. Instead of observers saying, "She is overinterested in dirt," they will say, "She has become a skillful painter."

I have tried to make clear the important resemblances and distinctions between the defense mechanisms of reaction formation and of sublimation. In both, the instinct is permitted free discharge, but the end results are entirely different. In reaction formation the instinct attempts to avoid the prohibitions of the superego by forcing the ego to give in to it and be ruled by it. The ego attempts to hoodwink the superego by pretending that it is obeying in presenting to it not the instinct representations but their opposites. In many cases, particularly if the reaction formation is severe, the superego dimly perceives that there is some sort of deception, and punishes the ego for its behavior. The unhappy, unsuccessful life of the girl in the case I described is a good illustration of superego punishment. Even if the superego does not punish the ego, too large an amount of pregenital instinct is drained off and discharged through the reaction formations, so that there is too little left for adequate development of the genital stage. Although this stage is reached finally the development is a weak one. Reaction formations therefore are more of a hindrance than an asset in life adaptation. Sublimations utilize only the parts of the pregenital instincts which are not capable of going on to the genital stage. They utilize these partial instincts for the benefit of the ego and so enable the ego to avoid having to use energy to keep them in repression or to deal with them by other forms of defense mechanisms. The alteration in the ego enables it to be the master of the instinct after the inhibition of the aim has occurred. In sublimation the ego controls the instinct, whereas in reaction formation the instinct controls the ego. Like reaction formations sublimations are attempts to avoid the superego prohibitions. This is done by hoodwinking the superego by the change in aim, and although the end result is a discharge of instinct, the superego raises no objection. The hard work entailed in developing ego skills for the sublimation is perhaps the penalty exacted by the superego for the violation of its prohibitions.

It might be of interest at this point to contrast some other types of defense mechanisms with reaction formation and sublimation. The little boy at the age of three to six loves his mother passionately and desires to possess her for his very own. As a consequence he is very jealous of his father and in his feelings toward him bitter hatred and love are mingled. This conflict of feelings, added to his jealousy, makes him fear his father. The little girl of the same age loves her father passionately and has the same conflict of fear, jealousy, hatred, and love of her mother. These conflicting feelings toward the parent of the same sex are too strong to be borne and the child has to discover some solution to them. Depending on certain circumstances, one of a variety of solutions may be selected, a few of which I will discuss.

In 1909 Freud [12] reported the case of a five-year-old boy, Little Hans, who suddenly became afraid to go out on the street lest a horse bite him. A careful study showed that the boy's fear of being bitten by the horse was an attempted solution of his conflicting feelings toward his father. He first had repressed his feelings of passionate love for his mother, and his equally strong feelings of hatred for his father, into his unconscious. Then these feelings had become displaced from the parents as object onto the idea of a horse. The horse represented in his mind his jealousy of his father, his hatred for him, and his love for him. He had then projected the feelings of jealousy and hatred from the idea of the horse in his mind onto the real horses in the external world. Horses, therefore, were jealous of him and hated him and desired to bite him, as he desired to bite and destroy his father. So he developed his fear of horses. In this way he became rid of his feelings of jealous hatred toward his father. He did not hate his father, but the horse did, and then he reversed the object of the feelings, so that the horse did not hate his father, but hated him. Having done this he was safe from his feelings toward his father as long as he did not see a horse. When he did see one, his only conscious feeling was a fear of the horse.

I have chosen this example of the use of the animal in the solution of a conflict of feelings because two of the other examples also use animals. For my next example I quote two cases from Anna Freud: [13]

> Our study of the defensive processes revealed in the analysis of Little Hans would suggest that the fate of his neurosis was determined from the moment in which he displaced his aggressiveness and anxiety from

[12] Sigmund Freud, "Analysis of a Phobia in a Five-Year-Old Boy," *Collected Papers,* Vol. III, London, Hogarth Press and the Institute of Psycho-Analysis, 1933.

[13] Anna Freud, *The Ego and the Mechanisms of Defense,* New York, International Universities Press, 1946.

his father to horses. But this impression is deceptive. Such a substitution of an animal for a human object is not in itself a neurotic process; it occurs frequently in the normal development of children and, when it does occur, the results vary greatly.

For instance, a seven year old boy whom I analyzed used to amuse himself with the following phantasy. He owned a tame lion, which terrified everyone else and loved nobody but him. It came when he called it and followed him like a little dog, wherever he went. He looked after the lion, saw to its food and its comfort in general and in the evening made a bed for it in his own room. As is usual in daydreams carried on from day to day, the main phantasy became the basis of a number of agreeable episodes. For example, there was a particular daydream in which he went to a fancy dress ball and told all the people that the lion which he brought with him, was only a friend in disguise. This was untrue, for the "disguised friend" was really his lion. He delighted in imagining how terrified the people would be, if they guessed his secret. At the same time he felt that there was no real reason for their anxiety, for the lion was harmless so long as he kept it under control.

From the little boy's analysis it was easy to see that the lion was a substitute for the father, whom he, like Little Hans, hated and feared as a real rival in relation to his mother. In both children aggressiveness was transformed into anxiety and the affect was displaced from the father on to an animal. But their subsequent methods of dealing with their affects differed. Hans used his fear of horses as the basis of his neurosis, i.e. he imposed upon himself the renunciation of his instinctual desires, internalized the whole conflict and, in accordance with the mechanism of phobia, avoided situations of temptation. My patient managed things more comfortably for himself. Like Hans in the phantasy about the plumber, he simply denied a painful fact and in his lion phantasy turned it into its pleasurable opposite. He called the anxiety animal his friend, and its strength, instead of being a source of terror, was now at his service. The only indication that in the past the lion had been an anxiety object was the anxiety of the other people, as depicted in the imaginary episodes.[14]

Here is another animal phantasy, produced by a patient of ten years

[14] Berta Bornstein gives an account of the phantasies of a seven year old boy, in which good animals turned into evil ones in a similar way. Every evening the child would put his toy animals round his bed like tutelary deities, but he imagined that, in the night, they made common cause with a monster which wanted to attack him. [Anna Freud's note]

old. At a certain period in this boy's life, animals played an immensely important part; he would pass hours at a time in daydreams in which they figured, and he even kept written records of some of his imaginary episodes. In this phantasy he owned a huge circus and was also a lion tamer. The most savage wild beasts, which in a state of freedom were deadly enemies, were trained to live together in amity. My little patient tamed them, i.e. he taught them first not to attack one another and then not to attack human beings. When taming them, he never used a whip but went about amongst them unarmed.

All the episodes in which the animals figured centered in the following story. One day, during a performance in which they were taking part, a thief who was sitting amongst the public suddenly fired a pistol at him. Immediately the animals banded together to protect him and dragged the thief out of the crowd, being careful not to hurt anyone else. The rest of the phantasy was concerned with the way in which—always out of devotion to their master—they punished the thief. They kept him a prisoner, buried him and triumphantly made an enormous tower over him out of their own bodies. They then took him to their den, where he had to stay for three years. Before they finally released him, a long row of elephants beat him with their trunks, last of all threatening him with an uplifted finger (!) and warning him never to do it again. This he promised. "He won't do it any more, as long as I am with my beasts." After the description of all that the animals inflicted on the thief there was a curious postscript to this phantasy, containing the assurance that they fed him very well when he was their prisoner, so that he did not become weak.

In my seven year old patient's phantasy about the lion we had a bare indication of the working over of the ambivalent attitude towards the father. The circus phantasy goes considerably further in this respect. By the same process of reversal the dreaded father of reality is transformed into the protective beasts of the phantasy, but the dangerous father object himself reappears in the figure of the thief. In the story about the lion it was uncertain against whom the father substitute was really going to protect the child, whose ownership of the lion merely raised him in a general way in the estimation of other people. But in the circus phantasy it is quite clear that the father's strength, embodied in the wild beasts, served as a protection against the father himself. Once more, the stress laid on the former savageness of the animals indicated that in the past they were objects of anxiety. Their strength and adroitness, their trunks and the uplifted finger obviously were really associated with the father.

The child attached great importance to these attributes: in his phantasy he took them from the father whom he envied and, having assumed them himself, got the better of him. Thus the roles of the two were reversed. The father was warned "not to do it again" and had to ask for pardon. One remarkable point is that the promise of safety which the animals finally forced him to make to the boy depended on the latter's continued ownership of them. In the "postscript" about the feeding of the thief the other side of the ambivalent relation to the father finally triumphed. Evidently the daydreamer felt obliged to reassure himself that, in spite of all the aggressive acts, there was no need to fear for his father's life.

Case 16. Another case is that of a girl of nine. She was fascinated by horses, made quite a large collection of toy horses, with which she played, and was able to persuade her parents to give her riding lessons so that soon she became quite an expert rider. She wanted to own her own horse and was planning to go into the business of raising and training horses when she grew up. This planning was done carefully, for she had already learned a great deal about horses and their care.

In her fantasies, which were reproduced in her play, there were many dangerous animals—lions, tigers, boa constrictors, and crocodiles—and dangerous people—Indians, bandits. These frequently came to attack the owners of the horses and the horses themselves. A stallion always protected the owners and the horses by attacking and defeating the dangerous invaders. It was possible to understand from her that the dangerous animals represented her mother and her siblings, of whom she was jealous. The dangerous enemies were her own feelings of jealous hostility against her mother and siblings projected into the animals. She did not have a phobia about these animals, as Little Hans did. Instead of fearing her hostile feelings toward them, she simply projected the feelings. The stallion was her protection against them. In her fantasies the stallion also represented her father, whom she loved passionately. If he loved her as she did him and allowed her to possess him then she would have no reason for any jealousy of her mother and siblings. The horse was a projection of her possessive love for her father and her desire that he love her exclusively. As long as she could persuade herself that this was the case she did not need to fear her feelings of rivalry with the rest of the family. She had no phobia about the horse nor was any attribute of the horse based on hostility, as in the cases I have quoted from Anna Freud.

She was conscious of her feelings of love for her father, so that only the passionate possessiveness had been repressed. In repression, the aim of passionate possessiveness of the father was inhibited and changed into a desire to possess horses and look after them. Besides the inhibition of the aim and its desexualization there was also a change of object. Formerly she had desired her father to look after her exclusively, now she desired to look after her father exclusively. This idea was in her unconscious but was able to represent itself consciously in her avowed desire to look after horses exclusively. Thus instead of developing a phobia such as formed Little Hans' neurotic solution, or the fantasy of protective animals which Anna Freud's cases entertained, this patient found a solution through sublimation. Through this sublimation the conflicting feelings toward her rivals were raised into the sphere of competition with rivals about which she need have no conflict.

Had this girl attempted to solve her problem through a reaction formation there would have been no interest in horses. Instead she would have felt consciously indifferent to her father and very devoted and loving to her mother, so devoted perhaps as to be irritating. This devotion would have been the conscious expression of her unconscious hatred.

THE REASONS FOR THE SELECTION OF A PARTICULAR DEFENSE

We do not know why the defense mechanism of reaction formation is selected for a specific instinctual drive in one instance and the defense mechanism of sublimation in another. There is some evidence to indicate that, apart from repression, one individual tends to depend rather heavily on one main method of defense and another on a different one. In a study [15] of defense mechanisms in children in nursery school, I received the impression that the individual child was accus-

[15] Gerald H. J. Pearson, "The Chronically Aggressive Child," *Psychoanalytic Review*, 26, 1939.

successfully to use the instinctual energy at his disposal. In the past few years they have become more cognizant of the latter problem, but their efforts in this direction have been based more on rather uncertain intuitive understanding than on actual knowledge of the instinctual life. For example, progressive educators have become much concerned with developing "creativity" in the child. In the previous chapter I have discussed the fact that creativity is the end result of a conflict between the ego and the instinctual life in which the ego develops the defense mechanism of sublimation. In this chapter I will discuss what facts psychoanalysis has to offer for a better understanding of the relation between creativity and education. In order to consider this subject realistically it is necessary first to examine what is meant by creativity and what the philosophy and social implications of academic education are.

Creativity is a sublimation, but all sublimations are not creative. The learning of arithmetic is also a sublimation, but it is not creative. In order to understand what is meant by creativity it seems desirable to contrast the fate of the instinctual impulses in play, in work, and in creative art. Play is the *direct* expression of an instinctual impulse which is permitted because there is a leave of absence from the superego during the play pretense. Work is a sublimated expression of an instinctual impulse but the sublimation is influenced by other factors, like imitation, identification, and so on. Creative art is a sublimated expression of an instinctual impulse but it implies doing something new. Also, the sublimated activity usually has a value element.

The school exists in our culture, basically, for three reasons. In the capitalistic economic system of free enterprise the child must learn skills through which he eventually will be able to earn a living for himself and his family. Among these skills are the use of language, as in reading, writing, spelling, and grammar, and the use of numbers in arithmetic, algebra, geometry, and allied subjects. This learning can be done only through a school system, because the skills necessary for earning a living in our highly complex civilization are too numerous to be learned except by special methods and through instruction by specially trained persons. Partly to help him earn a living, but chiefly to enable him to know as much as possible about all the phenomena he perceives in his daily life, the child must learn about the real world in which he lives, not only those parts of it that come under his personal observation but also the parts which he is far away from and may never see. These skills involve such studies as geography, astronomy, and biology. These two groups of skills are essential to the individual's ability to remain alive and to carry on the race. Also, he needs to learn about previous human experiences and the history of the world. Here are included history, anthropology, geology, and the humanities, the ideas and concepts of men in the past. He has to learn how to integrate all this knowledge for use in his daily living.

The curriculum of the grammar, junior high, and high schools in the United States is devised to conform to the standards laid down by the college and university boards. It consists of the so-called major subjects: English, mathematics, history, geography, science, foreign languages—either ancient or modern; and minor subjects: arts, music, shop, physical education, and dramatics. For a number of years there has been a tendency in the grammar school to combine the subjects of history and geography into one, called social studies, and to slant the emphasis from the history of the past to the history of the present. There always has been a tendency in the study of history to focus largely—in fact, almost exclusively—on the national history. Recently there has been a trend toward the de-emphasis of ancient languages in favor of the modern languages of Western Europe. The trend of progressive education has been away from the knowledge of the past and from emphasis on the major subjects toward a more intense interest in the so-called creative arts. Generally, the progressive schools have paid little or no attention to physical education. This has occurred partly because of their opposition to competitive sports and partly because general experience indicates that people interested in creative arts usually are not interested in physical sports, and vice versa. As the progressive schools tend to select teachers whose interests are in the arts, the teacher interested in sports is seldom found on the staff.

The type of curriculum generally found in our schools has a historical background. Adamson [1] states that the reason why for centuries all formal schooling in Western Europe has had a literary foundation and superstructure is that it originated in Rome, where grammar and

[1] John William Adamson, *The Illiterate Anglo-Saxon and Other Essays on Education Medieval and Modern,* Cambridge, the University Press, 1946.

rhetoric were the basis of education. Quintilian early in the fifth century organized the curriculum into seven arts.

Trivium
- grammar—language, literature
- rhetoric
- dialectic—philosophy, formal logic

Quadrivium
- geometry
- arithmetic—properties of numbers
- astronomy—astrology
- music—mathematical and physical study of sound

Grammar was the usual entrance to all the arts and to the professional studies of theologians and physicians. The literary, bookish type of education established within the Latin civilization was maintained and became the system of the medieval schools. The university was a guild. The teachers and students, sojourners in a population frequently hostile, formed associations for their mutual benefit from which colleges developed. It was not the business of the schools to instruct in the three R's. Elementary schools originated as a result of the demands of commerce and industry for junior clerks and workmen who could read and write the vernacular and make out and understand a bill. These schools were distinct from grammar schools and grew up in commercial and industrial centers, first in Italy and Germany. Originally religion was closely connected with education. It was no small part of true education to teach a man to act in accordance with his duty to God and his fellows. The book *De Disciplina Scholarium,* published in the twelfth century, gives the medieval concepts of education. During preschool education the delights of children were to be examined. Actual schooling began at the age of seven. For this the child was to be physically fit. The course was not to involve undue exposure to heat and cold. There could be frugal indulgence in food and drink, and the child was to have no lack of clothing. The laborious struggle of learning the alphabet and the meaning of words was not to be abandoned within two or three years. After the school rudiments had been learned, the next step was the study of logic. A good pupil had three qualities. He was attentive in hearing and docile in understanding and had good will in retaining. There were four hindrances to learning: truancy, a riotous disposition, unrestrained luxury and indulgence in sensuality, and feebleness of mind.

In our day, the avowed purpose of the curriculum is to give the child a general knowledge of the world in the present and, to a less extent, in the past, so that his intellectual curiosity will be stimulated and he will experience pleasure in continuing to learn more and more throughout his life. The hope is to fit him in this way to be a good citizen and to develop sublimations for his repressed infantile drives. Basically, however, the curriculum is slanted toward fitting him to operate successfully in our present culture, particularly toward equipping him to be self-supporting. For this purpose, skills in English and in mathematics are deemed of paramount importance—the former because it is the basis for all our means of communication, the latter because in our culture measurements and money require knowledge of the principles of computation.

Proficiency in these basic skills—reading, writing, and the use of numbers—is also considered essential in our culture for the acquisition of all the secondary skills, whether these are acquired for their occupational value, for the gratification of intellectual curiosity, or purely for pleasure. But though the acquisition of the basic skills is necessary because of our cultural development, it is not a biological necessity. This is the reason that the child often considers unreasonable the demand of the adult that he learn them. Consequently, this cultural requirement produces many conflicts between the child and the adult and many conflicts between groups of educators concerning how the teaching should be done.

COMMUNICATION

The basic means of communication is speech, which the child acquires automatically through his identification with his parents, long before he reaches school age. In this way he learns a set of arbitrary symbols which represent his visual and tactile perception of the world around him and of himself. Along with the symbols he learns the emotional values attached to them through the gestures which accompany speech and through the inflection, tone, pitch, of speech itself. The symbols and their emotional values are learned mostly through hearing and slightly through sight. This part of the learning process is passive-receptive. The attachment of the symbols with their emotional values to the child's own concepts and perceptions—which have their own emotional values—is an active process, as is the use of speech as a means of communication.

The use of speech as a means of communication has been until lately limited by time and space—the person to be communicated with had to be within the present sound of the communicator's voice. The invention of the telegraph, the telephone, and the radio have overcome these spatial limitations. They act to extend widely the use of speech as a means of communication—the communicator still using it actively, the recipient relying on his hearing to receive it. By the invention of the recording machine the temporal limitations have been overcome. The process of communication by records is still motor-active, auditory-passive, but the record also forms an extension of memory—for memory is the function which overcomes temporal limitations.

The invention of transmitting and recording machines is very recent. Before their invention, the temporal and spatial limitations of speech as a means of communication were overcome chiefly through writing, whose beginnings are lost in prehistory. It is necessary to use additional skills to translate the spoken, heard word into writing. The heard and spoken symbol has to be reproduced manually in a way that can be seen. This means the training of the associations between the auditory areas and the visual-motor areas governing the use of the hands. The auditory word symbol has to be perceived as a visual symbol and then reproduced in writing. Written speech readily overcomes the limitations of space and, by forcing an extension of memory, the limitations of time. It is actively motor and visual. The recipient has to be visually passive-receptive. It is this additional enlistment of hand and eye in the use of visual symbols to represent auditory ones which makes special instruction in learning these skills necessary, whereas because of the imitation and identification of the child with the adult, no special instruction is needed for learning the use of the ear-mouth combination in spoken speech. As I mentioned earlier, it is with the learning of the skills of reading and writing that most of the child's basic scholastic education is concerned, and it is here that the greatest problems arise.

To teach reading, writing, and the basic rules of mathematical calculation, such as tables, traditional educators have employed largely the repetition of activities of ear, eye, and hand; the enlistment of rote memory through drills and the like; and the pleasure-pain principle, through praise, reward, and censure. Progressive educators have turned away from these methods, preferring to wait until the child develops a desire to learn to read and write, and then combine this desire with pleasurable situations and the use of the circumstances of his daily life in order to teach him.

There seems to be a trend toward reducing the importance of learning the skills of reading, writing, and the basic technics of computation in favor of other branches of the curriculum—particularly of the arts and crafts—which do not require the knowledge of these skills. It is possible that the progressive educators are more aware than traditional educators of the present trends in culture—particularly the culture of Western Europe and America. It is only in this culture that the importance of reading and writing for everyone, the need for general literacy, has been stressed, and it seems at present that even here the emphasis on reading and writing has reached its peak. The importance of writing as a means of communicating with friends has diminished greatly since its heyday in the eighteenth and nineteenth centuries. No longer are long essaylike letters common. If one has something to communicate, he utilizes the telegraph or the telephone.

VOCATIONAL USES OF KNOWLEDGE

It is valuable to consider the use that the American citizen makes of the knowledge he has learned at school. In order to do this, it is necessary to group the population according to its various occupations, for as I said earlier, knowledge learned in school is taught primarily for its occupational value, and only secondarily for its gratification of intellectual curiosity and for pleasure.

FARMERS AND OTHERS ENGAGED IN AGRICULTURAL PURSUITS

At the present time, the farmer needs a basic knowledge of arithmetical computation technics, particularly those involved in using money. He keeps certain records in writing in order to economize on the use of his memory. He may read an agricultural journal or book which requires a minimal knowledge of the basic sciences. His occupation, therefore, requires a small degree of skill in the three R's and a very little of the knowledge he has learned in school. In his role as a citizen, to satisfy his interest in the world, and for pleasure, he reads newspapers, magazines, and books. His reading, however—whether it serves as a source of needed information, to gratify intellectual curiosity about his occupation, his community, his state, his nation, his religion or the past, or simply to give pleasure alone—is being displaced by the radio, television, movies, and records, and by the increased facilities of transportation, which enable him to see other parts of the world instead of reading about them. The increasing use of even the present rather crude computation machines will relieve him from the necessity for more than the most rudimentary knowledge of figures.

HOUSEWIVES

In her occupation, the housewife uses even less of the knowledge obtained at school than does the farmer. A knowledge of how to make change and add sums of money is all the mathematics she needs. Ability to read and to record recipes is necessary. Her intellectual curiosity is more and more gratified by the radio, television, and movies, and today even magazines rely more on pictures to present their contents than on the printed text.

In a country where the scholastic education of both sexes is compulsory, often up to the age of eighteen, the use that the girl can make of her education in her biological role of wife and mother seems very slight indeed. Every little girl desires to identify with her mother and has the ambitional fantasy of taking her mother's place when she grows up. Her scholastic education does not contribute a great deal toward developing skills for the better realization of this fantasy. In fact at present there seems to be little relation between the two. Much of the daily routine of the wife and mother is accomplished rather quickly through the use of laborsaving devices, which she demands from the beginning of her marriage in order to have the same comforts as her mother did, because she has to live out the fantasy of taking her mother's place. So she has a great deal of idle time on her hands. I wonder if it is not a combination of this idle time, her unused education, and the fact that these laborsaving devices are expensive that makes her want to earn part of the income of the family. I wonder, too, if they are not responsible for the discontent with the female role which seems to be increasing among civilized women, for the increasing drive to be male, for the increasing criticism of the husband, and for the feeling that he is inferior.

SKILLED AND SEMISKILLED MECHANICS

The mechanic's actual use of school knowledge is much the same as that of the farmer and the housewife. Diagrams, pictures, and the like have taken the place of written descriptions. For example, visual education has risen to great prominence in training a mechanic in the process of understanding and servicing an internal-combustion engine.

WHITE-COLLAR WORKERS

The so-called white-collar workers—businessmen, clerks, stenographers, salesmen, i.e., those whose livelihood depends on the exchange of goods rather than on production—at present use school knowledge and the basic three R's to a much greater extent than do members of the three previously mentioned occupational groups. There is much necessity for recorded communications and for records. However, it is easy to surmise that with the increase in recording machines, particularly those which record on a flexible plastic record that can be made in duplicate or triplicate, so that one copy can be mailed, and with the increase and perfection of computing machines, particularly if the results are recorded on records, the use of reading, writing, and arithmetic among this group will be vastly reduced. The only difficulty at present lies in the fact that to refer to a particular section in a record requires that the whole record be played through, whereas one can look up the section in a written record without bothering about the rest of the material.

PROFESSIONAL PERSONS

The various professions depend a great deal more on the knowledge of the past than do the other groups. So far, the written word is the medium which permits ready access to this knowledge. Also, certain professions, such as science and engineering, require a knowledge of mathematics. In most respects, however, the use of reading, writing, and arithmetic by professional people is much like that of members of the previous group.

It is evident that machines—recording machines, computing machines, radio, and television—are rapidly replacing reading and writing as methods of overcoming the limitations of space and time in communication. It is only in the sphere in which they are used as extensions of memory that machines have not been perfected to the point where they can replace the three R's. No one can say that this cannot be done in the next few years, but it may be wondered whether the auditory sensory system can tolerate their constant use and perform as well as the visual system does. The use of glasses, and therefore perhaps the need for them, has increased rapidly in the past century. There is evidence to prove that sound can have a destructive effect on the human body, and this effect is much more striking than is the effect of light impulses.

Perhaps in the next few years reading, writing, and arithmetic will become practically unnecessary. Education, then, will have to place less emphasis on the acquisition of these skills and more on the skills needed in using the recording and computing machines. This will necessitate a complete revision of the curriculum, particularly in the lower schools.

It should also be noted that there is a strong tendency in the Western world to replace various national languages by English, so that the learning of French, Spanish, and German—the usual modern languages required in the scholastic education of the American child—is rapidly becoming unnecessary. It may be necessary in the near future for children to learn one or more of the Oriental, Eastern European, or Near Eastern languages, but as in the past, English probably will remain the lingua franca. Latin and Greek have already disappeared from most school curricula. In other directions, change is apparent. Home economics is becoming obsolete. The great increase in prepared and partly prepared foods has removed any real need for anybody to know how to cook. Clothes can be bought which are cheaper and better styled and made than those that are homemade, so sewing is no longer a necessary skill.

The use of machines, such as those that make it possible to run an entire auto assembly line without the presence of a human being, means a great deal more leisure time for human beings. Perhaps another important change in the curriculum will be the introduction of opportunities for learning the use of sublimations to absorb this leisure. These sublimations undoubtedly will have to be more active than those presented by the radio, television, movies, and the observation of professional athletics. Otherwise adult life will become very boring. It is important also to remember that modern medicine is increasing the span of life and the physical abilities of persons beyond the age of sixty. As the sexual life becomes less active there is a tendency to regress to pregenital gratifications, as is seen in the so-called second childhood. In order to avoid the degenerative phases of this regression it is well that each person of sixty years or more have a number of real skills for the sublimation of his pregenital drives.

The more progressive schools, and even many of the traditional ones, are recognizing this need and are hurrying to fill in the gap by introducing instruction in the creative arts—painting, drawing, modeling, and dramatics. In some schools these subjects seem to assume as much importance, perhaps more, than do the humanities. In many ways this seems a pity, for the humanities contain knowledge that can be shared by all, whereas the successful use of the arts is, for reasons I am going to discuss, limited to certain individuals.

WHAT IS AN ARTIST?

What is an artist—whatever the specific field in which he practices? Certain people seem to have more artistic or musical or mechanical ability than the average person, and certain people seem to be very deficient in these abilities. It seems probable that a part of the reason for this difference lies in specific differences in brain structure, perhaps in the degree of development of certain cortical areas and in the degree of complexity of certain cortical-subcortical association pathways. This, as yet, has not been demonstrated anatomically. Some findings are significant. Psychotic children almost invariably show in their infancy a great terror of loud noises or even of any noise. Later these children compensate for this by becoming extremely interested in music, and usually show remarkable ability. Although this also has not been proven experimentally, it seems reasonable to believe that they have hyperacusis because their auditory centers and association pathways are better developed than those of the average child. There is definite need for further investigation into this matter, particularly as auditory hallucinations are so common in adult psychotics.

The probability, however, that differences among various people's artistic and other special abilities may result from anatomical differences gives only a partial explanation. Psychoanalysts are aware of the fact that often these abilities are inhibited by defenses against pregenital instinctual drives. Not infrequently, after a patient's defenses against his anal-erotic, sadistic, and exhibitionistic drives have been analyzed, he will become interested in music or painting or woodworking as a hobby. His performance, although perhaps not of the highest caliber, may nevertheless be very pleasing and creditable. This happens so often that I believe all persons actually have the ability to produce pleasing and creditable results along artistic or mechanical lines, but the ability lies dormant because of certain inhibiting effects resulting from the training processes used in early childhood. If the ego defenses, usually of the type of reaction formations, are very rigid, the fear of the expression of the instincts is very great and therefore the ability to produce artistically is below average. Such defenses can even prevent an individual whose ability along artistic, musical, or mechanical lines is greater than the average, because of differences in brain structure, from using this ability successfully. It is well known that the psychoanalysis of such people makes it possible for them to improve their productions.

Up to this point I have been discussing the artistic and other special abilities of ordinary people, not of the true creative artist. The creative artist has a particular type of personality which causes him to occupy himself with creative art. Freud [2] says: "The artist is originally a man who turns from reality because he cannot come to terms with the demands for the renunciation of individual satisfaction as it is first made, and who then in phantasy-life allows full play to his erotic and ambitious wishes. But he finds a way of return from this world of phantasy back to reality; with his special gifts he moulds his phantasies into a new kind of reality. . . . Thus by a certain path he actually becomes the hero, king, creator, favourite he desired to be, without pursuing the circuitous path of creating real alterations in the outer world." This presupposes that there are only certain individuals who, besides being capable of attaining great success in a chosen artistic field, also can obtain psychologically real pleasure from the field of art. These will be persons who for definite reasons have not accepted reality as much as most people do, but have circumvented it through the mechanism of daydreams. But this circumvention has not resulted from any damage to their ability to test reality, nor has it been of a degree that would interfere with their reality testing; therefore it will be found in only a very few people, as the result of certain specific influences in their early lives.

THE INTRAPSYCHIC BASIS OF CREATIVE ART

I have said earlier that creative art is a sublimation. Rickman [3] states that owing to the conflict of the underlying forces of love and hate, and ambivalence toward a single object, and to the unbearable nature of our unconscious ideas, our minds disguise the crude and horrible so that these will not disfigure the more gracious intentions of our thoughts. We call things ugly because they have an appearance or aspect which causes dread or horror, such as is aroused, for instance, by the visual perceptions of deformity or squalor, because they are offensive or unpleasant to taste or smell, or because they are suggestive of terrible danger. He cites Peto's experiments in regard to the devel-

[2] Sigmund Freud, "Formulations Regarding the Two Principles in Mental Functioning," *Collected Papers,* Vol. IV, London, Hogarth Press and the Institute of Psycho-Analysis, 1934.

[3] John Rickman, "On the Nature of Ugliness and the Creative Impulse," *International Journal of Psychoanalysis,* 21, 1940.

opment of feelings of disgust toward unpleasant smells. Peto studied the reactions of three hundred children aged from one month to sixteen years to "unpleasant" odors and was able to classify them into three groups. In the first group, composed of children of five and under, eighty-nine out of ninety-two found no smells disagreeable. In the second group, composed of children from five to six years of age, nineteen out of thirty-nine showed disgust with the same smells. In the third group, composed of children six years old and over, one hundred and twenty-seven out of one hundred and sixty-four showed strong disgust. To the younger children smells were not as "ugly" as to the older ones. There are many adults who dislike mutilated classical statues and consider them "ugly." Similarly, there are children who dislike or will not use broken toys.[4] In these instances the subject identifies himself with the broken object. He has thought of himself as a mutilated person and has wished to retaliate on the mutilator, or he has identified the statue with someone whom in his thoughts he has wished to mutilate. Rickman believes that the sight of these mutilations reawakens fantasies of hostility and of the desire to mutilate. These fantasies are more disturbing than the defects in the object itself. The fantasy of aggressive action remains unconscious, and the fear and horror of it become attached to the external object, so that the person does not realize his secret wish. Once the wish fantasy of mutilation has been brought to consciousness and its origin traced in its relation to loved persons, mutilated statues can be enjoyed as artistic compositions.

He found that when there seemed to be a limitation of interest to certain periods or cultures, there was a connection between the individual's conception of the culture or the period, and the fantasies which served as the background of his mental life. Like all psychoanalysts, I have seen this myself in a number of cases. One adolescent boy developed a great interest in *The Idylls of the King* when he

[4] This often seems to be true of children who cannot write *E* correctly, but reverse it. Such children also tend to reverse *S, B, D,* 6, 9, and 7. In my own experience I found *E* and *S* the most difficult letters to learn to write. My own first name, Gerald, means "strong with a spear" and I knew this from an early age. In the second grade I had great difficulty in spelling it because I usually wrote it as "Gearld." I believe I did this to avoid recognition of my hostility to my father, the *r* in "Gerald" being an attacking point.

began to develop heterosexual love. At the same time he developed a desire to fence and do combat as a knight. Another boy, who was concerned greatly with the period of his life when his sister was adopted, showed a devouring interest in the France of Louis XIV and XV. According to him, at that time men's clothes were more like women's clothes are today. If he had lived at that time he would have been more like the girl the parents seemed so pleased with. They would have liked him as much as he thought they liked his sister, and he would still have been a boy. Also, the period came to an end with a massacre, so this preferred sister would end that way too—but he would not be the person who committed the killing. In contrast, there are patients who show a reaction formation against interest in their own past by developing a lack of interest in the historical past, even to the extent of repressing such knowledge from consciousness. This is an attempt to repudiate any interest in their childhood, particularly in their relation to the parents and the parental ideology, and often it is combined with an insistence on the importance of social betterment today.

Rickman points out that the dream work and art work are the same. Dreams differ from one another in respect to the degree to which the manifest content shows the influence of the primary thought processes or of the secondary thought process. Also they can be classified with respect to their objects. There are dreams for oneself alone, dreams for a particular person, and daydreams in common for a group playing a particular game. The artist works for an inner audience, his superego. For the artist, this consists not only of the parental images but also of what he has learned from art school. Just as the child's work must gain his teacher's approval and as the child learns from that approval, so the artist's work has to be judged by his instructors, and as a result he incorporates the instruction and the images of his teachers into his superego. This superego influences his technic. It guides the hand but does not free the spirit.

This is true for the acquisition of all skills. The superego guides the hand—in short, it permits the ego to allow the instinctual drives access to motility. In this way the use of knowledge becomes for the artist a weapon to deal with reality, and is a phallic ability. His choice of subject is influenced by what he has absorbed from the cultured people of his generation during his formative years. In general, colleagues have an influence on learning, and on the subjects the person likes to learn. This brings competition and group approval into the process of learning.

In one's work one has to obtain the approval of inner objects which are compounds of external experience and inner fantasy. To the child's fantasy, a line is a parent figure. Another line crossing it is the other parent or a knife hewing the first in two. The pencil is a magic wand giving the child power to do good or ill to the figures according to the mood of the moment. This is a primitive expression of what the infantile artist feels, which has no relation to what he sees. When a higher stage of graphic skill is reached, there is a desire to bring objects in the outer world under the domination of the magic pencil.

There are three phases in creative art. In Phase 1, art is an expression in magical action of primitive impulses directed against external objects. In Phase 2, attention is paid to the depiction of the *form* of the external object because of an interest driven by anxiety as to the fate of its inner counterpart, or because the treatment of details is governed by past object interest. In Phase 3, the element of composition develops as a result of increasing capacity to separate elements in the combined parent figure. This is a phase in which the interaction between external and internal objects ceases to be wholly magical and acquires some of the characteristics of thought. Composition is the synthesis of elements which the mind has torn asunder, an effort at construction after a mental act of destruction. Art takes away the sense of guilt which arises from the fact that death wishes are streaming toward and stifling the good object. Creative activity in art is a way of abolishing the idea of death. Similarly, children's play at construction often is a defense against the mental act of destruction of the self as a retaliation for the desire to destroy.

Lee,[5] who has published the majority of recent articles on the psychoanalysis of creative art, agrees with Rickman. He says that the creative artist from time to time has to relax the function of pity in order to permit some expression of his destructive rage. When this happens, he suffers from a marked feeling of guilt which easily could

[5] Harry B. Lee, "Projective Features of Contemplative Artistic Experience," *American Journal of Orthopsychiatry,* 19, 1949.

result in a neurotic depression. Through the substitute reaction formations of inspiration and creativeness, the depressed artist makes restitution for the destruction contemplated by his rage and at the same time sues for the return of love and approval from his conscience. In relation to poetry, Lee [6] quotes Bull, who says that poetry is an oral-erotic play of chewing and sucking nice words and phrases. Freud, Rank, and Sachs regard it as a sublimation. According to Lee's analysis, poetry is produced to undo aggressive impulses. Artistic creativity is really a compulsive need to create form, and so it is a reaction formation against deeply repressed hostile drives. The particular form of the activity, and the subject matter, are not dependent on the reaction formation but express unconscious wishes and are sublimations of pregenital instinctual drives—oral, anal, peeping, exhibitionist, and the like. If there is too much conflict, not about the drive that is being sublimated nor about the repressed hostility, but about the solution of the edipus situation, the presence of such a conflict influences the content of the production. For example, it seems obvious that Browning's tendency to select as his heroes fictional characters who to some extent always fail in their ambitions reflects an unsolved portion of Browning's own edipus situation.

The drive to creative activity, based on a very great fear and sense of guilt about hostile impulses, and the form that the creative activity takes, based on sublimations of specific unexpended pregenital drives, are the results of specific experiences in the individual's life. The ability to use this combination effectively in reality to such an extent that it can be made a source of livelihood depends on a specific constitutional endowment in the individual. As I said earlier, this particular combination of forces will be found in only a few people, who because of their work will be considered exceptional.

Real creativity cannot be "taught" as is commonly thought by many educators. In *The New York Times Magazine* of August 31, 1952, Mr. Victor D'Amico, that day's guest columnist, who is Director of the Department of Education and the People's Art Center of the Museum of Modern Art, writes:

[6] Harry B. Lee, "Poetry Production as a Supplemental Emergency Defense against Anxiety," *Psychoanalytic Quarterly,* 7, 1938.

For a quarter of a century the idea has been growing that creative art experience has value for individuals of all ages but most especially to the growing child. Nevertheless, the idea is far from being carefully realized because of the confusion about what art really does for children and how it is best made available to them.

Art, in the opinion of many, should be the "Fourth R" of education. In my opinion, [he states,] it is more basic than the other traditional three, and the child can less afford to be without it because art contributes to his emotional and spiritual growth. Creative training will help to enrich a child through his increased sensitivity to living and at the same time will serve as insulation against the growing tension of our time. Obviously, with this as our goal, there is no place today for the "genius myth"—the idea that certain children, with perhaps more interest and aptitude, are the elite where art is concerned and therefore deserve better attention.

Neither is there a place, when increased creativity and deeper sensitivity is the goal of art training, for lessons which stress copying; for contests which pit one child against another; for coloring books with just one admonition: Keep inside the lines. The emphasis on the finished product, rather than the creative process—an emphasis which mass production has made commonplace—is also out of line with this newer thinking.

It may seem unfair to place the responsibility for the child's creative growth upon the parent, but the child begins his creative life at home under the guidance of the parent, and parents together can influence what goes on in school. Because the young child cherishes every word and act of his parents, the taste which the parents exhibit, the home environment will govern his taste. His parents' faith in his creative growth is of greatest consequence. They encourage or discourage his creative urges; they understand or fail to understand his art expression.

On the basis of the careful and detailed studies from which I have quoted, I cannot agree with him. Ability in creative art is the result of certain definite intrapsychic conflicts. It simply exists or does not exist and if it does not exist it cannot be inculcated. This does not mean that children should not be given the opportunity to work in all manner of media. They should be allowed to select the media they prefer. They also should be encouraged, but not compelled, to use the other media. In this way, a few of the more superficial inhibitions which have resulted from their early training may be removed. But doing this is not developing creativity. It is simply giving them the opportunity for free expression. At the same time they need instruction in the proper skills for the medium they prefer.

The creative arts arise as sublimations of pregenital instinctual desires which are not expendable in other ways. I have mentioned that these are specific for the individual. An individual with the need to sublimate exhibitionism may turn to dramatics. Another has no such unexpended exhibitionism and therefore dramatics have no appeal and are out of the question for him. Instead, his unexpended pregenital desire may be for peeping, and he will need to sublimate this. Each individual has his own specific drive or drives which he must sublimate, and he cannot become interested in activities which do not sublimate these particular drives. Ideally, the work of the teacher could be made easier and more profitable by the development of tests for discovering in the young child the drives which need sublimation, as I mentioned in an earlier chapter, but I do not believe that this will ever be practical. In any case the creative arts will not be useful to occupy leisure time in the technological world except for a very few persons.

TWO TYPES OF SUBLIMATION

To fill the increased amount of leisure what other forms of sublimation should be added to the curriculum? From my experience, I would conclude that there may be two types of sublimation. One is the sublimation of unexpended pregenital drives. I have already discussed this fully. It might be called sublimation proper. The other type directs the interest toward subjects which are related to an important early experience, for the purpose of mastering a psychic trauma which occurred during the particular incident.

A man had a great interest in history, particularly the history of wars and the details of the strategy and tactics of battles. He was a physician—not a surgeon—and except for serving in the Medical Corps he had had no occupational connection with military matters. He also had other hobbies, but he was especially widely read in, and enjoyed reading, the detailed descriptions of troop movements in warfare. Psychoanalysis showed that this interest originated in repressed memories of the primal scene, which he had observed around the age of three years and to which he had reacted with a great deal of emotion and conflict. The release of the memory of these traumatic incidents from repression allowed him to understand the origin of his interest but did not decrease his interest in his hobby—in fact it tended to increase it. Here, a very traumatic experience which afterward had quite an effect on his entire life was partly mastered through an interest the mechanism of which resembles a sublimation.

Another man had a great interest in and desire to possess antique furniture. He was not in the business of buying and selling, or of restoring, antiques, but as a hobby he spent a great deal of his spare time scouring the countryside for antiques and restoring them after he purchased them. He was very proud of his collection. In his psychoanalysis this interest was seen to be connected with a conflict—whether to spend his time studying for his legal work or working on his antiques. Both the interest and the conflict were traceable to his conscious adolescent fantasies. His most frequent fantasy, at that time, had been that he was engaged as a houseman for a prominent family living in an old home. This fantasy was accompanied by a forcible and rapid beating of his heart. A second fantasy was that he owned an old large house—all of which belonged to him—but despite this fact he was unable to persuade a woman who lived there to rent him a room. At the time he had these fantasies he had ambitions to enter college and study law. It can be seen readily that both these fantasies and his interest in antiques reveal a view of himself as one who though really a member of a noble family, entitled to all the ancestral possessions, was being treated as a hired hand and a stranger. This was the way he had felt at the age of about four years, when his younger brother was born. The interest in antiques and in old houses was an attempt to master the painful trauma of the brother's birth by trying to reproduce the time before the brother was born. The interest in antiques resembles a sublimation.

Fishing was one man's very absorbing hobby, but apparently he cared only about the number of fish he caught and was not very interested in what became of the fish after he caught them. He was the oldest child and the only boy in a family of six. When he was a child his mother permitted his younger sisters to play with and even break his toys. Even if these were the toys he valued most, she would not permit him to express any anger either physically or verbally. His next sibling was born when he was about eighteen months old. For a short time before his mother's confinement and for months afterward, he cried incessantly and his mother allowed him to cry it out. Eventually the crying stopped and later on he apparently loved this sister very much. In his psychoanalysis it was discovered that his interest in fishing—which also had a number of other determinants—basically represented his desire to get rid of his sisters. In his unconscious, the fishing pole represented his penis, the line, the frenum to the underside of the corona, the fish, his sisters, and the pulling of them out of the water, the desire to send his sisters back where they came from. Here the fishing resembles a sublimation. This second type of sublimation I would designate as the sublimation of a trauma.

FURNISHING THE CHILD WITH OPPORTUNITIES FOR SUBLIMATION

Modern adolescents frequently use baseball terms to designate certain types of sex play, so it appears that baseball is a sublimation of certain forepleasure activities which are carried over from the pregenital stages of the sexual development. Wood and metal working is sometimes a direct identification with a father who has a hobby of wood or metal working which his son can observe, sometimes a sublimation of sadism. Collecting is well known to be a sublimation of anal erotism. Interest in possessing and driving cars is a sublimation of interest in possessing and manipulating the penis. Interest in gas engines is a sublimation of the frightening curiosity as to the location of the female penis, and of interest in the insides of the body, in the process of sexual intercourse, and in the creation of babies.

The great number and diversity of sublimations shows clearly that they are not limited to the artistic fields, as many educators seem to think, but encompass all fields of human endeavor—artistic, recreational, occupational, and cultural. A sublimation from any one of these fields is as valuable as any other, because each gratifies some aim-inhibited pregenital drive and channels it into a useful activity.

The wide diversity of human activities in the machine age gives the educator many ways to fill the gaps in the school curriculum caused by the elimination of obsolete subjects. He can offer the child activities, both vocational and recreational, which will fit into his need for sublimations and so will be interesting and of real value. Already the skills required in sports like baseball, football, hockey, and tennis are being taught in many schools—although the progressive schools are woefully deficient along these lines as compared with the more traditional ones. A greater amount of time is being devoted to shop, even to the teaching of driving and the mechanics of the automobile, in many high schools. This study could be enlarged to include the mechanics of flying and of airplanes. Again, such studies are not so common in the progressive schools as they are in the traditional schools.

There is a tendency to regard the arts as the real examples of sublimations and to forget that many of the subjects mentioned earlier in this chapter—those concerned with the study of the real world and of previous human experience—are real and valuable sublimations also. This is particularly true of the humanities, which are actually more useful for sublimations for the majority of the pupils than are the arts, yet which, in the progressive schools, are more and more being relegated to a minor role in the school curriculum. Actually, because of the rapid changes of the machine age, they should be considered as more and more important parts of the curriculum. Also, though arts and dramatics have their place, the inclusion in the curriculum of skills used in recreation—in fishing, hunting, shooting, golf, baseball, and the like, particularly in those recreations which can be followed regardless of the changes in physical ability which occur with age—would be valuable for persons whose sublimatory needs require them, like the man whose sublimation was fishing. I realize that these additions to the curriculum would require more specialization on the part of teachers, and the employment of more teachers, but this will be necessary if the schools are to function adequately.

No educator can inculcate creativity. The most that the educator can do is to give the child the opportunity to see whether any subject, including the arts, will furnish a medium for the sublimation of that specific pupil's drives. This is important at all stages of the child's development. A little boy of three observed his mother blacken the stove.

Later he obtained the stove blackening and smeared it on the walls of one of the rooms, stating proudly that he was a painter. Instead of punishing him for his actions, it would be well at that point to introduce him to water colors and finger paints. At each step in the process of psychosexual development the child should be provided with activities and materials which he can use in the service of his sublimations. I have mentioned some of the activities and materials that are used in the sublimation of anal-erotic impulses. For the aggressive impulses of the phallic period, children need to be furnished with the proper tools to play war, cops and robbers, cowboys and Indians, and so on, and with adequate tools and places for destruction and construction. The sublimation of the deep disappointment felt by the little girl because she does not possess a penis can be helped by encouragement of her interest in frilly feminine clothes, hairdos, cooking and housekeeping, and dolls. It would take too much space to describe the various activities which serve as sublimations for each of the pregenital drives and for each stage of psychosexual development. I wish, however, to emphasize one more point. In each of these activities the child should be helped by instruction in the skills involved—skills which the child, at that particular time, is only too willing to learn. For example the interest in dolls, as the gratification of the fantasy of the little girl that she has a baby, can be utilized well in teaching her how to look after her doll as if it were a real baby. This instruction could cover the whole question of really feeding, bathing, handling, clothing, playing with, and disciplining the baby —all of which the child is avid to learn—so that when she grows up and has a child of her own she automatically will have all the necessary skills at her disposal. The educator who understands well the psychosexual development of the child and the points at which sublimations of pregenital drives begin, can use this knowledge in deciding when to teach the child the skills of a particular sublimation; but he will also have to recognize that parts of these skills have to be learned through hard, unpleasant effort and that he must encourage the child to undertake and carry to completion the difficult parts of each task.

CHAPTER XI

The Relation of the Reality Principle to Education

SO FAR I have discussed the relation of the ego to the external world through the perceptive system, the relation of the ego to the instinctual life, and the defenses it develops for a gratification of the instinctual life better than the simple relief of tension through discharge. The defenses prevent the immediate discharge of the instinctual energy, and so they impose frustrations on the individual and for a period of time increase his inner feelings of tension. This is necessary for the eventual attainment of real gratification. Therefore, the ego has to undertake another task—to try to make the desire for pleasure conform to the demands of reality.

There are two basic principles of psychic functioning which though often in conflict with each other operate in the mind at the same time. One of these is the pleasure-pain principle, with which the human being is born and which basically continues to act throughout the rest of his life. Always, basically, the human being turns toward anything which gives him pleasure and away from anything which gives him pain. The other is the reality principle, which is imposed on him through the influence of reality and which causes him to subordinate his desire to obtain pleasure and avoid pain to the limitations imposed by the possibility of real gratification (time and space, real ability, and so on). The reality principle is developed by slow stages during childhood, but a great deal of the child's life, particularly before adolescence, is passed under the supremacy of the pleasure principle.

THE PLEASURE-PAIN PRINCIPLE

Years ago Hilton [1] pointed out the fact that pain is an important biological mechanism whose purpose is to induce rest of the painful part and so allow the lesion which is affecting it to heal. It is important also to recognize that there are specific pain fibers in the nerves and spinal cord and specific pain sensory endings in the skin, whose function is to inform us of painful sensations so that we can avoid their cause. When these pain endings or fibers are destroyed by disease or injury, the particular part of the body where the pain anesthesia is located is constantly being injured and the injuries pass unnoticed until visible signs, such as ulcerations, appear. That there is a real need to perceive pain resulting from causes in the external world, in order that they may be avoided, is emphasized by the fact that there are no analogous specific pleasure fibers in the nerves or the spinal cord. Although everyone understands the desire to experience pleasure and avoid pain as a bodily phenomenon, many are not as aware that all mental processes also are governed by the pleasure-pain principle. Freud [2] described the subservience of psychic processes to the pleasure principle as follows: All psychic processes originate in a state of tension and follow a path to the goal of relaxation of tension. Pleasure, therefore, is a decrease in the quantity of excitation, while pain is an increase in its quantity. The purpose of the psychic apparatus is to keep the quantity of excitation as low as possible. It has within it a tendency to stability. Other forces in the psyche are opposed to the tendency to pleasure. The desire for pleasure receives its first check from the external world and from the instinct of self-preservation, and these checks are subsequently replaced by the reality principle which presupposes later gratification. However, the pleasure principle remains the mode of operation of the sex impulses and in this regard may overcome the reality principle. The second check of the desire for pleasure comes from conflicts and dissociations in the psychic apparatus. Not all instincts are allowed to develop to the same stage.

[1] John Hilton, *Rest and Pain,* New York, William Wood and Company, 1879.

[2] Sigmund Freud, *Beyond the Pleasure Principle,* London, International Psychoanalytical Press, 1922.

Some of the instincts prove irreconcilable in their demands and aims with others, which are more ego syntonic. The former, therefore, are split off, repressed, and cut off from gratification. If they succeed in fighting their way to gratification, the success is felt by the ego as pain, not pleasure. Pain is felt when there is a perception of the urge of unsatisfied instincts, or when there is a perception of physical distress or of something which arouses painful anticipations and is dangerous in the external world. The reaction to the claims of impulses may be guided correctly by the pleasure principle modified by the reality principle, and reactions to the threat of external dangers may impose a still more far-reaching limitation on the pleasure principle.

Anna Freud [3] lists a number of defenses against pain. If the pain arises from internal sources the defenses will be repression, reaction formation, or inhibition. If the pain arises from external sources the defenses will be denial, fantasy formation, or ego restriction. Fantasy formation is based on denial, since fantasy originally is a reversal of the real facts into their opposite. Denial and fantasy formation are employed in situations which give painful impressions and from which it is impossible to escape. When the ego refuses to encounter a situation, the defense is known as ego restriction. She points out that there are three types of children in modern schools: those who are intelligent, interested, and diligent; those who are intellectually duller and are hard to interest and induce to work; and those who are intelligent and well developed but cannot be induced to take part in regular lessons or games and behave as if they were intimidated. If these last-mentioned children fail in a task or game they show a permanent disinclination to repeat the attempt. They content themselves with being onlookers and so become bored because of this idleness and begin to quarrel with others. These children cannot compare themselves with other children because the comparison causes them to suffer too much pain. The real cause of their excessive pain lies in the memory of the pain they suffered earlier when they compared the size of their genitals with that of their father's, and in the memory of the hopeless rivalry of the edipus situation, when they had to accept the disagreeable realization of sexual differences. Children in the la-

[3] Anna Freud, *The Ego and the Mechanisms of Defense,* New York, International Universities Press, 1946.

tency period may attach more importance to the avoidance of anxiety or pain than to the direct or indirect gratification of instinct. In many cases, if they lack external guidance their choice of occupation is determined not by their gifts and capacities for sublimation but by the hope of protecting themselves as quickly as possible from anxiety and pain. Anna Freud goes on to say that the importance of the infantile ego's determination to avoid pain has not been appreciated in educational theory. The conflict between different methods of education concerns the question of how far it is the task of the educator to induce children, even of the tenderest years, to devote all their efforts to assimilating reality and how far it is permissible to encourage them to turn from reality and construct a world of fantasy. In fact, a real goal of education is to increase the child's tolerance to frustration. Those who can accept adversity will be happier people.

Before I go on to discuss reality and the reality principle, the psychic sense of reality, I think it is important to discuss another principle that operates in the human psyche. This is the repetition compulsion, the desire simply to repeat a previous experience whether it was a pleasurable one or not. It is seen in a marked degree in the symptoms of the war neuroses. Often in children's play an attempt is seen to repeat actively a painful passive experience. In psychoanalytic treatment patients often show a desire to repeat rather than to remember. All these are examples of the repetition compulsion. The repetition compulsion is not a form of defense of the ego against the instincts. It is an activity of the id and is done not for pleasure but simply to satisfy itself. It is more primitive, more elementary, and more instinctive than the pleasure principle.

THE REALITY PRINCIPLE

In direct antithesis to the often rather useless and sometimes harmful repetition compulsion and to the pleasure-pain principle stand the demands of reality and the reality principle. There are two kinds of reality, external and internal: the reality which exists outside the individual and the reality of the individual himself. Each kind consists of several parts. External reality consists, first, of the physical world and its properties, the three dimensions of space, the variations in temperature, moisture, consistency, and so on. Second, it consists of the changes and alterations man has imposed on the physical world—housing, clothing, means of transportation, and so on. Third, it consists of the customs, mores, and manners developed to make group life possible, of the concepts which man has evolved to make his life more economical and convenient, such as money, national frontiers, government, time, and the rest. In respect to the concept of time, Hughlings Jackson believed that the heartbeat had a cortical representation, from which the psychic concept of time developed. I see no reason to reject this hypothesis. Fourth, there is the social group itself, made up of individuals, each with his own needs, desires, hostilities, and loves, and of the tendency of these needs and desires to clash with those of other individuals. All these components of external reality, except the needs, desires, loves and hates of human beings, are to some extent subject to change. Some of these changes, such as storms, weather, and the formation of deserts in previously fertile areas, are beyond present human ability to control. Some are subject to human control; a gradual decrease in space, for example, has resulted from the development of more speedy means of transportation, and alterations in legal enactments occur as the result of rather slow, almost evolutionary social changes.

Internal reality is the reality of the individual himself. First, he has a physical body which has certain needs—for food, drink, sexual gratification, oxygen, a specific temperature range—and which will cease to exist entirely, or as a going concern, if these needs are not gratified. Also, the physical body is liable to be painfully, irreparably, or fatally injured if exposed to sudden changes in space, to physical substances such as weapons and fire, or to the invasion of poisons, toxins, or bacteria. And eventually the physical body will wear out and die regardless of what the individual does or does not do.

Second, the individual's physical make-up has certain characteristics—such as height, weight, color of eyes, level of intellectual ability, level of muscular ability, tendency to early baldness—which are probably inherited and which limit or increase his ability to deal with external and perhaps with internal reality. The individual has to accept these characteristics even if they are limiting, because he cannot change them, just as he has to put up with the parts of external reality which he cannot change.

I have already spoken of the individual's internal reality: his urges and needs—to love, to hate, to remain alive—and above all, the strongest possible desire to obtain pleasure and comfort and avoid pain, and a strong compulsion to repeat former experiences. These needs and desires are constantly demanding gratification.

These are the main components of both external and internal reality, and it can readily be seen that there is a clash between external and internal reality and, especially, that both external and internal reality are frequently opposed to the needs and desires of the individual, particularly to his desire to obtain pleasure constantly and to avoid pain at all times. It is the task of the ego to adjust this conflict as well as possible. In order to do this the ego has to use three definite abilities: the ability to use the perceptive apparatus to maintain contact with the external world and with reality, the ability to anticipate the future, and the ability to test reality. I have discussed the use of the perceptive system to maintain contact with the external world and with reality. All adults, from time to time, show a strong tendency not to maintain contact with reality and not to perceive what is going on around them. Of course some adults show this much more than others do. Children show less ability to perceive reality than do adults.

The capacity to plan ahead and thus anticipate the future is an important part of maintaining contact with reality. A large degree of the capacity to adjust to reality is based on the possession of a concept of the future. I will suffer the discomfort of frustration now, in order to have a better and more pleasurable gratification later. The ability to anticipate the future seems to be a function of the frontal lobes. If the frontal lobes are damaged or if their projection fibers are cut, the ability to anticipate the future is lost.

The function of reality testing has two parts. To protect the organism, the ego observes the external world, preserves a true meaning of it, and eliminates any element in this picture contributed from internal sources. Zilboorg [4] states that originally the images of the outside world do not produce representations but remain images and are

[4] Gregory Zilboorg, "The Sense of Reality," *Psychoanalytic Quarterly*, 10, 1941.

taken for objects in themselves. Libidinal charges are concentrated not on the images but on the associated fantasies. To the very young, as to the primitive, external phenomena are simply appearances that report something to the individual, so external reality is animistic—a projection of the child's desires. As a common illustration he cites the fact that human beings tend to see man as a unique phenomenon, different from other animals. This is not a real fact but an unrealistic point of view, the result of the constant pressure of the idealized hedonism of the human being, and so it subserves the pleasure principle. If you watch a small child, you will find that he has a tendency to consider everything in terms of himself. To him, everything is an extension of his body. This can be seen readily in the following example. A child was very frightened of a toy elephant which someone had given him. His parents directed his attention to the fact that the elephant's trunk served as a hand to put food into the mouth. The child started to imitate those motions of the hand and the mouth and soon lost his fear. He had accepted the elephant as part of himself.

As the child grows older he begins to compare things with himself and by comparing things with himself he begins to test reality. His ego also has to perceive the need of an instinctual urge for discharge and, perceiving that need, to determine whether in the light of the present reality adequate gratification can be obtained or whether the gratification should be postponed to a time when it will be more certain and therefore greater. The struggle between, on the one hand, the instinctual desires and the desires for immediate and constant pleasure and, on the other, the reality-testing function of the ego is observed early in the transference situation in psychoanalysis. The patient comes to psychoanalysis interested in finding out what is the matter with him. He is interested in the analyst as a person who can help him to understand his problems. This attitude is quite realistic. One day, quite suddenly, he no longer is interested in his illness, his problems, or his need to become well. He no longer is interested in the analyst as a person who can help him to get well. He begins to make unrealistic demands on the analyst and becomes furious if these demands are not gratified immediately. It seems as if he prefers present pleasures and no longer has any interest in his future well-being or the real gratification of his desires at a later date. In this he resembles the small child who demands to have what he wants when he wants it. The reality-testing function of the ego disappears in the transference situation and is temporarily replaced by the pleasure principle.

What are the steps in the development of the sense of reality, i.e., of the reality principle? Ferenczi[5] has contributed much to our knowledge of the sense of reality and of its development. If reality is pleasant, as it often may be, it is accepted readily. Only if it is unpleasant does a conflict arise. In the latter instance there are several methods of resolving the conflict. No human being ever entirely accepts all unpleasant reality. For example, no person accepts the reality of his own death. Anyone examining carefully his ideas about his own death will find that they are concerned almost entirely with what will happen after he dies, as if he were going to remain alive and be a spectator of events after his death. In fact, certain wealthy men arrange their wills in such a way that they have the entire disposal of their fortune for a generation or longer after they have died. In making such a will the testator is attempting to remain alive after his death and so is not accepting the reality of his death.

Faced by an unpleasant external reality, the individual may attempt to change it. If it happens that the furnace in a house has broken down, the owner will have to build a fire in the fireplace. This entails some labor which though it may be unpleasant is less unpleasant than shivering in a cold house. Changing the unpleasant external reality, if possible, is probably the most effective method of resolving the conflict. It is not used, however, as often as it could be. Instead, an individual may attempt to resolve the conflict by denying the existence of the unpleasant reality. This is well illustrated by the complete indifference of many Americans to the existence of atomic bombs. Instead of denying the existence of an unpleasant reality, an individual may accept its existence but deny the unpleasantness. The poverty-stricken Negro who sings, "I got plenty of nothing and nothing's plenty for me," is a case in point. Or an individual may deny the unpleasantness piece by piece, and so gradually adjust himself to the situation.

One universal method of dealing with an unpleasant reality, a

[5] Sandor Ferenczi, "Stages in the Development of the Sense of Reality," *Sex in Psychoanalysis,* New York, Robert Brunner, 1950; Sandor Ferenczi, "The Problem of the Acceptance of Unpleasant Ideas: Advances in Knowledge of the Sense of Reality," *Further Contributions to Theory and Technique of Psychoanalysis,* London, Hogarth Press and the Institute of Psycho-Analysis, 1926.

method which eventually leads to a real attempt to change that reality, has two steps. First, the individual denies the existence of the unpleasant reality; then, by denying the denial, he is able to accept it. A most striking historical instance of this has been pointed out by Dr. Robert Waelder.[6] For centuries mankind wanted a perpetual-motion machine, as a denial of the unpleasant fact that motion requires the expenditure of energy. At long last people became convinced that such a machine could not be built. They had to deny their denial of the laws of physics. Almost immediately there occurred the invention of machinery powered by steam, gasoline, oil, and electricity, in which the laws of physics were accepted and, moreover, utilized. Another very simple example of this mechanism follows: I may hate the reality of having to get up in the morning. In order to deny the unpleasant reality of having to do so, I may begin by getting up early and convincing myself that I like it. Thus I deny the unpleasantness. Later, perhaps, I can bring myself to deny that I like to get up and so simply accept the fact that I have to get up, whether I like it or not. In brief, the immature ego with its desire for pleasure only attempts to repulse an unpleasant idea. As repulsion cannot be effective because the idea is not a physical phenomenon but a phenomenon in the mind, the ego next tends to deny its existence. This is the stage of negation. Parents of little children, and even of children in the latency period, often consider this first stage as deceitfulness and lying and are worried that their child will grow up to be a pathological liar. If they would recognize that this negation of unpleasant ideas is simply a step toward eventual truthfulness they would be less upset when they met its manifestations. The stage of negation does not work effectively, so the ego attempts to repress the idea. However, the idea still remains, although repressed. It is necessary therefore that it emerge from repression and be accepted, and this is what usually happens.

MEASURES THAT THE EDUCATOR CAN USE TO HELP THE CHILD DEVELOP A SENSE OF REALITY

How can the educator help the child, who desires only pleasure, eventually to recognize reality even though it is unpleasant, and either

[6] In a lecture at the Annual Meeting of the Mental Health Clinic of Reading, Pennsylvania.

change it, if possible, or accept it? The child's ability to do this develops in two successive stages, both of which he passes through gradually. The first stage may be called the stage of learning the nature of external and, particularly, internal reality and of developing skills to handle it. The child at birth, and for some years after, suffers from a lack of development of his motor abilities. He has to learn gradually that he is a going concern, that he has sensations and feelings, some pleasant, some unpleasant, and that he has a slowly increasing ability to avoid or to do something about the unpleasant feelings. He needs, above all, opportunity and help to learn that he has pleasurable feelings in himself and that he can do things that will increase his bodily pleasures. At the same time he has to be protected from the many unpleasant aspects of external reality. The baby needs to be fondled, kissed, hugged, and held; he has to have all his sensations gently stimulated. The slightly older child needs to learn that he can gain pleasure from his body by his own efforts and activities, and he must obtain assurance of his parents' happiness about these efforts. These needs of the child are better understood now than formerly, because most parents are interested in helping the child to self-expression and to self-assurance. Parents, however, often believe that the procedure of allowing the young child freedom to learn about himself and to express himself may be overdone, and they may attempt to impose unnecessary restrictions in training. In this they forget about the existence of external and, particularly, internal reality. The child and parents live in an environment where there are at least three persons, father, mother, and child. Each of these persons has his own needs, desires, and rights, and just as the needs, desires, and rights of the child impinge on those of the parents, so those of the parents impinge on the child. He often finds these impingements unpleasant, and in order to abolish this discomfort he has the tendency of trying to change himself instead of trying to change his environment. As a matter of fact, society and his parents assist him in this process because they tend to call any attempt on his part to change the unpleasantness of his environment delinquency. In Samoa, if a child resents the expression of the parents' rights, desires, and needs, he can go next door and live with another family for several months. If he did this in America, he would be haled into juvenile court. The child tries extremely hard to imitate his parents, to the point of being exactly like them. In this way he strives to lessen the unpleasantness of reality, to solve the conflict between his desire for pleasure and the demands of reality. His desire to cling to the pleasure principle gradually decreases, and he becomes able to postpone his desire for immediate gratification and to alter some part of this desire in order to have the desire itself realistically gratified.

During this period, i.e., from birth to about the age of seven, it is necessary that the child be helped to develop real confidence in himself as a going concern able to deal with reality, especially his own reality, without denying its unpleasant features. Thus it is better to err a little on the side of indulgence than on the side of training, to say Do more often than Don't, and to let the impact of culture be assimilated by the child gradually, so that he can develop skills to deal with the unpleasant aspects of external reality. It has been customary to believe that the parent may err through too much indulgence. This is true, but it is true also that a parent can err as much or perhaps more by overemphasizing the demands of culture and training, thereby developing a lack of self-confidence in the child and increasing his use of mechanisms for denying reality or its unpleasantness. As a result, the child does not develop the ability to try to change reality.

The first stage of the development of an ability to deal with reality therefore lies in the gradual increase of the child's capacity to learn about and to realize his internal reality. Every help should be given him in this regard, or better still, there should be as few impediments as possible to the increase of such knowledge. During the same stage there is very slow acceptance of the less unpleasant portion of external reality.

The second stage in the child's adaptation to reality lies in the development of his ability to accept the more unpleasant parts of both external and internal reality, so that, if possible, he will desire to deal with it himself. There are many situations which may contribute to this development. For example, time is an increasingly important part of civilized culture. The child has to learn to get to school on time. If, during the early years of his life, he has had the example of parents who are aware of the cultural importance of time, he needs little training in this regard. If he has not accepted the parents' pattern it is better to allow reality to teach him its importance than it is for the parents to assume his responsibilities. It is better for the child to be late, and to experience the humiliation of arriving late for school and the disfavor expressed by the teacher and the group at such tardiness, than for the parents to take the responsibility for seeing that he gets there on time. A similar situation occurs with school work. His school work is *his* school work. If he does not do as he is expected he must suffer the real humiliations that his behavior causes. The parents should not shield him from these results either by doing his work for him or by nagging or forcing him to do it himself.

There seems to be a tendency to try to make the school curriculum too pleasant for the child, particularly as he grows older. In some places this tendency is so marked that he is even allowed to pick the subjects he will study. It is true that the learning of many subjects requires real hard work, to the point of unpleasantness. The older child should be willing to undergo such work for the satisfaction of having mastered a new skill. As a matter of fact, the developmental procedure that takes place in sports is an excellent example of what education could do. The grammar-school boy notices the acclaim which is accorded the college football player. He desires this acclaim and therefore engages in the rough and tumble of corner-lot football. However, he tries to carry the ball all the time and has no thought of learning team play. As a result, he develops his skill in handling the ball, but the hard exigency that every other player has the same desire and that anarchy and the loss of the game will result from such behavior, gradually causes him to be more interested in what he really can contribute to the winning of the game. Slowly he assimilates the unpleasant reality that only by team play can the game be won and that team play often means the subordination of his own desire to be the only star performer.

Another example of the need for allowing reality to teach the child to accept its unpleasant aspects lies in the field of money. It is good for the child to have perfect freedom in his use of his allowance, with the understanding, of course, that the allowance is adequate for his age, sex, and social situation, and that once it is all spent there is no more money forthcoming till the next allowance day. Such a procedure teaches him the reality value of the concept of money. He does not learn this at all if the parents inform him how he should spend it or insist on controlling his expenditures. It is good, also, for the adolescent girl to be allowed to select her own clothes, within the proper price range. If she selects foolishly once and has to live with the results of her folly, she will be more sensible the next time as she will have only herself to blame.

It is the task of the educator to show the child that he must accomplish his task by himself, that it is difficult, and that the adult will encourage and help him as much as possible. Here are two examples of what I mean. A little Indian boy was with his grandfather. He wanted to open the flap on the door of the tepee but found it very difficult to do. He asked his grandfather to do it for him. The grandfather refused. Instead he showed the child how to do it and encouraged him to continue until eventually he was successful. If a timid child desires to learn to swim the adult will say to him, "Yes, you want to learn to swim. At first you will be afraid of the water but you will have to overcome that fear. I will show you what to do and I will not allow you to get hurt. But you must continue to put my instructions into action until you really have learned to swim." Both of these examples illustrate how the educator can help the child to adjust to reality and develop the reality principle.

At about the age of seven the human being should begin to learn by trial and error to accept and master the unpleasant parts of reality. I believe that at present this necessity is being neglected as compared with those which govern the first seven years of life. A couple quarrel after a few months of married life, and the wife or husband, instead of attempting to make an adjustment to the inevitable clash of personalities, runs home to the parents and is received with open arms. Little or no real attempt is made by the parents to close the door to the child and suggest that he or she go back and see if the difference cannot be patched up. Or the young married couple seeks a divorce at the first indication of unpleasantness in the new interpersonal relationship instead of being willing to try honestly to work out the difficulty in adjustment. When an adolescent is not doing well in a good school he may want to change schools in order to avoid the difficulty, not realizing that the difficulty lies within himself and not in the school. Many parents will permit him to do so and in this way shelter him from the unpleasantness of reality.

Real life is hard, but it can be made pleasurable if the individual will do something about the unpleasantnesses. He can do so only if he has learned that he can do something but not everything, or not everything at once, and then in the light of this knowledge changes unpleasantnesses where possible and accepts the fact that unchangeable unpleasantnesses exist. Such an attitude is a sign of real maturity. The unchangeable unpleasantnesses of reality can be accepted if the individual has self-confidence, that is, if he knows that he has something to *give* which is needed by other people. With this knowledge he faces the unpleasantnesses without unreasonable hesitation or unreasonable fears.

Educators, whether parents or teachers, need to recognize the two steps in the adaptation to reality: first the pleasure principle and then the reality principle; first the negation of unpleasant ideas and then the acceptance of unpleasant ideas; first the gratification of internal reality and therefore the knowledge of it and then the acceptance of external reality. These two steps gradually merge one into another, but the first part of each pair needs to be realized first and the child must be assisted gradually to emerge from it into the second part.

CHAPTER XII

A Summary of the Contributions of Psychoanalytic Ego Psychology to the Education of the Child

It is desirable at this point to pause and summarize what has been said in the previous chapters about the psychoanalytic contributions to our knowledge of the learning process and the education of the ego and to determine how this knowledge can best be applied to the education of the child.

The most important contribution of psychoanalysis has been knowledge of the unconscious, its processes and ways of working, of the paramount role played by the instincts in human life and psychic activity, and of the influences of intrapsychic conflicts—conflicts between the demands of the instincts for discharge and the demands of the external world, between the desire for pleasure and the possibilities of reality, and between the demands of the instincts and the cultural and environmental prohibitions crystallized in that part of the psyche known as the superego. It is the task of the ego to synthesize and integrate all of these demands into a smoothly working entity which will permit adequate instinctual gratification. Therefore, up to this point, I have been discussing the relation of the functions of the ego to the education of the child.

The importance of the knowledge of these concepts for the educator and for the construction of any system of education is well demonstrated by a consideration of their influence on the learning process. Every individual has to learn that he is affected by two fields of influence—the external world, which he perceives through his avenues of sensory intake, i.e., through his perceptive system, and the inner world of instincts. The influence of the latter far outshadows the influence of the former so that if there is a conflict between the perceptions of the external world and the presence of the instincts, the latter takes precedence over the former. Only as they become combined with the perceptions of the instincts, do the perceptions of the external world receive any attention. If the instincts are not sufficiently gratified, their clamor for gratification obliterates the perceptions from the external world. An adequate combination cannot take place unless the child receives sufficient sensory stimuli from the external world and unless his ability to tolerate a certain amount of instinctual tension is developed. As motor activity is the ideal way for the gratification of instinct, the young baby's motor helplessness hampers him in obtaining adequate gratification.

In order that the very young baby develop an ego, a layer to mediate between and combine the perceptions from the external world and the strivings of the instinctual drives for gratification and discharge, it is essential that the educator—at this age, the parent—be aware of the vital need for specific procedures which will help the ego of the child develop. First and foremost, at this age, his instinctual needs must be gratified, at first as completely as possible and as soon as they appear. An example of this is the present plan of permitting a reasonable self-demand feeding schedule. Then very gradually the child will be introduced to the experience of tolerating minute degrees of ungratified instinct demand and its accompanying feeling of anxiety. In this way, he gradually learns what his instinct demands feel like and so begins to learn about his inner needs. This process of mild, but very gradually increasing, frustration goes on year by year during the *prelatent* period, with the educator constantly being aware that both too much frustration and too much gratification will hamper the process of combination and therefore impede the adequate development of the ego. This is the scientific basis for the commonly observed empirical fact that neither the spoiled child nor the fretful child seems able to learn. At the same time, the baby needs a great deal of sensory stimulation of a pleasurable character, alternating with frequent intervals of rest. He needs this in order to direct his attention to the outside world and to increase his perceptions of it. An optimum degree of sensual stimulation aids the process of combination and therefore the development of the ego. Too little sensual stimulation prevents this. If this situation occurs, the instinctual pressures are combined, if at all, only with disjointed and chaotic fragments of perception, and the result is a distorted fantasy perception of the external world. In this case, the child pays little attention to his surroundings and learns very little about them. A similar result occurs if the perceptions of the external world are associated with unpleasant feelings and experiences. If the child is stimulated too much, there is an increase in instinctual tensions, which become so great that the child tries to disregard the external impressions. He becomes fatigued, combination does not occur, and he does not learn.

THE ROLE OF MOTOR ACTIVITY

I mentioned earlier that motor activity is the most adequate method of instinctual discharge. In the young baby this takes the form of aimless movements. Later on these aimless movements change to a more purposeful type, although frequently some of the motor activity of the child—running, jumping, talking—appears to be aimless. This activity is necessary for instinct discharge and if it is unnecessarily hindered there is increased instinct tension and the development of the ego is hindered.

The researches of Fries, Mahler, and Levy [1] indicate that basically a tendency to lethargy or a tendency to increased motor activity is the result of constitutional factors. The constitutionally motor-minded child has to be educated (managed) differently from the lethargically-minded child. The former as a baby needs to be held firmly and comfortably when his activity gets too great but he also needs much more space in which to play freely. The latter needs to be stimulated into activity. If the motor-minded child has too many restrictions placed upon his motor activity by prolonged illness, by insufficient play space,

[1] Margaret Fries, "Psychosomatic Relationships between Mother and Infant," *Psychosomatic Medicine,* 6, 1944; Margaret S. Mahler, "Tics and Impulsions in Children: A Study of Motility," *Psychoanalytic Quarterly,* 13, 1944; David M. Levy, "On the Problem of Movement Restraint," *American Journal of Orthopsychiatry,* 14, 1944.

or by parental restrictions often due to the parents' fear that the child may be injured, fidgetiness and often tics result. I believe also that such restrictions will hinder the process of combination, of learning, and of ego development in a motor-minded child. It is of vital importance that the need for instinctual release through motor activity be recognized in the prelatent period by parents and by nursery-school and kindergarten teachers. However, as the child, including the motor-minded child, enters the latency period he tends to appear less active, so that sometimes even the most motor-minded child seems able to conform to the traditional type of classroom behavior except for his fidgetiness. His attempts, particularly the attempts of the very motor-minded child, to adjust to this situation, where motor action is more or less forbidden, result not only in fidgetiness but also in a diminution of the capacity to learn and in an increase of really purposeless activity outside of school.

The purpose of the overtraditional classroom—the school setup where a properly managed classroom is one in which "you can hear a pin drop"—originated in the desire of the educator to help the child accept reality, a very desirable and necessary part of the educational development of the child. The method of carrying out this purpose, however, did not take into account the fact that the development of the reality principle in the mind and the consequent acceptance of reality is obtained best by slow degrees, in order to subordinate the pleasure principle at the level necessary for a successful life. Contrariwise, the progressive schools often forget as frequently that it is desirable and necessary to help the child to accept reality as quickly as *possible*. Although the extreme type of traditional school, such as I have just mentioned, exists only infrequently at the present time, the routine of many of the usual schools is still too sedentary for the motor-minded child. In order to prevent the development in such a child of fidgetiness, increased purposeless motor activity, and increased learning difficulty it is desirable to consider carefully, before he is entered, the degree to which motor activity is permitted in the school and in the classroom of the chosen school. These children develop better in the progressive type of school, where much freedom of movement and speech is permitted at all times. Even the average child will learn better if he has frequent opportunities for movement and speech during the school day. There is a general tendency in most of the schools I have observed to place the athletic and motor part of the program at the end of the school day. I realize this is done in order to organize the roster more easily, but I question whether ease of administration is more important than the need to serve the child's learning ability. It might be better to have the athletic program interposed between the halves of the academic program. It certainly would help to have fewer restrictions on movement and speech in the classroom.

I have noticed that the gymnasium period is dreaded by many children. In fact, it is not unusual for children to try to avoid it with all kinds of excuses, some moderately reasonable, some very fantastic. It seems to me that there may be two important reasons for this attitude. Gymnasium work and what used to be called physical culture require constant and industrious application in order to acquire the co-ordination and rhythm of the skilled performer. A few children acquire this more readily than the majority and it is very humiliating to the less skilled children to have the evidence of their inferiority paraded before them. From watching children on corner lots, I have come to believe that perhaps definite instruction in the specific skills of various games—batting, catching, and pitching in baseball; punting, kicking, passing, and receiving in football; stance, swing, and putt in golf; tennis strokes; technics of basketball, bowling, boxing, wrestling, swimming, dancing, fishing, hockey, whatever game the individual child selected—would accomplish more toward the development of co-ordination and rhythm than the usual physical training of the gymnasium, and it would also enable the child to learn a recreational sport which he could continue in adult life.

Early adolescents normally go through phases of extreme modesty and extreme exhibitionism and, at intervals, feel very upset if exposed to much nudity of themselves or of others. At times during these phases they absent themselves from the physical-education classes in order to feel more comfortable. Reluctance to take part in such classes at these times should be respected.

I have seen a number of children—most frequently young adolescents—who were reluctant to attend gymnasium classes because they were afraid of being hurt by the sadistic homosexual play which occurs in unsupervised locker and shower rooms. There always are a few boys who take delight in grabbing at the genitals of their weaker, more timid companions or even in hitting their genitals very hard. Some of these attackers are simply maliciously sadistic and derive pleasure from the pain and terror they cause. Some are trying to demonstrate by these actions how masculine they are, either because they are very frightened of genital injury themselves or are struggling against latent passive homosexual drives. Others are overt homosexuals. Teachers of physical education should be more aware of these problems than, in my experience, they have shown themselves to be, and should supervise these situations more carefully, protect the boys who are being attacked, and arrange that the attackers be studied and therapy instituted if advisable.

All of these situations contribute to the reluctance to attend physical-education classes found so frequently among average children. These classes also often precipitate the outbreak of the symptoms of a frank neurosis in the child who is already neurotic or furnish the opportunity for an increase in the delinquency of the delinquent child. Teachers who specialize in physical education need the opportunity for consultation about the individual pupils with a trained child psychoanalyst, more frequently than do the members of any other teaching specialty. In my experience they avail themselves of it less. I believe this occurs because in the domain of physical education the opposition between the philosophy of education and that of therapy is highlighted. This opposition of philosophies is often the result of ignorance. The teacher of physical education believes that a timid or fearful child can be educated to be more courageous; he does not know that in an individual case the fearfulness may be the symptom of a neurosis which can never be cured by educational measures. The psychoanalyst may believe that the fearfulness in a specific child is the symptom of a neurosis and may attempt to cure it by therapy when all the child requires is training in being courageous. I believe that the teacher who specializes in physical education has more need for extensive training in the basic principles of human behavior as discovered by psychoanalytic research than has the teacher in any teaching specialty.

For an adequate development of the ego the child needs the optimum amount of sensory stimulation and the optimum opportunity for motor activity for his particular constitution. This is especially true for the first seven years of life, but it also holds for the latency period and for adolescence. It is the duty of the educator—the parent in the first few years, the parent and the teacher in the succeeding years—to provide as many opportunities for activity as are possible in *reality*. Also, when the child starts school it is the responsibility of the teacher to learn from the parents whether these opportunities have been restricted, either by necessity or by parental mismanagement, during the preschool years. If this has occurred, the teacher must see that greater opportunities than would be permissible with a child who has not been so restricted are available to this particular child in the school setting. This historical information should be obtained at the time that the child first enters school and should be included in the child's records.

It is important that the child during the preschool period also have an optimum opportunity to gratify his pleasure-pain principle, and, at the same time, that he be kept in touch with reality in gradually increasing doses. In the first seven years the impact of reality should be introduced gradually—usually in the form of the rights of each member of the family in their daily living. After the child enters school, it is the responsibility of the teacher much more than of the parent to help him increasingly to accept the unpleasant aspects of reality. Here again this must be accomplished through the carefully graduated dosage of the facts which confront one living in a real world with its limitations of space, time, customs, and manners, so that the child learns slowly but definitely that there are unpleasant tasks which must be accomplished if he hopes for future realistic gratifications and pleasures. The very strict traditional school forced the child to accept unpleasant realities too early and too abruptly. This did not help his ego development much, but it helped it more than does the very progressive school which enables the child to avoid as much of unpleasant reality as possible. Either plan, carried to extremes, does a great disservice to the adequate development of the child's ego, because it interferes with the establishment of the reality principle in the mind.

DAYDREAMS AND FANTASIES

I mentioned earlier that when the motor-minded child is forced to be sedentary for too long a period, he may try to relieve his tension through fidgetiness. This of course disturbs the teacher, who tries to make him control his restlessness. In his attempt to do this, he begins to deflect his attention from his own unpleasant feelings, which are the result of the motor restrictions and are more uncomfortable than he really knows. In order to keep his attention deflected from his partly conscious and partly unconscious discomfort, he deflects it also from his surroundings, including the scholastic subjects to be learned, and turns it to the gratification supplied by daydreams. A boy—who in his later life demonstrated his motor-mindedness by his mechanical interests and his proficiency in athletics—got into trouble with his teacher in the first weeks of school because he spent his entire time drawing trains and paid little or no attention to what the class was being taught. These drawings depicted his conscious daydreams of being an engineer and driving a train. He had always been active because he was motor-minded and as he was unable to tolerate the inactivity of the classroom he resorted to the pleasure he found in daydreams.

Of course not all daydreaming is the result of the restriction of motor activity in motor-minded children. Any external situation which is unpleasant, or any external or internal restrictions on instinctual desires, may produce daydreams, particularly in those children who have not learned to tolerate some amount of discomfort or anxiety. At the present time all teachers are aware that a tendency to daydream so marked that it interferes with the learning of school subjects indicates a pathological situation which needs study and management, but I do not think that they understand much about the psychology of daydreams. The term *daydream* should be used *only* for conscious fantasies. Such conscious daydreams are not necessarily pathological and may arise from any one of several sources. If I have an ambitional impulse—whether I am aware of its presence in my mind or not—I may find myself planning, daydreaming, about doing a certain project or about how to work out its details. The daydream arises as a conscious representation of an ambitional impulse and its purpose is to enable me to plan the methods of working out my project. When this has been done I recognize that I should work out my project in actual life. The daydreaming becomes pathological only if I spend my time planning, i.e., daydreaming, and do nothing to make the daydream become real.

As I mentioned in a previous chapter, the artist refuses to coordinate all his fantasies with reality but instead retains some of them as fantasies. The fantasy itself remains in the unconscious but, through representations, appears in consciousness as stories or as ideas which can be represented through the visual arts. The conscious process of working out these stories or ideas in the mind is that of daydreaming. After this working out, the daydream furnishes the basis for the story, poem, picture, or sculpture which the artist then creates.

In the first type of daydream, I simply plan the expression of an instinctual drive. I do not withdraw from my relation to reality and the reality-testing function of my ego is unchanged. In the second type, the artist withdraws somewhat from reality to absorption in unconscious fantasies, but the reality-testing function of his ego is undisturbed. If I have worked hard over a long period of time I will find myself planning, daydreaming, about my vacation. This daydream arises as a warning to me that I need a rest and a change of scene in order not to throw too great a burden on the functions of my ego and it has the same purpose as the first type has, i.e., to warn me that I had better really do something about my situation. This third type has the same basis and purpose as the daydream of the motor-minded child whose motor activity is restricted unreasonably. A great deal of daydreaming of this type results from unpleasant environmental situations about which the individual can do nothing. A certain amount results from internally imposed restrictions—usually emanating from the superego—which are more strict than is really necessary. If the excessive daydreaming arises because of the unpleasant environment, which for real reasons cannot be altered, the relation to reality and the reality-testing function of the ego are maintained unchanged, unless the unpleasant environment remains unaltered for too long a period. In that case both the relation to reality and the reality-testing function of the ego will become defective. An extreme, but excellent, fictional illustration of this is the case of Dr. Manette in Dickens' *Tale of Two Cities*. If the excessive daydreaming arises because the superego imposes too many or too unreasonable restrictions on the ego, the relation to reality and the reality-testing function of the ego may become disturbed. At this point the conscious daydreams often become a conscious manifestation of an absorption with unconscious fantasies. I will refer to this situation later.

It is the duty of the teacher who finds one or more children so involved in daydreaming that their capacity to learn is actually diminished, to investigate carefully the whole classroom situation—the classroom routines, his own attitude toward these children, his interest in the subject material he is teaching, and his teaching methods—to find out why the situation is so unpleasant to these children. This is a better first step in dealing with the problem than to say that there is something pathological in the child. As a second step, it is important to investigate why this particular child finds the classroom situation so unpleasant. In the example of the boy who drew trains the teacher was not considering the special motor-mindedness of this particular child and was not altering the routine sufficiently to accommodate it to him. A child may find the classroom situation unpleasant because his I.Q. is far above or below the class average. Here again the classroom routine must be altered especially to accommodate this particular child, else excessive daydreaming may take place. The child whose excessive daydreaming is the result of too severe or too numerous internal—usually superego—restrictions needs these restrictions relieved. This can be accomplished only through therapy. However, the teacher should consider this possibility only as a last resort. All children, but particularly those in the prelatent period and in adolescence, are faced with certain unchangeable realities. They may have wishes and daydreams about what they will do when they are grown-up but they cannot put these daydreams into action because they are neither physiologically or psychologically ready to do so. A certain amount of their time must be spent in daydreaming and allowance has to be made for it by the educator. Their relation to reality and the reality-testing functions of the ego are not disturbed. Particularly in adolescence this tendency to become lost in daydreams from time to time and for varying periods of time to the extent of temporarily reducing the capacity to learn, is a normal phenomenon. However, if the tendency to daydream becomes so excessive that it really interferes over a long period with the capacity to learn, a pathological process connected with unconscious fantasies is taking place. Such a child needs investigation and probably therapy by a skilled child psychoanalyst.

The term *fantasy* is best restricted to the phenomenon of unconscious fantasies. The nature of these is well illustrated by hysterical symptoms. A man constantly dreads that his legs will give way under him and that he will collapse. This dread is the conscious representation of an unconscious fantasy that his father will be kind to him and look after him—will carry him if he is overworked or tired, as he did when the patient was a child. The fantasy arises as a wish that he were little and helpless and that his father would have to look after him. A woman whose sexual life is unsatisfying dreads to walk on the street alone lest something terrible happen to her. Her dread of walking on the street is a fear of her unconscious fantasy that if she were a streetwalker she would be satisfied sexually. Her symptoms therefore represent the gratification of an instinctual wish and the superego punishment for this wish. As the wish is gratified in fantasy a great deal of energy is bound up in the fantasy, so the individual is impoverished in the efforts he consciously would like to make in his real life. He may have many conscious daydreams of any or all of the types I have mentioned but these daydreams fail in their purpose because there is not enough energy at their disposal to put them into action, for the energy is being discharged constantly through the unconscious fantasy. The fact that in this way the energy is discharged so freely attracts more and more instinctual energy to this method of discharge and consequently leaves little under the control of the ego. What energy is left has to be utilized by the ego to keep the energy-filled fantasy repressed and unconscious. When a child's energy is so absorbed by an unconscious fantasy he has little left at the disposal of his ego for learning. He also has a very disturbed relation with reality, and the reality-testing function of his ego is very disabled. Such children sit in school and learn little. They have conscious daydreams, but the content of these only points indirectly to the presence of an unconscious fantasy. It is not that they restrict their ego because of fear of the superego, but that their energies are absorbed into obtaining discharge through the unconscious fantasy. Their condition is quite pathological. They cannot be helped through any type of educational procedure or by any alteration the teacher can make in classroom routines. They are amenable only to therapeutic measures.

EDUCATION AND THE STAGES OF THE CHILD'S DEVELOPMENT

Nowhere in this book have I entered into a full discussion of the stages of psychosexual development of the child, because these stages —the oral, anal-sadistic, and phallic—and their manifestations are well known to anyone who has read the psychoanalytic literature since Freud [2] first published his *Three Contributions to the Theory of Sex* and even to many people who have read either the more recent psychoanalytic literature [3] or the popular adaptations of it.[4]

Parents and nursery-school teachers particularly need to have more knowledge of the phenomenon of repression—the fact that repression is an essential part of development and that if attempts are made to prevent it the child's development will suffer. This is as important as the knowledge that unreasonable degrees of repression also hamper development. They should know that a certain degree of the defense mechanism of reaction formation is necessary but that it is desirable, if possible, to direct the child toward sublimation rather than reaction formation. As both sublimations and reaction formations are methods of dealing with pregenital impulses, the educator must recognize several facts concerning pregenital development. If any stage of pregenital development is allowed to progress for an optimum period and if its termination takes place gradually, the pregenital impulses which do not continue into the next stage of development are more available

[2] Sigmund Freud, *Three Contributions to the Theory of Sex,* New York and Washington, Nervous and Mental Disease Publishing Co., 1930.

[3] Richard Sterba, *An Introduction to the Psychoanalytic Theory of the Libido,* New York and Washington, Nervous and Mental Disease Publishing Co., 1942.

[4] O. Spurgeon English and Gerald H. J. Pearson, *Emotional Problems of Living,* New York, W. W. Norton & Company, 1945; Siegfried Bernfeld, *The Psychology of the Infant,* London, Kegan Paul, 1929; Erik Erikson, *Childhood and Society,* New York, W. W. Norton & Company, 1950.

for sublimation than for reaction formation. If the optimum period of any stage of development is curtailed or if the child is forced to relinquish its pleasures too suddenly, a great deal of energy will be fixed to this stage and reaction formations will become the only means of defense. If any stage is allowed to continue long past the optimum period, it will have to be terminated suddenly and reaction formations against the instinctual impulses of that stage will develop. If there is an easy progression from one stage of optimum length to another, sublimations are more likely to result than reaction formations. In order to help the tendency toward sublimation, substitutes for the instinct pleasures should be provided for the child. Certain illustrations suggest how this is done. At the time of toilet training, opportunity should be provided for the child to play with mud pies, finger paints, and the like. These opportunities should be continued after toilet training has been achieved. The mud pies should later be replaced by wet, then dry, sand—and, still later, no objection should be raised to the collection first, of useless treasures and later, of useful treasures such as coins, stamps, and so on. When a small girl comes to the age of wanting to have a baby she should have the opportunity to play with dolls. When she is in conflict about penis envy she should have the opportunity of knowing all the importance of being a girl. During the latency period, the boy should have opportunities to play warlike games. These are only some examples which indicate the importance to the educator of understanding the stages of libidinal development and utilizing this knowledge practically to help the particular child toward the sublimations which he needs most. This understanding is essential in connection with the tendency to impose creative arts on children in order to "teach them creativity." The understanding educator will provide opportunities for the use of the creative arts but will not insist that every child take part in them all.

Finally, every educator should recognize the great importance of helping the child gradually to place himself under the supremacy of the reality principle rather than the pleasure-pain principle. Particularly in the latency period, this is the role of the professional educator more than of the parent. Every opportunity to test reality is useful in helping the child solve his intrapsychic conflicts. During the latency period there should be ample opportunities for unsupervised and unrestricted play so that each child may have the chance to work out his specific conflicts in the make-believe of play. In reality, human life consists more of hard and tedious work than of pleasurable experience and if the individual wishes to lead a pleasurable life he must develop the capacity to accept and adjust to reality—to the realities of the physical world, the needs and desires of other people in this world, and the customs and mores of the culture in which he lives. Only when the individual has this capacity will he be able to attempt to change any part of the environment—the physical world, the other members of his social group, or the prevailing customs and mores.

I have pointed out that disturbances during the oral period may result in learning difficulties. When a child enters school his teacher should find out whether he has had such disturbances and what their nature and extent was. He will then be prepared to note whether the child has greater difficulty in learning than the average child; if he does, the teacher may have to use different methods of instruction. If these fail, he will understand the need for consultation about this particular child's problems with a psychoanalyst who specializes in the treatment of children.

It is a general rule in classrooms, both progressive and traditional, that children must not eat while they work because eating interferes with learning and paying attention. On the surface this idea seems at variance with ordinary human experience. It is true that a person does not think as well as usual after eating a large meal, but it also is true that group discussions on any subject proceed better and with more real interest and profit when accompanied by smoking or nibbling. The nibbling helps to replace the gradual lowering of the sugar content of the blood which results from the increased metabolism necessary for hard intellectual labor. The Coca-Cola advertisers show their awareness of this need in their slogan: "The pause"—for drinking Coca-Cola (a drink high in sugar content)—"that refreshes." The prohibition against eating in the classroom, therefore, looks like a superstition—which it undoubtedly is—but like all superstitions it contains more than a grain of truth. Psychoanalytic researches have proven the close relationship between the desire to eat and to suck and the learning process. As I mentioned in an earlier chapter, traumatic experiences in connection with eating and sucking, early in life, damage the later ability to learn. The teacher's unconscious knowledge of the connection between eating and learning is the basis in fact for the superstition. It becomes a mere superstition because the factual knowledge has been lifted out of context, for it is only very early traumatic experiences in eating and sucking—those occurring the first year—that affect the development of the capacity to learn. This never happens in a child of school age.

Eating together has always been recognized as a part of the communion of souls. This is excellently illustrated in the Christian ritual of the Communion. It is illustrated also when the child brings an apple for the teacher—if the teacher eats the apple, she will be in communion with him and will love him. The fact that an article of food is brought, not something else, indicates that the gift is more than a mere bribe. The sharing of food expresses the desire to be close to another person—to love him and be loved by him. Solitary eating may indicate a refusal to enter into such a sharing. There is often a real antithesis between solitary eating and genital love, something like the relative lack of sexual desire and object relationship found in the glutton. When the child wishes to occupy most of his classroom time in eating or sucking, it may indicate that he is not able to love the teacher or to desire to be loved by him. When this happens the child does not learn.

The most important contribution made by psychoanalysis to the field of education is the knowledge that mutual love between teacher and child—a positive object relationship—is the first step in the use of the mechanisms of identification and incorporation, by which all learning actually takes place, and the corollary knowledge that feelings of hatred and fear, whether one-sided or mutual, interfere with the learning process. In the child in the latency period and in adolescence this positive object relationship wavers among three levels. Basically, there is the earliest level of object relationship, which has the aim of introjection of the object, which results in incorporation and identification. In latency, adolescence, and adult life, the presence of this form of object relationship is often regarded as pathological. For example, it is often found that an adult woman who behaves in a so-called masculine manner and who either is an overt homosexual or has very strong unconscious homosexual desires may present this picture because she is identifying with her father. During her edipus conflict she developed terror—for whatever reasons—of her heterosexual desires for her father, and in order to solve the conflict between her terror and her heterosexual desires she regressed to the earlier form of object relationship, i.e., identification. Her adult behavior, therefore, is a mask for her passive-receptive feminine heterosexual desires, which she dreads. Her identification with her father is a pathological defense, as is her regression from the level of genital object love to identification. Although identification as a form of object relationship is always regressive, usually neither the regression nor the identification is a pathological defense. They are simply defenses which are necessary in reality. As direct genital sexual desires cannot be sublimated and as it is neither possible nor desirable to gratify them directly with everybody with whom one has a genital object relationship, three nonpathological courses are left open: the sexual element may be repressed into the unconscious and retained there, it may be repressed and then redirected into conscious feelings of friendliness and companionship,[5] or repression may be followed by regression to the earlier form of object relationship, identification. None of these methods of defense can be considered pathological, because all of them are attempts at adaptation to reality and do not result from implacable internalized superego prohibitions, such as those which caused the pathological defenses of regression and identification in the case of the woman I mentioned earlier.

Second, there is a phallic object relationship, in which the child desires a sexual relationship, that is, desires to have his body penetrate or be penetrated by the body of the teacher and thereby to possess the latter completely. This relationship is not at the level of real genitality, but is centered solely on the union of the genitals without much regard for emotional reactions or feelings, because at the phallic level of development, the chief aim of the sexual instinct is to possess and penetrate or be penetrated by the genitals of the love object. As this is the ultimate goal of the biological process of reproduction, this desire cannot be sublimated. At the phallic level of development, the

[5] This really is a sublimation. The sexual aim is inhibited and the instinct obtains discharge in a nonsexual way. It then would be a sublimation of a pregenital phallic impulse, because genital sexual impulses cannot be sublimated.

pregenital impulses have been only partially subordinated to the supremacy of the genitals—so that they appear in the sexual act only as sexual forepleasure—and parts of each pregenital impulse have not yet been sublimated. Sadism has not yet been changed into a desire for mastery and tender care, nor masochism into a desire for being mastered and tenderly cared for. Other important changes have not yet occurred: of the desire to look and be looked at into aesthetic respect and admiration; of hatred and jealousy into competitiveness; of the desire to be fed and supported into the desire to feed, support, and look after; of the desire to be independent into the desire to be partly independent and partly dependent, and partly to have others dependent on oneself; and of the desire to be given pleasure into the desire to give pleasure. Ambivalence, selfishness, and altruism have not attained a reasonable balance. Homosexuality has not developed into friendship, and heterosexuality has not developed into genital love and mutual companionship and tenderness. The pregenital impulses are still demanding gratification for and discharge of their energy through achievement of their direct aims, contradictory as these may be in reality and to each other, and substitute methods of gratification and discharge have been consolidated only slightly. The organizing, integrating, and synthesizing functions of the ego, although present and active, are still weak in the face of the instincts and of reality. A constant state of conflict exists. When the child at the phallic level of development is overwhelmed by his feelings, his capacity to learn undergoes marked fluctuations. This unleashing of feeling at the phallic level of development, subordinating, as it does, other levels of love, is well known to everybody as the "crush."

Lastly, there is a genital object relationship, in which the student admires and respects the teacher, desires the same feelings from him, and wishes that he were old enough and capable enough to have the teacher as a real friend or marital companion—depending on the sex of the teacher and student. This goal cannot actually be achieved until late adolescence or early adult life and then may result in the formation of a lifelong friendship and companionship or, sometimes, in marriage.

As I have said, the child in the latency period and early adolescence learns because he loves the teacher and desires the teacher to love him, that is, he has a positive object relationship with him. This positive object relationship will have components from all three levels of the development of object relationships. Learning takes place best when the dominant levels are those of identification and of genital object relationships. The presence of too much of the phallic level interferes with it. This type of interference is often seen in adolescence. When the adolescent falls in love either with the teacher or with someone else he tends to spend his time mooning about his love, and he can direct little or no attention to other matters in his daily life. This is an expression of love at the phallic level. This amorous phenomenon is seen often in analysis. A female patient of a male analyst will declare verbally her tremendous love for him and will make impossible demands for sexual relations with him regardless of the practical and emotional results of the gratification of these demands. Her declarations are purely at the phallic level, for, if she loved the analyst at the genital level, she would try to win his respect and admiration through her compliance with the rules of analysis and her real efforts toward cure of the illness for which she came to analysis. Similarly in the adolescent, love at the genital level may urge him to learn as much as possible so as to be successful in his competition with his rivals and to be certain of greater admiration, respect, and love from his love object.

SELECTION AND TRAINING OF THE TEACHER

The knowledge of the importance of love, of a positive object relationship between the child and the teacher as a basis for learning through introjection and identification, throws into strong relief the extreme care with which teachers for children should be selected. The child who learns incorporates not only what the teacher teaches but all aspects of the teacher's personality. If the teacher has an extremely rigid obsessional character, the child will incorporate that. If the teacher has a delinquent character, or is sadistic, or too inhibited, the child will incorporate that. These incorporations may be of benefit to the child, if they are the opposite of his parents' characters, which he has incorporated earlier. They can be harmful if they reinforce the pathological character of the parents. From the standpoint of the process of identification, therefore, it is necessary that the teacher be a desirable model. The child is going to be overwhelmed at times by the feelings of the phallic level of object relationship. The teacher who, himself, is still operating on the phallic level because his internal prohibitions or his real environment prevent him from attaining the genital level, will unconsciously encourage the emergence of the phallic level in the child. At this point identification disappears and the child ceases to learn. Such a teacher may be notorious for the crushes which develop in his classroom.

Since the relationship between the teacher and the child forms such an important part of the educational procedure and of the character development of the child, it becomes very evident that the teacher himself must have an adequate personality. It seems to me that a teacher should be as carefully, if not more carefully, selected than a psychoanalyst is. The analyst is concerned only with the treatment of neurotic or psychotic patients, usually adults, and if treatment results in their being less neurotic or psychotic and eases their sufferings, and helps them to be more successful in life, he has accomplished a great deal. The teacher has a greater responsibility: he has the job of aiding the personality development of nonneurotic children and his influence can be helpful or harmful. In order to become a practicing psychoanalyst the student must undergo a personal psychoanalysis. Since Freud first attempted a psychoanalysis of himself—an attempt which resulted in his classic *Interpretation of Dreams*—all instructors in psychoanalysis have believed that the foundation of the curriculum is the analysis of the student, and that the personal analysis is a basic and indispensable preparation for psychoanalytic training. In this analysis the prospective student undergoes a penetrating psychological study of himself. He is expected to explore resolutely and thoroughly the unconscious reaches of his mind, to trace his development back to the formative experiences of his childhood, and to arrive at a better knowledge and more realistic appraisal of himself as an individual and as a product of a given period and culture. He is expected to overcome his personal difficulties and to acquire a greater measure of self-direction and psychological and critical independence, and a more mature outlook upon life. After the analysis has been completed he is instructed in the theory, technic, and practice of psychoanalysis. If this is necessary for a psychoanalyst, it seems to be at least as necessary, for the reasons I have stated, for the training of teachers, particularly teachers in nursery schools and kindergartens, and, at least, the early grammar-school grades. It is perhaps not so essential for the teachers of junior-high-school and high-school grades but it would be valuable for them also. However, under present conditions and from a practical standpoint this seems an impossible ideal. There is only a relatively small number of practicing psychoanalysts. Psychoanalysis itself is expensive and therefore usually beyond the financial reach of most late adolescents and young adults—those at the age in which teacher training takes place. Neither the government—even though at the present time it is allocating moderate sums of money for mental hygiene—nor the foundations which are interested in education or mental hygiene recognize the importance of a personal psychoanalysis as part of teacher training. Some method of subsidy or the establishment of scholarships for the psychoanalysis of student teachers seems the only practical method of including a personal psychoanalysis as part of the curriculum for the training of teachers. The Institute of the Philadelphia Association for Psychoanalysis has long endeavored to find the resources to supply a few scholarships of this sort, and it has been ready to help any teacher who has undergone or is undergoing a personal psychoanalysis by adding to his professional knowledge the information about children which has been gained through psychoanalytic research. In the 1920's and 1930's many Viennese teachers were psychoanalyzed and received some instruction in psychoanalytic knowledge. This has been true to a lesser degree in London, New York, Boston, and Chicago. In fact all psychoanalytic training institutes are very much interested in helping teachers as much as possible. It is to be hoped that these efforts—which are only a drop in the bucket at present—will be increased in the future and will be supplemented by demands from the faculties of teacher-training institutions for an increasing number of personal psychoanalyses for their student teachers.

However, the concept of a personal psychoanalysis as part of the training of all student teachers exists at present only as a wish, and like all wishes is subject to the reality principle. Resources have to be found to implement it, if it is to be translated from the realm of wishes into practical reality.

Psychoanalytic knowledge, however, can suggest some rough criteria for personality and character development by which teachers could be selected. A good teacher must have imagination. He must have intuition, which is an unconscious ability to sense what is happening in another person's emotional life and in another person's unconscious. This means the unconscious capacity to put oneself in the other person's place. Perhaps all people have this capacity, but not all will permit themselves to be influenced by it. Sometimes, after a psychoanalysis, a person who had seemed completely devoid of intuition will begin to show a certain degree of it. There are others who are not influenced in this way by psychoanalysis and still others who show a marked degree of intuition before their psychoanalysis and whose intuitive capacity does not seem to be affected by the analysis. These findings seem to indicate that the capacity for intuition arises from some constitutional trait. Some people have it and some people do not. Some of those who have it are unable to use it for neurotic reasons. Others, despite their neurotic problems, are capable of using it even to a high degree.

A teacher needs empathy. This ability differs from intuition. It is the unconscious capacity not only to put oneself in the other person's place, to recognize consciously what the other person's unconscious feelings and ideas are, but also, at the same time, to help the other person with his problems. Empathy or psychological insight bears some relationship to intuition and like intuition seems to be a constitutional trait. Whatever its basis, it is increased by experience. We all understand better what another person is feeling if we ourselves have gone through a similar experience. I do not know of any tests which will determine the presence or absence of imagination, intuition, and empathy. I know that during psychoanalysis it is relatively easy for the analyst, after a number of sessions, to know whether a patient is imaginative, intuitive, or empathic. His conclusion is not reached through the uncovering of the patient's unconscious, but is a clinical judgment formed through listening to him. I believe if the instructors of student teachers directed their attention to finding out whether the individual student was imaginative, intuitive, and empathic, they would soon be aware consciously of the presence, the degree of the presence, or the absence, of these traits in their pupils.

There are also more objective criteria for the selection of a teacher and these can be applied with relative certainty. A teacher should have an adequate social life. This social life should not be limited to the company of other members of the same profession. In such a social life, as everyone knows, the conversation and discussions too often are confined to "shop talk." Because of this shop talk real social relationships are prevented. If the student teacher's social life is limited, then it is necessary to learn whether this is the result of real limitations, financial, situational, and the like, or whether there are neurotic inhibitions. The individual with neurotic inhibitions will not make a good teacher.

A teacher should have an adequate recreational life. Teachers, more than the members of any other professional group except psychoanalysts, are exposed to the instinctual temptations arising from the unconscious of those with whom their work is concerned, in this instance their pupils. Children are freer than adults in their direct expressions of hatred, envy, destructiveness, jealousy—particularly sibling rivalry—ridicule, cruelty, anger, uncleanliness, sexual curiosity, exhibitionism, oral erotism, masochism, and the rest, and this relative freedom offers a great unconscious temptation to the teacher to do likewise. The teacher's defense mechanisms—particularly that of repression—therefore have to work overtime in order to prevent him from descending completely to the level of the children. If he did, he would cease to be a good teacher because he would cease to be an adult and would become embroiled and overwhelmed by the emotional problems of the pupils. If the defense mechanisms work overtime, they may become too rigid and the gulf which separates child from adult then becomes unbridgeable because the rigid defenses do not allow the teacher to continue to understand the children and their reactions. The pupils start to "get on his nerves" and he is compelled more and more to force them to cease what they are doing, lest his own unconscious drives suddenly erupt and overwhelm him. This is neither a helpful nor a healthful atmosphere for the child. Besides the constant struggle to control the instinctual drives stimulated by the behavior of the children, the teacher undergoes the constant intrapsychic struggles that are inevitable in any institutional setup like a school. These center around jealousy of colleagues, whether this be unconsciously heterosexual or homosexual, fear of and desire to be favored by superiors, or hatred of and rebellion against superiors, and inclusion in or exclusion from cliques.

All of these difficult situations impose a severe burden on the teacher's capacity to adjust. Therefore he needs more real recreation than do other people. This must be a specific type of recreation—the type which allows the direct expression of instinctual drives in play. A frequent change of scene may be necessary (as it is for everybody) but touring the American or European continent for cultural reasons with a group of teachers will not supply the necessary release and relaxation. Aggressive competitive games—the more childish the better—dancing, smoking, social drinking, sun-bathing, and the ordinary pursuits of the mountain and seashore are more necessary for teachers than they are for other people. Any recreational pursuit which tends in the direction of children's play is very valuable. I am only making a practical application of the old adage, A little nonsense now and then is relished by the wisest men. In brief, anything that allows the direct expression of pregenital impulses in the form of play forms a desirable basis for the teacher's recreational life. Again, if his recreational life seems to be limited it is necessary to ascertain whether this limitation is due to reality or to neurotic reasons. If it has a neurotic basis, he will not make a good teacher. It is essential also that school boards and personnel directors of schools understand that a teacher will be a better teacher if he is allowed opportunities for such recreations. The community or school board which demands that the teachers at all times be perfect examples of complete and total inhibition of all expressions of instinct will find eventually that their children will not learn, that their character and personality development is impeded, and that the proportion of improper discipline in the school system and of nervous breakdowns among the teaching staff has increased greatly.

It is desirable that a teacher have interests outside of his profession. In examining candidates applying for admission to the training course of a psychoanalytic institute, inquiries of this nature are made as a matter of routine, for it has been found that a physician whose interests are centered entirely on medicine suffers from a neurotic character restriction. He has unconsciously restricted his ego in order to defend himself against his instinctual drives and he avoids intrapsychic conflict by using large amounts of energy—which otherwise would be available for his daily life—to cement his repressions. It is well known also that when a child plays the same game over and over, seldom, if ever, changing the content of his play, he is definitely neurotic and finds his intrapsychic conflicts insoluble. In using this last illustration I am not implying that interests and recreation are identical. Far from it—recreation offers an opportunity for the direct expression of instinctual desires and the discharge of their energy in play, while interests are the result of sublimation. The more interests a person has, the more of his pregenital instinctual drives have been sublimated and thus become a source of value beyond the simple value of discharge of tension. If the student teacher's interests are limited, it is necessary to ascertain whether this limitation has been imposed by reality or whether it is the result of the defense mechanism of ego restriction. A person with a restricted ego is not going to provide a desirable model with whom the children can identify.

It is desirable that the student teacher have the capacity for an adequate sexual life. Genital sexual desires cannot be sublimated, they must be gratified directly. If this does not occur the intrapsychic equilibrium is upset and in certain cases pathological defense mechanisms develop which later may produce neurotic symptoms, in the form of a neurotic illness or a neurotic character disorder. There is no question that a married teacher will be a better teacher and a better model for his pupils than an unmarried one. I realize that certain school systems are opposed to this idea, partly because a married person is entitled to a higher salary—which many school boards are reluctant to pay—and partly because if the teacher is a woman she will have to be given leaves of absence, from time to time, because of pregnancies. These are not valid objections and certainly do not counterbalance in any way the benefit to the pupils of a teacher whose sexual life is adequate. It is an interesting philosophy which says that the persons to whom children, who are the future of the nation and the world, are entrusted should be paid only a small salary and which raises objections to any demand that these salaries be increased. Lest any reader of this statement raise the accusation that I am not considering morals, I have no hesitation in stating that I see no reason why an adequate genital sexual life cannot be attained within the existing moral patterns.

If the student teacher appears to lack the capacity for a future sexual life it is necessary to ascertain whether this seeming inadequacy is the result of a real external limitation or of the student's moral or religious principles or whether it is self-imposed because of neurotic conflicts. If it arises out of the need to avoid a neurotic conflict, the individual will not be a good teacher.

In the past few pages I have been saying simply that the good teacher will be one who has psychic flexibility which expresses itself in all phases of his life, and only the student who shows such flexibility should be selected for teacher training. I have stressed the need to determine whether a limitation in a teacher's life is the result of intrapsychic problems or of environmental limitations. Intrapsychic problems can be changed only by therapy, but environmental limitations are amenable to correction through a better understanding on the part of the parents, school boards, and the community in general. There are several of these limitations which need attention and change at the present time. In order to attract better people to the teaching profession the salary scale will have to be increased. The person who teaches nursery school, kindergarten, and the elementary grades has to be more highly selected than the one who teaches in high school, and therefore he is entitled to a higher salary. The powers that be should see that the teacher, particularly the teacher of young children, has opportunity for an adequate social, recreational, and sexual life and for pursuing his extra-professional interests. The foregoing applies to all teachers but it is especially applicable to people, whether teachers or houseparents, who are in charge of children living in various types of institutions—boarding schools, orphanages, detention homes, reform schools, and the like. Such people need an even greater opportunity for social, recreational, and sexual life than do teachers in day schools—and these opportunities are usually woefully inadequate. This lack of opportunity and the low salary scale deter really desirable people from taking such positions. This is especially unfortunate because children in orphanages and in detention homes need the care and guidance which can be furnished only by well-integrated persons with a high degree of insight.

Discussion of the criteria for the selection of student teachers raises the question of why a person selects teaching as a profession. I realize that there are certain social, economic, and family pressures which contribute to the choice, but these influences are not the whole story. There must be psychological determinants but, so far, I know of no study of these determinants. Psychoanalysis as yet has not done much detailed research into the unconscious determinants of the various occupations, even of the occupation of psychoanalysis itself. The Committee on the Psychoanalysis of Children and Adolescents of the American Psychoanalytic Association attempted to ascertain why a psychoanalyst decided to specialize in the psychoanalysis of children, but they were forced to terminate their discussions for the present because they lacked sufficient data. However, they agreed that people with certain conflicts tended, before psychoanalysis, to try to solve these conflicts by working with children rather than with adults. These conflicts were as follows: 1. An unconscious fear of their own unconscious hostile and sexual impulses toward other adults and of the unconscious hostile and sexual impulses of other adults toward them. Consciously they controlled their fear by marked feelings of inferiority which made them feel very uncomfortable with adults but more comfortable with children, of whom they were not so afraid because they felt able to dominate them. 2. An unconscious desire to get even with their siblings, whom they hated, and to put the latter in their place. Consciously they felt most comfortable when placed in a situation where they could direct, control, and dominate *other* children. 3. A usually unconscious but sometimes conscious hatred of their parents and of the way their parents had brought them up. At some time in their childhood such adults had consciously said to themselves, "I do not like the way I am treated. When I grow up I will treat my children in exactly the opposite way." Later this determination might be repressed into the unconscious but, whether conscious or unconscious, it served as the guide by which they dealt with children. In some instances it led to a desirable ideal, but because of its unconscious sources, it could be a guide fraught with danger to the child in the care of such an adult. 4. An unconscious conflict about having children of their own, either because of fear of the physiological processes of impregnation, conception, pregnancy, and childbirth, and of the responsibilities of parenthood, or because of the persistence of the childhood fear of the desire to take the place of the pregnant mother or the impregnating father. Adults with such unconscious conflicts tend to have no children of their own and instead desire to manage other people's children and, in fact, to try to take these children away from their parents. The need to solve one of these unconscious conflicts is not a good basis for working with children. The Committee believed that unless these conflicts could be analyzed the person should not be permitted to work with children. As student teachers usually are not psychoanalyzed, there is no way at present of knowing how many select the profession of teaching as a solution for similar unconscious conflicts. It is only after years of teaching that the effect on the children begins to be obvious. In the meantime, such teachers have a deleterious effect on the development of many of their pupils. I see no way of discovering such student teachers unless all are required to have an investigation of their unconscious by a psychoanalyst. Perhaps a rough screening could be carried out by means of projective tests such as the Rorschach and Thematic Apperception tests and those students whose test results showed indications of such unconscious conflicts could be further studied by a psychoanalyst. If such unconscious conflicts were present to a marked degree, the student should be advised to change his profession or, if he wished to continue, to have a therapeutic psychoanalysis.

The Committee believed that there was evidence to support the following concept. Psychoanalysts who desired to specialize in the psychoanalysis of children seemed to have had a definite kind of history. In their early childhood they had felt rejected by their mothers, often because of the birth of another sibling. In order to assuage their suffering they had turned to another woman in the family who was a person with a marked intuitive knowledge of children's feelings. They had then identified with this woman and through this identification developed an interest in helping children and a capacity intuitively to understand their problems and conflicts. Such a motivation usually resulted in the ability to handle children successfully. Much more research is needed on the problem of the unconscious motivations that underlie the desire to work with children either therapeutically or educationally. Here the educational psychologist and the psychoanalyst need to work close together—which they have not done up to this time.

All-important as the selection of the student teacher should be, it needs to be supplemented by the education of the student to be a teacher. He must learn the methods of teaching in general, and those best suited for teaching certain subjects. At least as important, if not more so, is the necessity for the student teacher to acquire a thorough knowledge and understanding of children, particularly of their emotional life and the phases of their psychosexual development. Too frequently this need is passed over lightly or even omitted in teacher-training curricula. Courses are given in child development, but there has been a general tendency to neglect the data compiled from psychoanalytic researches which have developed as a result of Freud's *Three Contributions to the Theory of Sex*. The teacher needs intensive instruction about the processes of development of the libido, the ego, and the superego during the oral, anal-sadistic, and phallic phases, in the latency period, and through puberty and adolescence, as well as instruction about the usual behavior of the child during these periods. To teach only from the standpoint of the educational psychologists, such as Gesell, is to present only the outward appearance without the dynamic reasons for the behavior. Both must be learned if the teacher is to have a real understanding of the child.

SOME EDUCATIONAL PROBLEMS

Besides having to know and understand the psychosexual development of the child, the teacher should also be aware of certain problems which seem to be problems of the ego more than of libido development.

There has been an increasing tendency among progressive educators, both in schools and in camps, to remove all elements of competition from the education of the child. This has come as a reaction against the overuse of competition in some of the traditional schools.

In the latter the prizes of scaling, grading, and so on were given to those children who showed the highest academic standing, regardless of their other accomplishments or of their intelligence level. A child with a lower I.Q. than others in his class might meet constant failure under this system and therefore be unhappy because he could acquire no sense of achievement, although he might be doing his absolute best. A child with a higher I.Q. might be rewarded constantly even if he did not actually work nearly as hard. Such procedures resulted in an increased amount of jealousy, resentment, and unhappiness. A child might do only moderately well scholastically but might be outstanding in social consciousness or in athletics and yet receive no recognition for these capacities. I believe Cecil Rhodes was among the first to attempt to remedy this difficulty. He required that the students to whom his scholarships were to be awarded must be outstanding not only scholastically but also athletically and socially. This was a more reasonable point of view. However, the progressive educators went too far in the opposite direction, doing away with all opportunities for competition in order to correct these abuses. They neglected to recognize the fact that competition is a culturally beneficial form of expression of the aggressive instincts, which is necessary if the expressions of hatred, jealousy, and resentment are to be reduced to their proper place in social life. There is no benefit in denying the existence of the aggressive instincts and trying to act as if they did not exist. Only by recognizing their presence can the educator help the child to find adequate beneficial and socially acceptable forms of expression for them. Despite the ideas of the progressive educators, children in progressive schools do compete with each other because it is natural for them to do so. Instead of removing all opportunities for competition, the educator should encourage it as a means of learning and perfecting ego skills, but it should be on a fair basis. Starting with several children who are equally endowed, beneficial competition within a group can be encouraged if the teacher really recognizes three principles: that the desire to compete successfully is natural, i.e., instinctual, in every child, that its expression can be utilized as a method of perfecting ego skills, and that it can be so utilized only if the competitors have equal basic endowment.

The child throughout the course of his development is torn by a constant battle between the need of his instincts to be discharged and the counterforces of reality, culture, the needs and desires of other people—all of which frequently are inimical to this discharge—and also by the struggle which results because his instincts themselves have antagonistic aims and therefore cannot be discharged simultaneously. The presence of these conflicts is indicated by the frequent occurrence of anxiety states, of temper tantrums, and of phobias in the child during the prelatent period. The anxiety state indicates to the child that he is in the grip of an instinct that is demanding gratification. The temper tantrum allows him to withdraw from reality and to come to some terms with his overstimulated instinctual desires. The phobia warns him to watch out that his instincts do not get beyond his control. Ever so often he has to relax his vigilance a little and seek respite through regression. This may be a regression in his libidinal development. He may revert for a short period to fingersucking, wetting or soiling himself, and so on. However, it may be a regression in his ego development, manifesting itself by a return of the primary processes of thinking when he indulges for a short period in nonsense, rhymes, and the like. This type of regression is observed very often as the edipus period draws to a close, although it occurs also at intervals before then and, though not to the same degree, later. The child gets discharge pleasure from repeating the same words or syllables over and over even if they are nonsensical. It seems to me that educators might make more use of this tendency in teaching the child ego skills—which he will have to learn anyway at some time. In spite of the efforts of progressive educators, there is only one effective method of learning arithmetic fundamentals such as tables, and that is by rote memory. The difficulty in the past has been that these were taught to the child of nine or ten, when such learning really is hard work and the only incentive to learn is to please the teacher. As the ego regressions to the primary processes occur most commonly in children of about six to eight, would it not be a good plan to use this period for the child to learn his tables? He would get the discharge pleasure he needs and at the same time the repetition would implant the facts of the tables in his memory, so that they would be readily available in the later years, when he needs them. Dates, names of states and their capitals, and other facts which must be learned by rote memory could be acquired in a similar way at the same time. Peller [6] says that at the beginning of the latency period, compulsive mechanisms are normally present and children strive for exactness and conventional standards which are independent of personal variables. As a result, the child of five or six has a greater interest in counting, weighing, measuring, and arranging than he has earlier or later. It is at this time, then, that these skills could be taught.

I am not educator enough to be very specific as to the application to the field of education of the facts about the child's development discovered by psychoanalytic researches. These are matters for the psychoanalytically trained educator. They open up a field of research and experiment by such persons toward what may be still better educational procedures.

[6] Lili E. Peller, "Incentives to Development and Means of Early Education," *The Psychoanalytic Study of the Child,* Vol. II, New York, International Universities Press, 1946.

PART THREE

Psychoanalysis and the Development of the Moral Sense

CHAPTER XIII

The Functions and Development of the Superego

In the introductory chapter I pointed out that education combines two processes—the learning process, by which the child or adult gathers knowledge of the world, past and present, and the training process, by which the child learns to live satisfactorily with other people and with himself. I mentioned also that the psychoanalyst has had more experience with the deleterious results of improper training along moral lines than he has had with any other parts of the field of education, so that psychoanalysis almost from its beginning has been able to make its most definite contributions in the field of education to knowledge of the training process. It was noteworthy, in the seminar group referred to in the Preface, that the psychoanalysts were interested mostly in what the educators could tell them about the learning process. This held little attraction for the educators, who insisted on discussing the methods by which the moral development of the child could be helped. At their request a number of sessions were devoted to the methods by which antagonistic, destructive, and cruel behavior could be handled; or, again, they would raise questions like the following: "Do our school practices, particularly for the younger boys and girls, assist the children in recognizing sexual differences and identifying themselves with their own sex? These practices are: the older boys and girls play team sports together on the playing field; in crafts, boys and girls use shop tools or sew or weave; boys and girls in the three-, four- and five-year-old groups use toilet facilities at the same time; slacks and dungarees are preferred dress by women and girls throughout the school, and in the nursery school and kindergarten, all children wear clothes that are predominantly male."

In the previous chapters I have tried to show that a very important task of education lies in helping the child to develop an ego which can integrate and synthesize his needs for instinctual discharge with the reality in which he lives. On the one hand the impulses to be discharged may be those "that impel the separate parts of living matter towards one another and hold them together" [1] and that may be directed to objects (as the sexual instincts are directed) or to the ego (as the self-preservative instincts—what Freud calls the life instincts or Eros—are directed); on the other hand, there are the impulses which are directed to the destruction of life, whether of external objects or of the self (what Freud calls the death instinct). The most recent working classification still divides the instincts into these two groups, which involve antithetic forces. The basic instincts are classified as follows:

The aim of the erotic instinct is the preservation of the life of the individual and of the species, directly through the development of abilities to look after oneself and through heterosexual genital object relations, and indirectly through creative, constructive, altruistic, and friendly sublimations.

The aim of the death instinct is to return from the animate into the inanimate, essentially to reinstate the status quo. Hartmann, Kris, and Loewenstein [2] have discussed fully the psychoanalytic concept of aggression. Aggressive impulses and their manifestations are the result of an innate primary aggressive drive. After describing the steps in the history of the present concepts of aggression, they contrast the behavior and the vicissitudes of the erotic and the aggressive drives. The activity of the libido of the erotic drives may be the opposite of inactivity or the opposite of passive receptivity, or it may be actively loving as opposed to passively being loved. Active aggression is a wish to harm. Passive aggression is a wish to be harmed

[1] Sigmund Freud, *Beyond the Pleasure Principle,* London, International Psychoanalytic Press, 1922.

[2] Heinz Hartmann, Ernst Kris, and Rudolph M. Loewenstein, "Notes on the Theory of Aggression," *The Psychoanalytic Study of the Child,* Vols. III–IV, New York, International Universities Press, 1949.

and this is accessible to observation as masochism, which is a fusion of aggressive and erotic drives. An absence of activity may express aggression. The tensions of the erotic drives follow specific time curves, while the discharge of aggression is less clearly structured. There is a question whether the satisfaction of purely destructive impulses can be felt as pleasure. However, certain outbursts of rage follow patterns of discharge similar to those of the libido in the oral and the anal phases of psychosexual development, and so may contain a pleasurable element. If there is pleasure in the satisfaction of purely destructive impulses, this pleasure may be due to narcissistic components.

The erotic drives are plastic, while aggression is rigid. The aims of an erotic impulse may be temporarily inhibited because of the restrictions imposed by the ego and superego or the erotic drives may be dammed up permanently with the result that substitute formations or sublimations occur. The aim of aggression is the total destruction of objects, animate and inanimate. If the individual restricts this aim by attempting to be satisfied with less, the aim of aggression is changed to a desire to battle with or dominate the object or to produce its disappearance. The modification of the aims of the aggressive drives is imposed because otherwise they would threaten the existence of an object which is loved, i.e., invested with libido. The aim may be modified in two ways. There may be a mere coexistence of two investments in which the erotic drives prevail over the aggressive, or there may be a fusion of the two drives.

There are several types of conflicts in which the aggressive aims are modified by the erotic drives. The two drives may be in conflict because both are directed to the same object. This is an instinctual conflict. The reaction of the object to the aggressive drives may endanger the subject's existence. This is a conflict with reality. Danger may be anticipated by the ego if the latter in part is identified with the object, and therefore the ego will be opposed to the completion of the act. This is a structural conflict involving the superego.

Some defense mechanisms seem to be more efficient in dealing with erotic drives; others deal more efficiently with aggressive impulses. Besides the modification of the impact of aggression by the influence of the libido, three other processes are used to achieve a similar result. The aggression may be displaced to other objects. The aims of the aggressive impulses may be restricted. Or the aggression may be sublimated.

The means and ends of aggression are as follows: An objective danger invites the discharge of aggression in flight or fight. It is *only* through the latter that a real discharge takes place. The aggressive energy not used in fight may be internalized in the superego and result in a feeling of guilt. It may be neutralized in the ego without interfering with the integrity of the individual; or it may become internalized in the ego without neutralization, in which case it may result in self-destruction. The strength of the ego is seen in the capacity to neutralize large quantities of aggression. A weak ego means the internalization of large amounts of nonneutralized aggressive energy. Neutralized deaggressivized psychic energy does not lead to self-destruction but supplies the ego and the superego with motor power and equips the ego for its function in action. The displacement, restriction, or sublimation of aggression is a most important prerequisite of mental integration and of the mastery of the environment. Aggression is linked to the muscular apparatus of the ego because the ego organization controls motility. The musculature and the motility apparatus for the discharge of aggression contribute to the differentiation between the self and the environment and, through action, to change of the environment.

Aggression is related to deprivation. "A hungry man is an angry man." Therefore modifications of the aggressive impulses are more necessary than similar modifications of the erotic impulses because the full discharge of the former would endanger the desired object. A permanent object relation depends on the capacity to bear frustration and this means the ability to sublimate the aggression.

It is common knowledge that any interruption of a child's activity evokes an aggressive response. The child without outlets tends to become naughty because of regression. This is greatest during the period when activity is being learned. At the stage of development when aggressive behavior is addressed to the object, the child expects the object to yield. If he does not get it, he becomes dissatisfied with the usefulness of his aggressive outbursts as a method of controlling the object and gives them up. Aggressive outbursts usually are silenced by the parents. If the parent *does not impose* such restraint carefully and reasonably, the child's only method of dealing with his aggression is to internalize it. This will give him increased guilt feelings and will cause the development of a rigorous superego or a masochistic ego.

The two basic instinct groups seldom, if ever, appear in pure form. They are usually seen in varying degrees of mixture of one with the other, and they are mixed also with the striving for pleasure and the avoidance of pain and with the compulsion to repeat former experiences whether pleasurable or not. These combinations produce the secondary pairing of opposing forms of instinct expression in relation to objects and to the external world. The more striking of these are activity and passive receptivity in relation to objects and to the world, sadistic and masochistic behavior toward objects and toward the world, and bisexuality—the presence of both heterosexual and homosexual desires in every individual. All of these, because they all contain elements of both the erotic and the aggressive instincts, i.e., of loving and hating, produce the well-known phenomenon of ambivalence—the capacity to love and hate the same object at the same time.

The death instincts, compounded with the erotic instincts, show themselves through destructive and aggressive impulses toward objects and toward the world, directly as feelings of hatred, anger, jealousy, resentment, and antagonism and as the destructive actions which may accompany such feelings; and indirectly as competition, rivalry, ambition, and the drives to success, to cultural advances in the social organization, and to the conquest, exploration, and subjugation of the physical world, particularly of such elements as disease, climate, storms and floods, which interfere with the life and comfort of the human being—in short, to the achievement of security.

Against the demands of the instincts are opposed the demands of the external world, whether these demands are made by the real physical world, by the needs of other human beings for instinctual discharge, or by the mores, customs, and manners of the social organization in which the individual lives and under which he grew up. It is as much the function of the ego to take cognizance of the mores, customs, and manners of the social organization in which it finds itself as it is to take cognizance of the real physical world. It is the function of the ego to arrange for adequate instinctual discharge in the light of its knowledge of the demands of society, which basically are opposed to the discharge and gratification of the instincts. The ego can do this in several ways. It can remove the individual from this social organization into another where there is less hindrance to instinctual gratification. It can attempt to change the customs and mores either through a sudden rebellion—which usually is not feasible—or through the slow process of education, so that they will offer less hindrance to instinctual gratification. It can find fully adequate opportunities for instinctual gratification within the limits imposed by the mores. This is usually possible in any culture even though in every culture there will always be certain rebellious members who deny the possibility. Such persons are not real revolutionists or even real rebels but are quite badly integrated individuals who are attempting to find a reasonable alibi for an unconscious intrapsychic conflict of their own. Extensive clinical experience has shown that the symptoms of the illnesses from which the neurotic, the psychotic, and the person with a character neurosis suffer are the result of an attempt to solve an intrapsychic conflict between the need for instinctual gratification and an unconscious intrapsychic sense of morality, and not between the desire for instinctual gratification and the mores, customs, and manners of the culture in which the individual lives. This unconscious intrapsychic morality is known as the superego.

THE SUPEREGO

The superego has both unconscious and conscious components. The conscious part is known familiarly as the conscience. Most people are aware of the conscience because its feelings are conscious and their presence and functions can be recognized introspectively. The conscience is a censor of morals. Everyone has conscious ideals for himself and is aware that he tends to compare his behavior and feelings with these ideals and to feel pleased or displeased with himself depending on how close he approximates them. However, much of the superego is unconscious. This unconscious part also is a censor of morals. It is the seat of morality and its function is the control of the discharge of the instincts. It warns the ego by feelings of guilt and of diminished self-esteem that an instinct is demanding discharge of which it disapproves because it condemns either the instinct itself or the channels through which the discharge is to take place. It can do this because it stands apart from the ego and, being in much closer touch with the instincts than is the ego, is more aware of the instinctual demands. This is because it is derived from the object cathexis of the id with which it is connected phylogenetically. If the ego allows an instinct of which the superego disapproves to be discharged, the superego punishes the ego with feelings of remorse or of shame. The oldest moral phenomenon is repentance and love after a hostile act. If the hostile act cannot be carried out because the person toward whom the hostility is directed is also loved, the aggressive impulse becomes inturned and is directed against the ego, producing the feeling of guilt.

The superego therefore contains social feelings. The fear of punishment by the superego is the cause of the ego mechanisms of repression and resistance. These mechanisms arise in the following way. The little child fears that the parent will punish him by castration or loss of love if he allows his instinctual impulses full rein. So he tries to curb them. Later he becomes afraid that society will punish him in the same way. He develops social anxiety. Later the moral prohibitions become completely internalized as the superego and he fears its punishment. The superego enjoys a certain independence and it pursues its own ends because it has energy independent of the ego which it draws directly from the instincts and which contains libidinal and aggressive components in varying degrees of fusion. The superego demands are largely prohibitive in character. It says to the ego, "You must *not* do so-and-so or wish to do so-and-so because I do not like this action or this wish. If you do, I will punish you severely or will never love you again. I will indicate to you how you will feel under the punishment by giving you a small dose, that is, a painful feeling of guilt, as an example and a warning." The real behavior of the superego can be observed best in melancholia, where it rages in a very hostile fashion against the ego and forces the latter to use many mechanisms, besides repression, to avoid punishment. Some of these are the withdrawal of cathexis from some object systems or an increase of cathexis in other ego systems, the diffusion of libidinal and aggressive impulses, regression, the turning of an impulse from an object onto the self, and the change of the aims of an instinct from activity to passivity and from passivity to reflexivity. Although its demands are largely prohibitive, the superego also indicates to the ego that the latter must wish and act in certain ways. It says to the ego, "You ought to wish and act in this way. If you do not, I will punish you, look down upon you, and as an example of the punishment, I will make you *feel* you are an inferior person even though you are not inferior. This feeling of inferiority is only a pale example of how you will feel if you disobey me."

I wish to digress for a moment at this point. The terms "feelings of inferiority," "inferiority complex," and the like are frequently bandied about without any real understanding of what they signify. Realistic feelings of inferiority are seen, for instance, in physically handicapped persons. The usual reaction to such unpleasant feelings is to attempt to remove the feelings through compensatory activities and through the development and use of skills and assets which do not depend on physical ability. The so-called feelings of inferiority which may occur in persons who are not physically handicapped have the same origin as feelings of guilt. They are a sign that the ego is not living up to the demands of the superego. Such feelings are likely to develop in a child who is never able to please his parents, no matter how hard he tries, because they do not like him. When the parental images are internalized as his superego, the superego makes the same excessive demands as the parents did and indicates that the individual is not worthy. The feeling of inferiority has the same mechanisms as the feelings of lack of self-esteem, which I will discuss shortly. The ego therefore not only has to mediate between the instincts and reality—the instincts and the external world—and between the instincts themselves, but it must do all this in a manner that will meet the approval of the superego.

THE SOURCES OF THE SUPEREGO

The prohibitory demands of the superego arise from three sources. The most important arises from the solution of the edipus conflict.

The little boy hates his father as a rival because of his size and competency and because of his possession of the mother. He fears his father unnecessarily as the result of the projection onto his father of his own hatreds and jealousies. He loves his father passionately and solves the pain of this conflict of strong opposing feelings by introjecting—taking in and making part of his own psychic apparatus—the psychic image of his hated, feared, and loved father. This is not the real father but the projection onto the real father of the little boy's own feelings toward him. This introjected image stands as a guardian to the boy against his instinctual impulses, specifically his hatred of his father, his jealousy of him, his desire to be the father's sexual partner, and his desire to possess the mother sexually. In short, it stands as a taboo against acting out his wishes to murder his father and to fulfill his incestuous sexual desires toward his mother and sisters. Functioning in this way, it is a recapitulation of the course of development of the human being from his subhuman ancestors during the period that Freud has referred to as the time of the Primal Horde, the dim remembrance of which furnishes the motive for a great many folk legends and fairy tales. It reflects the phylogenetic conflicts of primitive man, as its chief prohibitions in the male are against incest and hostility to the father. It is a substitute for longing for the father and therefore it is the germ of all religions. Its severity depends on the character of the father, the intensity of the edipus situation, and the rapidity with which the edipus situation succumbs to repression.

A second source of the superego results from the incorporation of the parents', and later the teachers', real conscious and unconscious attitudes toward instinctual drives and toward reality. For the boy, the father's attitudes are the most important, for the girl, the mother's. At the risk of oversimplification I will use two examples as illustrations of what I mean. There are two brothers, an older and a younger, who pummel each other unmercifully. In this illustration, the instinctual drive actuating the behavior is aggression. Both boys may be taught forcibly that it is wrong to fight. Even though this instruction may be forgotten, i.e., repressed into the unconscious (as a matter of fact, particularly if this is so), it will continue to operate as a barrier to any expression of aggression and both boys will go through life unable to take any part in athletics, or to do acceptable work in school, and in adult life they will either be ambitionless or, if ambitious, unable to take part successfully in competition, whether vocational, recreational, or sexual. In this case, a superego too severely restrictive against the aggressive instinctual drives has been inculcated. The end result will be a lack of success in practical living and a constant feeling of inner discomfort. On the other hand, if both boys are *encouraged* to fight, they may grow up with the belief that the desirable way to get what they want is by the use of force. Here, a superego too permissive to aggressive instinctual drives, for practical living in a social organization, has been developed. The end result will be an individual who is disliked by other people and who offends against the codes and mores of society. He will not suffer inner discomfort but he will suffer at society's hands in retaliation for his behavior.

A girl is continually trying to see her older brother and her father nude. The drive actuating the girl's behavior is basically sexual, i.e., sexual curiosity. If the girl is taught forcibly that her sexual curiosity is wicked, when this teaching is repressed into the unconscious, it will make her attempts to obtain adequate and necessary sexual pleasure in her adult life futile. If she is overencouraged she may become a sexually uninhibited, somewhat perverted person.

The function of the superego is to serve as an automatic regulator of the expression of instinctual drives. If as a result of education it becomes too strict toward either the erotic or the aggressive drives, or both, the child will become neurotic, both in childhood and in adult life. If as a result of education it becomes too permissive toward either the erotic or the aggressive drives, the child will develop a character neurosis and will be unable to tolerate frustration and the discomfort and anxiety resulting from frustration. This functioning of the superego is intimately connected with education and the aims of education, particularly so-called character education.

A third source of the superego arises from the culture in which the child is reared. In the superego there operates the personal qualities of the parents and the traits of everything that has had a determining effect on parents, including the tastes and standards of their social class and the characteristics and traditions of the race from which they spring. The parents' attitudes toward the child, toward his behavior, and toward reality are themselves partly the product of their cultural milieu. Erikson [3] points out that the different methods of training a child in different cultures are directed to obtaining the ideal that the culture recognizes as desirable for all the adults. He illustrates this by contrasting the cultural ideals of the Sioux and of the Yurok and the training of the Sioux children and the Yurok children. At each stage of psychosexual development the training is conducted in a way which contributes to the formation of the desired type of character in the adult. While the superego itself is an internalization of the training of the child in a particular culture, the mores, customs, and manners of any particular culture are the projection into the external world of the codes of conduct of the superegos of the members of the group. Toynbee [4] says that mimesis is a generic feature of social life both in primitive societies and in civilization but it operates in different ways in these two species of societies. In static primitive societies, mimesis is directed toward the older generation of the living members, and toward the dead, in whom the "cake of custom" is incarnated; whereas in societies in the process of civilization the same faculty is directed toward the creative personalities who have broken ground. The historical development of the mores follows the same course as the development of the moral sense of the child. Breasted [5] described the historical course of the development of the moral sense. The earliest known evidence of human ability to draw a distinction between good and bad conduct appeared at the time of the founding of the First Dynasty by Menes in 3400 B.C. This early code said that if you are loved, you are good, if you are hated, you are bad. "Life is given to the peaceful"; i.e., he who is loved. "Death is given to the guilty"; i.e., he who is hated. Later the code changed to "He who is rich is good; he who is poor is bad." About 3000 B.C. the family was the primary unit in the rise and development of moral ideas, and filial piety was the best claim to virtue. In the moral code

[3] Erik H. Erikson, *Childhood and Society,* New York, W. W. Norton & Company, 1950.

[4] Arnold Toynbee, *A Study of History,* New York and London, Oxford University Press, 1947.

[5] James Henry Breasted, *The Dawn of Conscience,* New York, Charles Scribner's Sons, 1933.

of Ptah-hotep—about 2500 B.C.—the penalty for conjugal infidelity was death and there was much advice about not corrupting boys. By the time of the Middle Kingdom, a man's behavior was considered satisfactory if it received the approval of father, mother, brothers, and sisters. A social conscience had arisen.

When the unconscious superego has matured it can be changed in only four ways. A woman can change her political views, or, less easily, her religion, because she loves a man. She is able to do this because her love relationship is passive-receptive. A member of a group may project his superego onto a leader of the group whom he loves and then, because he has given over his superego to the leader, can follow the leader's dictates, often without regard to the characteristics of his own superego before he entered the group. There is some question as to the duration of the influence of the leader on the individual. Hypnosis imposes a parasitic superego, but its action is limited by the subject's real superego for if the demands of the hypnotist are too extreme, the patient wakes. In psychoanalysis the unconscious superego can be made conscious. Then the patient is able to subject it to the influence of reality.

THE PRECURSORS OF THE SUPEREGO

The superego is the heir of the edipus conflict. Its crystallization as a part of the personality occurs as the edipus conflict is solved. It is only after this crystallization that the child begins to govern his behavior through moral principles and begins to feel guilty if he violates his codes, and inferior if he does not live up to them. However, even before the edipus conflict is solved the child shows evidences of morality. If he behaves, or wishes to behave, in a way which he knows will not meet with approval from his environment, he suffers from unpleasant feelings—fear of the parent and of society, which are known respectively as objective anxiety and social anxiety. Unlike the superego, these moral controls have not solidified into a part of the personality. The child is quite capable of behaving in a moral way in front of the parents, and in an exactly opposite fashion if he is sure that the parents will not find out. In the latter instance he will not suffer any feelings of remorse, guilt, fear or shame *about his behavior,* although he may be afraid that the parents will find out about it. This objective anxiety is one of the precursors of the superego morality which will be imposed later.

Another precursor—one whose manifestations are closer to those of the superego—is illustrated by the morality learned by the child through toilet training. For a period the child acts as if he is under the influence of objective anxiety. He is clean as long as his mother is around, but if she goes away, he becomes untrained. Later, but long before the superego is crystallized, the child feels shame, embarrassment, and humiliation if he has bowel or bladder accidents even though his parents may be quite sympathetic with him. The toilet training he has learned from his parents has become incorporated, and his shame is the sign that he has offended, not his parents, but the incorporated toilet training. The incorporated toilet training has become part of his personality and stands in relation to his ego as the later superego does. Thus it is a true precursor of the superego.

Anna Freud [6] in discussing the children described by Sophie Dann and herself [7] points out that these children, placed in a concentration camp because they were foundlings and brought up there through the ages of one to four, showed a form of morality that is usually considered very unusual in such small children. They demanded that everyone share and share alike. Any benefits that were given to one of the group were shared by all. They wanted to be sure that all members of the group were present at and included in everything the group did, and they showed a high degree of empathy for the feelings and particularly for the sufferings of any single member. Anna Freud believes that this was a natural development and *did not result* from any training or example given by adults. She believes this is the same phenomenon as was observed by Dorothy Burlingame [8] in her study of twins. The latter concluded that the wish of the twins always to have the same thing, to share what they possessed, and to copy from one another originated from the wish of

[6] Anna Freud, Discussion with the Eastern Subcommittee on the Psychoanalysis of Children and Adolescents, Boston, Massachusetts, October 8, 1952.

[7] Anna Freud and Sophie Dann, "An Experiment in Group Upbringing," *The Psychoanalytic Study of the Child,* Vol. VI, New York, International Universities Press, 1951.

[8] Dorothy Burlingame, *Twins: A Study of Three Pairs of Identical Twins,* New York, International Universities Press, 1952.

each to have more than the other, to do better than the other, in other words to supersede the other. By sharing, the twins overcame this competition and reached the first stage of an altruistic development. At the same time sharing was the continuation of their former competition. The struggle was now centered around the desire to have not more, not less, but the same amount of anything. To have the same amount prevented the other from having more, and in this way a balance could be struck. The two mechanisms employed to overcome the jealousy of each other were identification, which produced a form of altruism, and fairness, as a reaction formation against competition. Together they produced harmony in the twin relationship.

Anna Freud and Sophie Dann believe that this type of morality would occur as part of the development of the ordinary child if it were not hindered by our cultural pattern of child training.

According to the results of child analysis and reconstructions from the analyses of adults, the child's relationship to his brothers and sisters is subordinated to his relationship to the parents, is, in fact, a function of it. Siblings are normally accessories to the parents, the relations to them being governed by attitudes of rivalry, envy, jealousy, and competition for the love of the parents. Aggression, which is inhibited toward the parents, is expressed freely toward brothers and sisters; sexual wishes, which cannot become manifest in the oedipal relationship, are lived out, passively or actively, with elder or younger brothers and sisters. The underlying relationship with siblings is thus a negative one (dating from infancy when all siblings were merely rivals for the mother's love), with an overlay of positive feelings when siblings are used for the discharge of libidinal trends deflected from the parents. Where the relations between the children of one family become finally manifestly positive, they do so according to the principles of group formation, on the basis of their common identification with the parents. The rival brother is tolerated as belonging to the mother; in special cases which lead to later homosexual attitudes the rival brother even becomes an object of identification as the mother's favorite. The child's first approach to the idea of justice is made during these developments of the brother-sister relationship, when the claim to be favored oneself is changed to the demand that no one should be favored, i.e., that there should be equal rights for everybody. Since contemporaries outside the family are treated like the siblings, these first relationships to the brothers and sisters become important factors in determining the individual's social attitudes.

It is well in line with these views when our material shows that the relations of the Bulldogs Bank children to each other were totally different from ordinary sibling attitudes. The children were without parents in the fullest sense of the word, i.e., not merely orphaned at the time of observation, but most of them without an early mother or father image in their unconscious minds to which their earliest libidinal strivings might have been attached. Consequently, their companions of the same age were their real love objects and their libidinal relations with them were of a direct nature, not merely the products of laborious reaction formation and defenses against hostility. This explains why the feelings of the six children toward each other show a warmth and spontaneity which is unheard of in ordinary relations between young contemporaries.

When working with the children of the Hampstead Nurseries one of the authors has described certain attitudes of helpfulness, cooperation, identification and friendship which appeared in a group of toddlers (between fifteen months and two and one half years of age) who had been temporarily deprived of their mother's care. The six Bulldogs Bank children, as the observations prove, show these attitudes in excess, the quantitative difference between them and the Hampstead Nursery group corresponding to the difference between total and partial absence of a parent relationship.

The high degree of identification with each other's need is known from one other relationship in early years, that of identical twins to each other. In a recent study of the subject Dorothy Burlingame demonstrates the emotional importance of twins to each other, the way in which the twin is treated as an extension of the self, cathected with narcissistic as well as object love. Identification with the twin prospers on the basis of common needs, common anxieties, common wishes, in short, on the similar reactions of two beings of the same age living in close proximity under the same external conditions. While in the case of twins the twin relationship conflicts with and has to adapt itself to the parent relationship, the attitude to the companion within our age group of orphans reigned supreme.

That the children were able to attach their libido to their companions and the group as such, bypassing as it were the parent relationship which is the normal way to social attitudes, deserves interest in relation to certain analytic assumptions. In recent analytic work the experiences of the first year of life, the importance of the relationship to the mother during the oral phase and the linking of these experiences with the beginnings of ego development have assumed great significance. Explorations in these directions have led to the belief, held by many authors, that every disturbance of the mother relationship during this vital phase is invariably a pathogenic factor of specific value. Grave defects in ego development, lack or loss of speech in the first years, withdrawnness, apathy, self destructive attitudes, psychotic manifestations, have all been ascribed to the so-called "rejection" by the mother, a comprehensive term which includes every disturbance within the mother relationship from loss of the mother through death, permanent or temporary separation, cruel or neglectful treatment, down to lack of understanding, ambivalence, preoccupation or lack of warmth on the mother's part.

The six Bulldogs Bank children are, without doubt, "rejected" infants in this sense of the term. They were deprived of mother love, oral satisfactions, stability in their relationships and their surroundings. They were passed from one hand to another during their first year, lived in an age group instead of a family during their second and third year, and were uprooted again three times during their fourth year. A description of the anomalies which this fate produced in their emotional life and of the retardations in certain ego attitudes (though much of these have to be ascribed to the additional material deprivations) is contained in the material. The children were hypersensitive, restless, aggressive, difficult to handle. They showed a heightened autoerotism and some of them the beginning of neurotic symptoms. But they were neither deficient, delinquent nor psychotic. They had found an alternative placement for their libido and, on the strength of this, had mastered some of their anxieties, and developed social attitudes. That they were able to acquire a new language in the midst of their upheavals, bears witness to a basically unharmed contact with their environment.

A further discussion [9] of this subject developed the following conclusions: The concentration camp presented a very unusual situation. The children were confined to a few rooms. The adults in charge changed frequently as, one by one, they were sent to the gas chamber. As these adults had nothing else to live for, it can be speculated that they went out of their way, even though half starved and

[9] Discussion held by the Eastern Subcommittee for the Psychoanalysis of Children and Adolescents, New York, November 15, 1952. (The full reports of these discussions are available in *Childhood Psychoses,* Transactions of the Eastern Subcommittee on the Psychoanalysis of Children and Adolescents 1952–1953, in the library of the Philadelphia Association for Psychoanalysis.)

hopeless about themselves, to see that the children remained alive and were not too conspicuous. These children would lead a life dominated by fear of extinction if they misbehaved themselves. They might not know the nature of the fear, but it would be present as a terrible nameless dread. They would tend to live in a community with a real community spirit, understanding how the others were feeling, sharing with one another, and needing the reassurance of the constant presence and comfort of one another, so that the nameless dread would not come upon them. This could be one explanation; but it does not suffice to explain their behavior at the times when there was no really frightening and dangerous environment. Miss Freud postulates that because the children in the concentration camp had no close attachment to a mother or a mother figure, such as occurs in the average home in Western culture, they were able to love one another and thereby to develop defenses, mostly reaction formations, against their antagonisms and jealousies. It is possible that a similar relationship develops among children in large families. Thus it may be possible, through the love felt for his peers, for the child to develop a social conscience quite independent of the superego and long before the superego has been crystallized.

This reopens the whole question of the value of nursery schools. It is still true that perhaps most mothers place their small children in nursery school either because they do not wish to look after them or because they wish, or need, to have a career as well as a family. Some mothers want their children to be in nursery school because the living conditions at home—in apartment houses, in urban business sections, or on isolated estates—prevent the child's having other children of his age to play with. Other mothers, wishing to bring their children up in an intelligent manner, have accepted the theory of educators that the nursery-school experience helps small children to develop better social relationships. It has been my opinion that the child has so much difficulty making an adjustment to his edipus conflict that he has no interest or energy at his disposal for the formation of adequate social relationships until the age of five or six, when he has come close to the solution of the edipus conflict, just as he has difficulty in learning academic subjects until the same time. I have believed that some recognition of this was responsible for the traditional choice of some time between the fifth and sixth years as the age for beginning school. So I have believed that nursery schools were a necessary evil which furnished the best solution known at present for children who would otherwise lack play space or playmates. I have believed also, and still believe, that nursery-school teachers should be selected as carefully as psychoanalytic students and consequently that their rate of pay should be as high if not higher than that of the best paid positions in the school system.

If, however, as Miss Freud speculates, a social conscience develops early in young children, if permitted, then nursery schools under very capable and well-trained teachers will have to be an essential part of American education. However, as yet this is only speculation. A great deal more study of this question is necessary. Particularly, psychoanalysts need to pool their observations on the childhood memories of patients who attended nursery school as little children. In the psychoanalysis of several such adult patients, and also of older neurotic children, I found that the patients tended to regard their being sent to nursery school as a rejection by the mother. They felt weak and helpless with other children who were slightly older. They had reaction formations of oversympathy, an overaccentuated need to share, and a tendency to put themselves out in order to do more for other people than was either necessary or wise. These reaction formations were not helpful in their lives, but caused them to be imposed on by others and to be rather timorous socially. At the same time, they did not show a very good social adjustment. Their jealousies were quite marked, but at the same time they seemed less afraid than most of other people's jealousy. Of course in each of these patients the nursery-school experience was only one of many influencing factors.

The type of morality shown by the children from the concentration camp may have occurred because these children were banded together by the fear of real dangers in the external world, because they were trained in this way by a succession of adults who looked after them, or because, as Miss Freud believed, this type of morality actually formed a stage in their development. If it really is a stage in development, this type of morality is not a superego type or even a precursor of the superego, but resembles much more the type of morality due to extensions of the ego boundary.

Although we are well acquainted with the relation of the superego to morality and with the facts of the development of the superego, the more recent studies on the development of the precursors of the superego are not as well known.

Glover [10] points out that the primary functional level, the central path between sensory and motor boundaries along which unbound instinctual charges advance or regress according to the pleasure principle, is a series of dynamic sequences representing and recording the flow and ebb of psychic excitation to reduce traumatic stress due to the damming up of excitation. At this stage the repetition compulsion is the first attempt at active autoplastic psychotherapy. The final form of the mental apparatus, i.e., the ego, the superego, and the id, is reached at the end of the edipus conflict. The stages between are not well known but could be studied by several methods. There could be an analysis of psychic stresses, i.e., of what happens when there is a damming up of instinct quantities, of what occurs as the result of the stimulus of reactive anxiety or the pressure of unconscious guilt. These influences would have to be considered during three stages—the time when the ego is not organized, the stage when the ego is more organized and employs specific defense mechanisms but is subject more to anxiety than to guilt, and the period when the superego stresses give rise to the purest forms of endopsychic conflict. They could be studied also through the isolation of defense mechanisms predominant at a particular phase, such as the primitive phase when regression and reflection of instincts predominate, and the phase during which a system of autocathexis is organized. Autocathexes in prolonged periods of early ego development are important because they are used in the control of frustration and the consequent damming up of excitations and in the development of the preconscious. Autocathexis occurs in response to traumatic stress rather than to conflict. Again, they could be studied through an examination of the development of the barriers between

[10] Edward Glover, "Functional Aspects of the Mental Apparatus," *International Journal of Psychoanalysis,* 31, 1950.

the unconscious and the conscious systems. These have several phases, from a primitive imaginal phase, where thinking is mainly symbolic in nature, to the time when conceptual thinking becomes predominant as the ego develops rapidly under the expansion of the preconscious system. At the earlier part of this stage, stress rather than conflict is important. At the end of this phase the influence of the superego begins to dominate organization of the mental apparatus. Finally, these early stages of development could be considered through a study of object relations and boundaries or through a clinical approach, i.e., the analysis of a developmental series of mental disorders. It is in this middle period referred to by Glover that the forces of morality dependent on ego boundaries and not dependent on the superego arise.

The ability to delineate an ego boundary depends on the development of a sense of self-esteem. Erikson [11] says that in modern civilization the image of man is expanding with the acquisition of inclusive information about new entities and identities and ideologies. This development is accompanied by reactionary spasms, where fear of loss of privilege arouses archaic fears of extinction and of loss of cultural identity. The social organization, i.e., public opinion, grants certain things to the infant in keeping him alive and ministering to his needs and so seduces him to want to live that way. It also denies instinctual gratification to the child and disapproves of his instinctual desires. In this way the child's self-love is injured. The child looks for models and tries to resemble them; if he succeeds, he achieves a self-esteem which is a not-too-convincing facsimile of his original narcissism and sense of omnipotence. A child just able to walk is driven to repeat and perfect the act of walking because of the libidinal pleasure of locomotor erotism, the need for mastery in the sense of Hendrick's work principle, and an awareness of his new status and station as "He who can walk," with the cultural connotations of "He who will go far," "He who will be upright," or "He who might go too far."

Through these trial-and-error methods the child grows to develop a conviction that his ego is learning effective steps toward a tangible

[11] Erik H. Erikson, "Ego Development and Historical Change," *The Psychoanalytic Study of the Child,* Vol. II, New York, International Universities Press, 1946.

collective future. They therefore contribute to the development of a realistic self-esteem which is different from the more narcissistic corroboration of infantile omnipotence. This realistic self-esteem develops into a defined ego within a social reality and gives the sense of ego identity. In its subjective aspect the sense of ego identity is the awareness, achieved by the ego's synthesizing methods, of the fact of self-sameness and continuity, and the knowledge that these methods are effective in safeguarding the sameness and continuity of one's meaning for others. Real education, while protecting the rights of others, must seize upon mobilized forces for playful learning. If a child feels that the environment tries to deprive him too radically of all forms of expression which permit him to exercise his new ego identity, he will resist with astounding strength, as if his life were imperiled, as his ego identity is. Education for an ego identity which receives strength from changing historical conditions, demands conscious acceptance on the part of adults of historical heterogeneity and enlightened efforts to provide childhood with a new fund of meaningful continuity.

The sense of ego identity has to work through the conflicts that are inherent at each stage of the psychosexual development. In the oral stage there is a conflict between basic trust and basic mistrust. Social trust is first demonstrated by the baby in ease of feeding, depth of sleep, and relaxation of his bowels. His first social achievement is the willingness to let his mother out of his sight without undue anxiety or rage. Mother has now acquired inner certainty for him as well as outer predictability. This depends on recognition that there is an inner population of remembered and anticipated sensations and images which are fairly correlated with an outer population of familiar and predictable things and people. Smiling shows this stage of development. Constant tasting and testing of the relationship between the inside and the outside meets a crucial test during the rages of the biting stage. Erupting teeth cause pain from within which is relieved by biting, but the outer funds withdraw from biting, which is the only action which promises relief. This experience of rage turning upon itself has to do with the masochistic tendency to get cold and cruel comfort in hurting oneself when the object has eluded the grasp. Out of this comes a primary sense of badness, the potential loss of all that is good, because we could not help destroying it inside and drove it away outside.

Clinically we find an absence of basic trust in infantile schizophrenia and a weakness of basic trust in adult schizoid persons and adult depressive persons. Projection with introjection originates from an early process of differentiation between inside and outside. In introjection we feel and act as if outer goodness had become inner certainty. In projection we endow significant people with the evil which is actually in us. The first task of the ego is the solution of the conflict between basic trust and basic mistrust.

The conflict in the anal stage is between autonymy and shame and doubt. Shame is inturned aggression. There is a desire to destroy the egos of the world. This is inturned and becomes a desire to be invisible and to destroy the object self which is being looked at. Visual shame precedes auditory guilt and is dependent on the consciousness of being upright and exposed. Doubt is dependent on the consciousness of having a front and a back. The back is the individual's dark continent, which can be magically dominated and invaded by those who would attack one's power of autonymy. Behind cannot be seen by the child but is dominated by the will of others. This basic sense of doubt about whatever one has left behind forms a substratum for verbal forms of compulsive doubting and for paranoiac fears concerning hidden persecutors and secret persecutions threatening from behind and from within the behind. These fears were originally his fears that he could not control the excretions within himself, which he could not see either when they were inside him or as they came out. The sense of omnipotence is a retrospective illusion, for now the child, endowed with more powerful muscular equipment, despairs of autonymy and allows himself oral rages and hallucinations.

The conflict in the phallic stage is that of initiative versus guilt. The initiative is expressed in boys through pleasure in phallic intrusive modes of attack and conquest, and in girls through aggressive forms of snatching, and bitchy possessiveness or the milder form of making oneself attractive and endearing.

In the latency period the conflict is between industry and inferiority. The child's development is disrupted if his family life has not prepared him for school life or if the school life fails to sustain promises of earlier stages. During adolescence the conflict is between identity and role diffusion. In late adolescence, it is between intimacy and isolation. In the adult, it is between generativity and stagnation and between ego integrity and despair. The solution of these various conflicts produces the sense of self-esteem. Of course the degree of self-esteem depends on the type of solution found.

Recently Phyllis Greenacre [12] has suggested another factor in the development of the superego besides the well-known ones I have just discussed—habit training, the solution of the edipus situation, and the reinforcement of the attainments of the edipal struggle by social influences. She points out that there is a distinct difference between the superego of the man and of the woman. The man usually is afraid of punishment, actually of castration, for breaches of morality. The woman usually is afraid of the loss of love for similar offenses. She believes this difference is due partly to the variations in anatomical structure—in the genital organs themselves and in general peripheral muscular development—and the individual's reaction to them.

In the boy the dominance of peripheral muscular skill and the exposed position of his genital organs tends to cause an especially strong struggle with masturbation and a greatly increased fear that he may lose his valued visible penis. The girl accepts castration as an accomplished fact; this attitude seems generally to imply that she has already been castrated, and she frequently hypothecates that this has resulted as a punishment for masturbation. This accounts for the greater struggle against masturbation in girls and the enormous enhancement in them of later guilt feelings in a situation of conflict, as though they had a hidden constant fund of guilt. From this source may arise some of the marked and diffuse, often aimless, conscientiousness and worrying tendencies which girls often show. The girl's greater concern with social relationships and with responsibility is derived mainly from the nature of her edipal struggle.

She must remain dependent in a very intimate body-comfort fashion on the mother at the same time that the beginning rivalry with the mother

[12] Phyllis Greenacre, "Anatomical Structure and Superego Development," *American Journal of Orthopsychiatry*, 18, 1948.

and the attraction to the father is setting in. She needs indeed a fine sense of social value to maintain a balance between the two, and with a greater natural ambivalence to the mother with whom she must presently identify in order to achieve a growing femininity. This necessarily grossly incomplete separation from the mother in the pre-oedipal period repeated in another form in the oedipal attachment to the father, recurs again in the characteristically ragged and disturbing mother-daughter struggle of adolescence.

Her type of conscience may be derived also in a small measure from the lack of a ready-made toy (penis) to play with.

CHAPTER XIV

The Task of Education in the Development of the Superego

IDEALLY the task of education is to help the development of a superego which will permit the gratification of instinctual drives in ways and at times which are acceptable to the culture, i.e., the manners and mores of the social organization in which the individual lives. This does not mean that the individual should always be content with those manners and mores—for these change from time to time and he may help toward making change possible—but until the change takes place, he himself should be able to live comfortably in the existing situation. Accomplishment of this task seems to have been recognized as the aim of education. I quote from a statement issued by a progressive school:[1] "The aims of nursery school teachers for promoting mental health are, to help children to be emotionally free, i.e., to like themselves (have confidence in themselves and self-respect), to have interests and be able to pursue them, to feel worth while, to feel success in relation to the approval of others and in relation to their own standards; to help children to be free to use their positive aggressive impulses and to control and redirect destructive impulses; to help children like, grow to understand and get along with people and to find their place with others." In short, the aim is for the children to have self-esteem, good object relations, self-control of their impulses, and the ability to redirect their impulses so they will be socially acceptable.

[1] Oak Lane Country Day School, Philadelphia, Pennsylvania.

How is this end best brought about? In discussing this problem I will use as my basis the question, asked by all educators, of the relation between indulgence and discipline.[2] We have seen that education depends basically on the interplay between the *persons* in the environment and the child, which enables the latter first to understand his own feelings and the inner drives which they represent, and then to perceive how he can use them in his life. This process takes place through the mechanisms of imitation and, later, identification, which at first is based on love, and later, in the formation of the superego, is based on the ambivalence between hatred and love. It is the interplay of the relationship between the child and other human beings which eventually develops real object relationships and the necessary defenses against the desire of the id for immediate discharge, and which later produces the capacity to obtain indirect satisfaction and discharge for those drives which cannot or may not in reality be discharged directly.

THE EARLY YEARS

The education of the child during the first period of development —which begins at birth and lasts until about the age of eighteen months—lies strictly in the hands of the parents, particularly of the mother. The educational problem during this period is to help the child to know himself as a *separate* individual, possessing feelings which are worthy of expression and desires and needs which are

[2] I am indebted for the material in this discussion particularly to the following articles:

Edward Glover, "Unconscious Functions of Education," *International Journal of Psychoanalysis*, 18, 1937.

Michael Balint, "Ego Strength and the Education of the Ego," *Psychoanalytic Quarterly*, 11, 1942.

Otto Fenichel, "The Means of Education," *The Psychoanalytic Study of the Child*, Vol. I, New York, International Universities Press, 1945.

Ernst Kris, "On Psychoanalysis and Education," *American Journal of Orthopsychiatry*, 18, 1948.

David P. Ausubel, "Negativism as a Phase of Ego Development," *American Journal of Orthopsychiatry*, 20, 1950.

Ernst Kris, "Notes on the Development and on Some Current Problems of Psychoanalytic Child Psychology," *The Psychoanalytic Study of the Child*, Vol. V, New York, International Universities Press, 1950.

worthy of gratification, and to realize that he is worthy in his own right of having them satisfied by a beneficent environment so that, in spite of his real helplessness, he can feel secure—in the proper sense of the term—about the discomforts aroused by his temporarily unsatisfied inner needs and the discomforts he perceives in his environment. At the same time, in order to learn to know himself he has to begin to realize that the feelings within himself—such as hunger and anxiety—are not always sources of pleasure, which he would like to believe, but are sometimes painful, and that there are sources of pleasure, out in the world, which are not within himself. In this stage of his development it seems as though he would like to believe that all sources of pleasure were within himself, as the feelings of pleasure are, and that all sources of pain and displeasure and the feelings of pain themselves were without himself and would be removed by the removal of his environment or of himself from it. This is well illustrated by the angry crying and aimless kicking and hitting that occur when the active baby is deprived of some desired comfort or pleasure and by the tendency of the inactive baby to fall asleep under similar circumstances. In the first situation the painful environment is to be removed, in the second, he removes himself from the unpleasant environment.

On the one hand, he has to learn that he has pleasurable feelings which arise within himself. On the other, he has to learn that he has unpleasurable feelings which arise within himself but which can be removed at this time by the actions of someone in the environment, later by his own actions. As he learns these facts he becomes able to see himself as an individual separate from his environment, particularly from his mother.

The child needs through experience to gain knowledge of the pleasurable sensations that come from gratification of his physical needs and from stimulation of his sensory pathways. He needs to know that his body is a source of pleasure. I have mentioned a number of times the importance of this and the ways in which he can be helped. The recognition that his body is a source of pleasure gives him self-confidence. If he never had any other experience, however, he would become only slightly aware that he is an individual separate from others, he would realize only slightly the need for any relationships with other people, and he would never learn any necessity for self-control. Recognition of these three realities implies also the recognition that his body can be a source of pain and of painful feelings of unsatisfaction, of instinctual tensions, and of dissatisfaction and displeasure. This knowledge he would avoid, if he could, by attempting in some way to deny that such feelings were his and by attempting to attribute them to the environment. The learning of this knowledge is painful and therefore conflicts with his desire for pleasure. At this point, it is the problems that are connected with this learning which need to be understood rather than the question of whether indulgence or training should be used in the management of the child.

The instinctual metabolic needs for food and drink are represented consciously by the painful feelings of hunger and thirst, which cause the baby to cry. In the first few weeks of life the time between his recognition of pain and its assuagement by the mother should be as short as possible. It is in this period that the so-called self-demand feeding schedule should be strictly followed. Its purpose is to increase his knowledge that his body is a source of pleasure. This must come *first.* During the same period he also needs a certain amount of pleasurable stimulation of the sensory end organs. He needs to be rocked gently, picked up and carried gently, bathed gently, and sung to softly, and to see his mother frequently. These pleasurable sensations must be given him by his mother because he is not able to obtain them himself, nor is he aware of their existence until they are revealed to him. Of course no matter how devoted the mother is to the baby there will be times when she does not understand what is the cause of his pain or when, due to her other activities, the time between his recognition of pain and her assuagement of it is longer than usual. It is this slightly lengthened interval that initiates his recognition that his pain is his and that the source of pleasure—his mother's breast and her ministrations—are not his but are available to him when he needs them. The establishment of the sequence of instinctual demand or conscious recognition of the somewhat painful representations of the demand—in the case of metabolic need, feelings of hunger and thirst, in the case of the sexual and other instincts, longing or somewhat feared anxiety—and the secure knowledge that the means of satisfaction will be available after an interval of time—very short in early childhood and gradually increasing as adulthood approaches—is the important factor in the development of the recognition that the individual is separate from other individuals (in psychoanalytic terminology, the recognition of ego boundaries) and of the ability to achieve self-control. The most important condition necessary for the child to learn this sequence is that he have the sure knowledge that the means of satisfaction will be available to him at some future time, a time not so far distant that he cannot tolerate the delay. This knowledge, added to his knowledge that he can obtain pleasure through and with his body, is the basis for self-confidence, which permits him to tolerate a certain amount of discomfort and to begin the slow process of the subordination of the pleasure principle to the reality principle which has been discussed in an earlier chapter.

The child's knowledge of assured later gratification depends on the amount of love that the parents actually have for him. How the fact that the parent loves the child is communicated to the baby is not well understood, but there is no question that it is. I believe that this fact is conveyed to the child from the time of birth through the parents' hands, tone of voice, and the like, and later on through the actions of each minute of the day, and of course to a much slighter degree by the parents' statements of love.

There is some question as to how early the baby recognizes other persons, specifically his parents, but there is considerable evidence to indicate that this begins somewhere about the end of the first month and increases quickly until there are definite indications that at the end of the fourth month there is some recognition of himself as a separate individual.

It is the awareness of displeasurable sensations and of the fact that these sensations can be relieved by someone else that helps the child to recognize himself as an individual and to give up his tendency to project all displeasure from himself into the external world and to introject all the pleasant parts of the external world into himself. However, he must receive the displeasurable sensations only in very small doses. He is helpless to do anything to relieve himself of the discomfort except through crying—which is only a means of communication—and through inco-ordinate movements of his hands and feet, and therefore a relatively small amount of discomfort appears to him to be larger than it would to an older child or adult. Because the discomfort feels great, he is easily overwhelmed by it and, at that point, he ceases to concern himself with it but instead attempts to project it outside himself.

It can be seen that the loving mother who is willing to give a great deal of time and attention to the infant and who will not permit him to be uncomfortable, as well as the present self-demand feeding schedules, really help the child to recognize that he is a separate individual and to become self-confident, because they allow the child to experience uncomfortable feelings only in very small doses. The ordinary routine duties and interests of a wife and a mother and the realities of space interfere with the constant immediate removal of unpleasurable feelings. There are very frequent times when the child cannot be fed or fondled, or rocked or carried or turned, the moment he wants to be. As an educational measure, there is a need not to increase these intervals between his recognition of a need and its satisfaction during the greater part of the first year of life.

The development of the ego boundary is accompanied by the development of a sense of self-esteem. The first determinant of self-esteem is the satisfaction acquired through all processes connected with feeding. Early disappointments, anxiety, helplessness in connection with feeding and digestion, cause a later sense of unhappiness, of inferiority, of worthlessness, as if badness existed in the self. If the primary self-esteem is secure and stable the child develops an adaptable ego; if it is insecure, a rigid ego structure develops which later under strain may cause regression to the basic insecurity of early childhood. It is therefore clear that the child's relationship with the mother and the mother's attitude toward the child are all-important. A large proportion of babies, instead of becoming happier at about four weeks, show a new type of crying in the afternoon and evening, which disappears at ten to twelve weeks. This increased demand for the mother occurs because the mother is turning away from the baby to more activity in her own existence. This annoys the baby; at the same time, the mother's desire to turn away from the baby makes her more anxious.

In the situations where children show a lack of differentiation of ego boundaries, their experience has been exactly the opposite of the experience outlined above. Spitz and Wolf[3] have shown that when object relations are constantly contradictory, object formation is made impossible and "rocking" results. When object relations change in an intermittent manner, as in cyclothymia or depressions, fecal play results. When object relations are normal, genital play results. In the histories of children who showed lack of differentiation of ego boundaries, the mothers themselves were found to be suffering from a depression, varying in degree from a mild depression to a psychotic one, from schizophrenia, varying in degree from a mild but definite schizoid personality to a psychosis, from a serious inability to love this particular child, or from a severe obsessional character which forced them to obey too literally restrictive and routinized advice about the management of the child. In certain other cases the child unfortunately had suffered unpreventable and severe pain and distress, so that it was not the careful daily exposure of the child to very small doses of discomfort through the ordinary circumstances of living which resulted in a lack of differentiation of ego boundaries, but the fact that he was subjected to massive doses of pain, fear, and prolonged lack of gratification.

As the baby begins to recognize himself as a separate person and to delimit the boundaries of his own ego he comes to desire love, pleasure, and satisfaction from his mother. He is pleased with her when he receives it and because he is pleased he begins to love her and to want to please her. In this reaction, there is still evidence of a lack of differentiation between himself and her. If he pleases her, he pleases himself and vice versa, but in addition there is a love for her as a separate person. I believe that we often underestimate the power of this love, and I believe also that its real strength is apparent in the first instances of self-control that appear. A good illustration is the child's relinquishing his cannibalistic fantasies, which I have described in an earlier chapter. Toward the end of the first year, because the fantasies themselves are not successful in accomplishing their purpose of making him forever free from discomfort, because

[3] René A. Spitz and Katherine M. Wolf, "Autoerotism," *The Psychoanalytic Study of the Child,* Vols. III–IV, New York, International Universities Press, 1949.

they result in fear of losing his mother and of consequent danger to his comfort, and because he also loves her and wants her to remain present, he tries to avoid having them. After a struggle, he erects in his mind a barrier of energy against the conscious knowledge of these fantasies. This barrier is the beginning of the distinction between the conscious and unconscious parts of his mind. Its energy is directed to having him not think of the fantasies. It therefore delineates the beginning of the ego—I will not think of these fantasies—from the id, where the fantasies continue to exist. It is erected because he fears retaliation for the fantasy and because he loves his mother and wishes to protect her from himself. This barrier, therefore, has a component resembling morality, which is based on the still not completely differentiated ego boundary. If he wishes a catastrophe on his mother it may fall on himself, and if he tries to make himself and his mother one, he may lose her. So because he loves her he keeps her alive. This thin barrier therefore divides the conscious from the unconscious, the ego from the id, and sets up over the ego an authority as to what it is and is not to think of. In this last capacity it serves as the early nucleus of the superego. The child will not be able to erect this barrier, or it will not be formed adequately, if because he is not confident that his needs will be met by his mother before he suffers too much pain and displeasure, he is not able to conceive of his mother as a separate individual toward whom he has feelings and desires.

If he has been not loved enough or has been too deprived, i.e., exposed to too large doses of discomfort, his destructive cannibalistic fantasies become more powerful and an excessive amount of energy is needed to keep them repressed. There is a lessening of the amount of energy at the disposal of his ego for other purposes, which results in a weakness of ego development. At the same time, too much energy is given to the prototype of the superego, which, so to speak, causes his ego to be too submissive to it. He then becomes too moral, but in an inactive way which forces him again to too much dependence on his mother and establishes a pattern of too much self-control. This results in a different type of person from the one in whom the ego boundaries remain ill-defined or absent. The clinical picture is not of psychosis, but of inactivity and inability to develop adequately.

Often, as I pointed out in an earlier chapter, it may result in serious learning difficulties later.

Educational procedures therefore lie in the hands of the parents, particularly of the mother, during this stage. Suitable education at this period results from the gratification of the child's needs and from the effect of the small doses of displeasure which arise by force of circumstances in the living together of three people—father, mother, and child. It is to be hoped that the end result will be a child confident of himself and of his environment, able to repress his fantasies as much as really is necessary and to govern his thinking, not his actions, for the purpose of expressing love toward other people who are his love objects. Such a child will have a definite ego boundary but at the same time will be able to extend that ego boundary to include his love objects, so that eventually he can perceive their feelings and desire that they have pleasure as he would like to have it himself, without losing the recognition that he and they are different persons.

Confident in himself because he is confident that his needs will be gratified, even if he has to tolerate a short period of discomfort, he has now reached the point where he is able to begin to do things for himself with his hands and with his legs. He can walk, and if he wants something he picks it up with his hands. These two abilities bring him into contact with two forces with whose presence he has had little experience—the real physical three-dimensional world, which in our culture, particularly in urban culture, is filled with real danger to his safety and his life, and the demands of his parents and of other human beings, demands which to him are unnecessary but which comprise the basis for our cultural life.

In our culture we have harnessed to our service dangerous forces, which if uncontrolled can maim or kill. We have made height our servant and have learned how to use and not tempt the forces of gravity. Houses have stairs, beds are no longer on the floor. The child can fall out of his crib, or off a chair, or down a flight of steps, or over a banister. Such falls will be painful and some of them may maim or kill him. He may be burned by the fires we keep harnessed in our houses, he may be poisoned by eating substances we keep at hand. He may be injured by eating pins, or glass beads, or their fragments.

He may be cut by sharp knives. He may be electrocuted by putting his finger into an electric outlet. I could go on endlessly with the dangers to his life both in and out of doors in our highly mechanized culture. Parents, rather than architects and engineers, do all in their power to protect him from getting into situations which will be dangerous to him. They install gates for stairs and keep dangerous objects out of his reach but they cannot protect him all the time, and even when they can protect him, the child has to learn the dangers from which he is being protected.

The child has to be warned to avoid these dangers, and almost without exception, the harassed parent applies some physical punishment at one time or another to enforce the warning, on the principle that a small amount of real pain will form a conditioned reflex which will prevent the child from suffering greater pain, perhaps accompanied by mutilation or death. The child, not having experienced the real consequences of his desire to investigate, tends to regard the forbidden object as a source of pleasure and feels that the parent is responsible for thwarting him. He feels that it is the parental disapproval that is dangerous or painful, not the forbidden object. Fortunately, he desires to please the parent and so learns to avoid the real danger in order not to lose the parent's love. Later on he will come to realize that certain actions are dangerous simply because he has been told so and will never investigate to see whether the warning is true or not. He first abstains to avoid the parents' disapproval, then takes what his parents tell him on faith, and this faith, amplified by the statements of other people, what he reads, and so on, governs his behavior almost automatically for the rest of his life. He has learned not by experience but simply by precept, and these precepts after a struggle have become part of his personality, even if the original precepts have been repressed into the unconscious. This is accomplished not only through his desire to love the parents and be loved by them, but also through his desire to imitate them, to be like them, and through this unconscious tendency, to identify with them.

It is interesting to observe how a precept becomes incorporated. The child puts out his hand toward a hot radiator. The mother says, "It will burn your hand," and often illustrates by gesture, putting her hand toward the radiator and drawing it back as she speaks. After this has been repeated several times the child starts playing a game. He reaches out to the radiator, says, "Burn," and draws his hand back. This is done for parental approval, which he usually gets, either directly or through the mother's repeating the same game with a pleased look on her face. As his hand has been close to the radiator he has felt a slight degree of heat, not unpleasant, in fact, pleasurable and so not a warning, i.e., a small amount of pain inflicted to avoid a great amount. The game is continued a number of times and then ceases. Sometime later, if he puts his hand out and feels a warm sensation, he will draw it back quickly, and if asked why he does so he will say, "It will burn me"—whether it would or not. Most of us, in the dark or encountering an unfamiliar object, will draw back our hands quickly if we feel a mild sensation of heat and will not proceed until we are sure we cannot get burned. The original precept has become incorporated, not through trial and error, but through parental admonition.

In our culture, the parents' precepts are often presented in moral terms. The parent tells the child that his desire to touch a dangerous object or to enter a dangerous situation is "bad." At first, the parent usually means by "bad" dangerous for the child. Later, to reinforce this precept, he may call the action "bad" because it frightens him by making him feel the child is defying him. "Bad" is also used in other situations, not dangerous to the child, in which he is rebelling against the parents' dictates, reasonable or unreasonable. The child is not able to distinguish between the two concepts—"bad" meaning dangerous and "bad" meaning immoral. So a moral value is connected with the instinctual drive for self-preservation. In short, in the child's mind the instinctual drive for self-preservation is equated with being moral, i.e., with being "good" and pleasing the parents. The energy from which the prototype of the superego draws, and from which later the superego will draw, is, therefore, the instinctual energy of self-preservation—preservation from the danger of not being loved, i.e., of being deserted, or from mutilation and death.

I do not think it is possible to avoid the moral implications of physical dangers, no matter how carefully the admonitions and precepts of the parents are worded. Somewhere in the depths of the egos of all of us, there is the feeling that if an external misfortune happens to us, it is because of some fault of ours. Freud says that the feeling of guilt, which stems from the superego, increases as a result of extreme misfortunes. It is not the external world or circumstances or other people that have misused us and against which we can fight: we are suffering because we are "bad." Such reactions are quite conscious in people with psychotic depressions. We may attempt to project the blame and to kick the chair on which we stub our toe in the dark or, like certain primitives, we may believe that all our illnesses and misfortunes are the result of malignant feelings toward us on the part of other people. This is simply the obverse of the concept that it is morally bad to be injured. The depressed patient accepts his responsibility, the primitive projects his own "badness" onto others. The latter reaction is possible because of the fact that the child at the age when he is learning to walk regards everything in his environment as animate. He cannot conceive of an inanimate object. Traces of this concept are seen in the fantasies of older children in which dolls, furniture, and the like come to life at night.

In his clumsiness, the child falls and hurts himself, or he hurts himself by knocking against a piece of furniture. This object is "bad" because it hurt him and if he is courageous he wants to fight back. If he is not courageous he may for some time refuse to walk again or to go near the piece of furniture. (I do not know whether these reactions really have to do with courage or not. It may be that the child who withdraws has concluded, because so many actions are forbidden, that a "bad" action of his has resulted in his punishment, and therefore repudiates the action. In this case the child would be lacking in self-confidence rather than courage, while the child who wants to retaliate would be more self-confident.) The object is "bad" not only because it hurt him but because he projects onto it his own hostile feelings and his desire to obtain pleasure from hurting others.

This whole process makes him lose the self-confidence which he had before. The world is not a pleasurable place, but is full of dangers and painful experiences with which he finds himself unable to cope. He finds also that his parents are not as completely capable of protecting him from pain as he thought they were. This whole discovery is made in consequence, usually, of his learning to stand, and his loss of confidence in himself and in his parents is felt consciously as shame, i.e., as lack of self-esteem. Conscious shame is useful for the human being, but its aim should be to insure a better relationship with other human beings. It is desirable that a set of values should be incorporated in the final organization of the superego such that when instinct representations arise which indicate that instinctual drives desire discharge that will violate adequate relationships with other human beings, the ego will suffer a feeling of shame, and the individual can then use his conscious judgment to avoid modes of expression of the instinct that would result in ridicule or dislike by other people. The original values that produce this sense of shame are those which I have discussed earlier; when they are incorporated, they form a thin layer of the prototype of the superego. Too much incorporation of this prototype and of the values on which it is based should be avoided. The child first attempts to re-establish his self-confidence by invoking his omnipotent wishes and hallucinating that he is all-powerful. This helps a little, but as it is based on an unrealistic wish, it leaves him still the prey of further misfortune. The real re-establishment of his self-confidence will come when he has acquired the skills necessary for dealing with the world, but these are learned slowly and only over many years. Educationally, therefore, the child needs some help at this point, and such help may be supplied in two ways which, fortunately, many parents use intuitively. The mother picks up the hurt child and kisses him, perhaps on the hurt spot. This kiss does not magically remove the pain, nor is this its purpose. The kiss is the sign that the mother loves him and the "bad" hurt spot, and therefore the "bad" is no longer "bad" but "good" and his self-esteem is re-established.

Often the mother hits the offending object—the floor, the chair—and comments on its "badness." At the same time she encourages the child to do likewise. The "badness," then, is not part of the child but part of the world, which the mother and he can punish. Again, this restores the child's confidence in himself and indicates to him that he can use his muscles to retaliate and remove a painful situation. This may seem to be pandering to the child's own omnipotent wishes, but actually it changes the procedure from a wish—which is a hallucination and does not deal with reality—to an action which, later, will be a learned way of approaching reality. Such methods may help to lead to the use of instinctual energy in the development of sublimations.

There are certain physicians who *are* physicians partly because as small children they were frightened and made uncomfortable through the pain of illness. If the child blames the doctor for the suffering, he will be furious at him and desire to make him suffer as he supposedly has made the child suffer. The child may become a doctor, through identification with the aggressor, so that he can control the amount of suffering meted out to others. If the child does not blame the doctor, he feels that there is a real but un-understood malignant fate in the world, which is causing him to suffer. Later he may become a doctor in order to destroy this ogre and relieve other people, and himself, from any future suffering.

With the child's increasing ability to walk and to use his hands, he is soon confronted definitely with the fact that other human beings have their own desires, which they consider their rights and privileges and which they will maintain even if in so doing they cause the child to suffer. He desires to touch and investigate everything in his environment but there are many objects which he is not permitted to touch and many more which he is not permitted to destroy, because they belong to other people. It is here that the knowledge of what is one's own and what belongs to others begins. Even in the upbringing of children under the Soviet government, where by precept and example the children from the earliest years are taught to share toys, though the toys may be "ours" certain other things are regarded by the child as "mine."

The task of education at this time is not to teach the child that he must not touch, that touching is forbidden. Rather, at first, the number of articles he may not touch should be reduced to a minimum to enable the parent to avoid using too many "don'ts." The child has difficulty in distinguishing between objects he may touch and those he may not, and if "don't" is used too often he may soon take the prohibition as applying to all touching, and in his mind (for intrapsyhic reasons, which have been intensively investigated by psychoanalysts and are well known) he may inhibit all investigative use of his hands or he may become frightened by pleasurable sensations in his genitals. The emphasis in the admonitions, therefore, should be on the distinctions between "mine" and "yours" rather than on touching.

From the time that the child can walk, up to and through the la-

fact that the progress from one stage to another must be made gradually. Also, he must understand the automatic educational effect of the process of living together with other people who respect the child's rights and privileges and, at the same time, respect their own rights and privileges. He must recognize that his duty as an educator is to help the child to acquire skills for dealing with the external world as quickly and completely as his physical development permits. If the educator is mindful of these three rules and also of the fact that the child, desiring to be like his parents, himself manfully struggles toward self-control, he will soon forget that there ever was such a problem as whether the child should be indulged or trained.

THE EDIPUS CONFLICT

The next and greatest step in the development of self-control and of morality lies in the solution of the severe conflict of the edipus period. Freud's original statement that the edipus complex is the nuclear complex of all the neuroses has been substantiated by all psychoanalytic research, and I do not need to discuss it in detail here. The struggle between the passionate sexual love for the parent of the opposite sex and the conflicting feelings of bitter hatred, intense fear, and passionate sexual love for the parent of the same sex, occupies most of the child's life during the period between three and seven years and ends in the erection in the mind of a new structure—the superego—which is the incorporated image of the loved, feared, and hated parent of the same sex. Basically, the superego stands in the unconscious as an observer who watches the instinct representations from the id. If they seem to have incestuous or parricidal aims, the superego warns the ego through feelings of anxiety or guilt, which may or may not become conscious, that unacceptable instincts are demanding discharge and that the ego, if it does not wish to suffer punishment through loss of love or castration, had better impose some defenses lest they break through into action. Therefore, the superego is basically prohibitory in nature, and it is actually a part of the human psyche which is a monument to the primitive struggles in the primal horde, out of which culture and civilization first developed. This superego develops as the outcome of the edipus struggle, although the fact that it will develop is predetermined. The inner moral codes, as well as the character and the personality of each individual, will depend on what the child has experienced within himself during the course of the edipus conflict. The difference between individuals which results will depend on the strength of the instincts, which varies somewhat from person to person, and the ways, perhaps also predetermined, in which the defenses have become organized to control them. To this core a number of other factors are added. These will include the actual daily attitudes and behavior of the parents toward the child, particularly those of the parent of the same sex. The personality and character of each of the parents, again particularly that of the parent of the same sex, will also be included. This means that the superego will be the heir of the cultural traditions of the social organization into which the child is born. All of the restrictions which the child has imposed on himself earlier, such as the results of his toilet training, now are embodied in the superego. This means that the so-called pregenital impulses, such as peeping, exhibitionism, sadism, and masochism, come under its ban, and because of this, they now arouse feelings of fear, disgust, and loathing in the ego, which defends itself against them either by sublimating them—turning peeping into nonsexual curiosity, exhibitionism into desire to be an actor, sadism into the socially acceptable forms of cruelty like butchering or surgery or into aggressive activities, and masochism into passive-receptive activity—or by developing reaction formations—lack of curiosity defending against peeping, modesty defending against exhibitionism, kindness and sympathy against cruelty, and unwillingness to be hurt against masochism. With the crystallization of the final superego, the pregenital impulses become cultured and civilized even if no specific training has been directed against them. As these pregenital impulses vary in strength, they will not all succumb to the superego prohibitions at the same time in the same individual, or at the same time for different individuals, but at some time during early latency the superego prohibitions will come to include them.

The superego also contains the memory traces of the child's experiences, particularly those in which he was frightened by the results of the expression of his instinct representations. "A burnt child dreads the fire," and the superego stands on guard to warn the child's ego when dangerous instinct representations are demanding expression.

The greater part of the superego is unconscious and its presence can be detected consciously in the ego only through the warning signals of anxiety, guilt, disgust, loathing, and the like. The conscious part, known commonly as the conscience, actually is very small and draws its energy from the unconscious part of the superego. The basic and greater part of the superego is the heir to the primal struggle, when the human being started to become civilized, and the content of the superego prohibitions arises from the way the child solves his edipus conflict by incorporating his fantasy picture of the parent of the same sex, as well as the picture of the actual parents. It is the actual experience of living together with his parents, not their precepts and admonitions, which is educationally important. Because of the importance of the wish to identify with the parents, their example, whether they are conscious of what they are doing or not, is the most powerful educational force in the moral development of the child. It may be sharpened and delineated a little more clearly through precept and admonition, and from time to time it necessarily will be if the parents respect their own rights and privileges. As a result of both of these incorporations, the superego is either reasonable and practical or unreasonable and impractical.

A great misapplication of psychoanalytic concepts was made when the idea was promulgated that the severity of the unconscious superego would be reduced if the child were raised in a completely permissive atmosphere. This view respected the rights and privileges of the child—which often had not been considered at all before this time—but neglected the equal rights and privileges of the parents. Instead of producing a more capable child this attempt produced a less capable one. In an early chapter I have described the personality and behavior of children reared in such an atmosphere. I want here to mention again only one striking characteristic. They have great difficulty learning skills, particularly academic skills. All education, whether it be moral education or the learning of academic subjects, is opposed to the free discharge of the instincts. Instincts and their representations have to be inhibited in order for the individual to utilize perceptions from the outside world. The child who is reared in a completely permissive atmosphere places fewer inhibitions on the discharge of his instincts and therefore has no dammed-up energy at his disposal for the purpose of learning. The degree of his intelligence makes no difference in this connection. As I remarked earlier, progressive schools at present are faced with the problem that children who have been reared in over-permissive homes do not learn, or even want to learn, and progressive methods have to be altered so that such children learn first to inhibit the discharge of their instincts. When this has been accomplished, they begin to want to learn, and are able to do so.

As I write this, however, I feel that my emphasis leans, perhaps, too much in the opposite direction from that of the main misapplication of psychoanalytic concepts in education. Actually, the educator of the growing child has to walk a narrow chalk line between training and indulgence. It is better that he walk a little on the side of indulgence but he will not go far wrong if he remembers that he, as well as the child, has rights and privileges.

So far I have been discussing the education of the child from birth to the age of about six or seven. During this period the child alternates between the free expression of his instincts—to the extent that he is physically capable, and by means of manifestations that are not appreciated by the adult—and the control mechanisms of phobias, labile emotional reactions, and temper tantrums. Particularly during the years of the edipus conflict—from three to six—the child's behavior is usually annoying. When I read over the discussion notes of the series of seminars mentioned in the Preface, I found that much of the discussion centered around the education of the child in this early period and often referred to the child in nursery school or in kindergarten. I believe that either educators are ignorant of the existence of the struggles of the edipus situation or they ignore its reality and do not realize that, apart from furnishing the child with a stable environment, they can do little to help him with his problems except in the ways I have just described. In fact, here professional educators can do practically nothing, for the outcome of the edipus situation depends on the parents. For example, I believe Neal [7] errs when he says that children should be sent to boarding schools at five, to help with the solution of the edipus complex. Also, they do not recognize that the child of six—

[7] A. S. Neal, *The Problem Teacher,* New York, International Universities Press, 1944.

helped along these lines by the professional educator than by the parents. The former must understand that at six or seven the child verbally rebels but secretly desires a strong hand over him to support him against his impulses. A mild rebellion against this need is found at nine and ten. In both of these phases the child will be helped by the educator who supports him instead of attempting to take the opposite attitude—the progressive-minded educator wishing to encourage "freedom" in the six- or seven-year-old, the traditional-minded educator wishing to suppress rebellion in the nine- or ten-year-old. The educator of the six- or seven-year-old can utilize the fascistic strivings of the child to help him to learn to tolerate present discomfort in the hope of future pleasure. The educator of the nine- or ten-year-old can allow the child's rebellion to be limited by reality, which includes the rights of others. Children in the latency period, when their activities are unsupervised by adults, themselves introduce this limitation. All group games are governed by hard-and-fast, self-imposed rules of a definite, obsessional character and the infraction of these rules is a major offense, which is swiftly punished by ostracism. Also, at about the nine- or ten-year-old level, the group decides whether the behavior of a particular individual is acceptable or not, and if it is not, the culprit is so informed in no uncertain terms. The mores of the group—however good or bad they may appear to the adult—and physical reality are the great educators during this period and the admonitions of the adults are listened to with tongue in cheek. The old adage, Experience is the best teacher, is predominantly valid for the child in the latency period.

Whatever adult admonitions are desirable, as adjuncts to the mutual respect between parents and child for each other's rights that living together entails, come better from the professional educator than from the parents, because the child is less involved in deep-seated conflicts with them than with his parents. Everyone observes that the child of the latency period is much better behaved, i.e., more cultured and civilized, away from home than at home, and that he has infinitely more respect for the opinions of adults other than his parents than he does for his parents. This attitude reaches its zenith during adolescence, whereas its nadir occurred during the prelatent period.

PARENT-TEACHER RELATIONSHIPS

From what I have said so far the reader can see that at no point is the problem of education the question of whether the educator should be permissive or restrictive. The problem is really whether the educator understands the psychological needs of the child. Many good teachers understand intuitively. Others have become good teachers as a result of training and experience even if their native intuition is slight. The best training, of course, is the unprejudiced and unbiased observation of children and of the way they operate among themselves when unsupervised.

The observation reported by psychoanalysts and psychiatrists that neuroses begin in childhood and are often the result of, or are connected with, adverse parental attitudes has produced a growing tendency among educators at the present time to feel, when they find a child who is having difficulties in adjustment or learning, that in order to help the child they should understand the home situation, which they believe they can alter through advice and precept. It seems to me that this is just a way of passing the buck. It is no longer usual for parents to interfere with the child's development through ignorance. Formerly this may have been true for the preschool child with respect to his sexual behavior, but such interference is not so frequent nowadays. True, a child's difficulties may result from the fact that his parents have misread and misapplied the psychoanalytic concepts about permissiveness, and the teacher may find it possible to correct the mistaken point of view of such parents. But more often the teacher tends to say, "This child comes from this type of home and unless the home situation is corrected, I can do nothing for the child." As I mentioned before, this is an obvious passing of the buck.

Recently there has been a strong tendency in progressive schools to encourage the parents to take an active part in the school program. The teacher frequently visits the home, particularly for meals. Committees of parents are formed to function as an integral part of the school administration. The parents are encouraged to visit the classrooms. They are asked to take an active part in the parent-teacher organization. Often, they are allowed to help in some of the housekeeping and other tasks of the school.

As a method of increasing community understanding of the philosophy of modern education, this procedure has merit, but it really contributes little to helping the teacher with the education of the child. The teacher's time and ability, to my mind, would be better directed to the education of the child in the classroom, particularly, to the real education of the child in academic skills and in our cultural lore.

In a similar fashion, in many schools the teacher and the parent periodically discuss the child's achievement and behavior in school, or a long detailed report is sent to the parents. These discussions or reports are concerned not so much with the child's academic progress as with the child's so-called character development. The child is reported as being too aggressive or not aggressive enough, as being too much a leader or too much a follower, as being too independent or too dependent. It would seem that the parent is expected to do something about these traits or at least to come and discuss with the teacher what to do about them. I am puzzled as to what the teachers expect the parents will be able to do about them or how they can be educated by the teacher to do more than they have been capable of doing themselves in the past. If the child is too disturbed to be helped by the teacher's educational methods, he is too disturbed to be helped by the type of change in the parental educational methods that could be suggested by a teacher. Instead, the parents need to seek psychiatric help either for their own problems or for those of the child. I believe that this type of report and discussion, if it does anything, only arouses the parents' anxieties because it undermines their self-confidence. That parents should be so interested in such type of report is the result of a cultural problem, which has arisen partly from the knowledge that neuroses begin in childhood and partly from the progressive schools' insistence that character development is of greater importance than intellectual achievement. As always happens when a concept is misunderstood this has resulted in a kind of caricature of desirable attitudes, with an increasing apprehensiveness on the part of parents, who at least in urban America have come to depend more on intellectual knowledge than on their intuitive understanding.

In some schools parents are interested even in policy-making and in the methods of teaching. This seems to me to be as ridiculous as for a parent of a sick child to decide what treatment the physician should prescribe. I believe these policies are based, in reality, on mutual fear and lack of respect between the parents and the schools. The parents, on the one hand, do not seem to respect the professional training and ability of the teacher—as is well illustrated by the community attitude toward teachers' salaries—and seem to feel that though untrained they are more capable than the teacher. At the same time, they seem to be attempting to force a large part of the responsibility for the rearing of the child onto the teacher's shoulders. This ambivalent attitude produces a very confusing relationship. Instead of respecting the teacher's professional skills and ability, the parent desires to control the child's life both at home and at school. This removes from the child the necessity of making his own adjustment to situations outside of the home, an adjustment which is a great help to his developing a sense of reality. It seems to me that the parent who is always at school having conferences with the teacher resembles the wife who runs both her home and her husband's business at the same time.

On the other hand, the schools, particularly the progressive schools, are afraid that the parents will not believe that their child is really being educated through the modern methods and that they will therefore withdraw their support from the school. In order to prevent this the schools have tended to encourage closer and closer contacts with parents.

The better progressive schools are now trying to limit this trend. It is a hopeful sign that more recently the numerous books for lay readers on psychiatry and mental mechanisms are less popular than they were several years ago.

It seems probable that a middle ground will be attained some day, in which the community will become really interested in, and understanding of, the need for well-trained, well-paid teachers and for producing funds for more research into methods of teaching—just as communities are interested at present in raising funds for the investigation and treatment of the diseases of children. Then they will be no more concerned with the particular methods used by the teacher, provided he is well chosen and trained, than they are concerned with the treatment methods used with the child by their pediatrician.

CHAPTER XV

The Functions and Development of the Ego Ideal

IN HIS description of the structure of the psyche Freud [1] used two names, the ego ideal and the superego, to designate the part of the personality I discussed in the last chapter. It is not clear whether he considered the terms synonymous or whether he was indicating that the superego has two parts with different functions. He stated that the superego is a deposit of early object choices and reaction formations against these choices. The outcome of the edipus situation depends on the comparative degrees of identification with the father and the mother. When the edipus conflict passes, there will be left a series of ambivalent identifications with the father and ambivalent identifications with the mother and a series of object relations to the mother and object relations to the father. The comparative strength of the identifications depends on the relative strength of the masculine and feminine sexual predisposition in the individual. The superego consists of a biological part (the relative strength of the two innate sexual trends), and an historical part containing the residues of the child's relationship with his father during the long period of helplessness which characterizes the development of the human child. Its severity depends on the character of the father, the intensity of the edipus conflict, and the rapidity with which it succumbed to repression. Freud went on to say that the ego ideal is the heir of the edipus situation. By it the ego masters the edipus complex. The ego ideal takes over all the

[1] Sigmund Freud, *The Ego and the Id*, London, Hogarth Press and the Institute of Psycho-Analysis, 1927.

traces of biological development (the archaic inheritance), becomes a substitute for the longing for the father (and therefore is the germ of all religions), and functions as the censor of morals (a conscience). The sense of guilt results from the tension which arises when the attainments of the ego fall short of the ideal set by the ego ideal. The ego ideal contains social feelings because individuals in a particular culture tend to have a common ego ideal. The principles of religious and moral restraint which appear in the ego ideal are the residues left by the final mastery of the edipus conflict, and the principles of social feeling are the residues of the struggle to overcome feelings of rivalry.

Although Freud did not state clearly that he postulated a real distinction between the superego and the ego ideal, a careful reading of Freud's discussion suggests that he made such a distinction. Many psychoanalysts do not agree that such a distinction exists and believe that the terms are synonymous. I believe that a distinction between the functions of the superego and of the ego ideal helps to clarify certain developmental facts and certain functions of the superego-ego ideal complex, particularly in their application in the field of education. As I have stated in the previous chapter, the superego is formed as the monument to the solution of the edipus conflict. Its function is to warn the ego that certain instinctual impulses must no longer be directed toward the parents. I would describe this function as a prohibitory force whose role is to say, "You must *not.*" However, from very early in his life, the child also admires his parents, particularly the parent of the same sex, wants to be like that parent, strives to be like him, and feels very unhappy and worthless when his strivings fall short of this goal. This desire for identification with the admired and loved parent sets a goal toward which the child is permitted to aspire and this goal is incorporated as part of his personality by the time the edipus situation is solved. When this occurs, there is not only a new part added to his mind which *forbids* him to desire certain gratifications and which, if he does not obey, threatens him with punishment—his superego—but there is also a new part added to his mind which permits and encourages him to strive toward certain attainments and makes him feel disapproval of himself if he does not live up to its expectations. This latter part I would designate as the ego ideal. The superego is the more basic and more punitive part of this new portion of the anatomy of his personality, has a tendency to be unchanging because it is mostly unconscious, and so is not amenable to the later influences of reality except when it can be made conscious. It remains the repository of the infantile relationship with the parents. On the other hand, the ego ideal, although a large part of it is unconscious, is influenced to a much greater degree by reality and by relationships with people outside the family. It has more to do with conscious social feelings and therefore is more amenable to change. This is observed in a number of situations, three of which I will mention. I have already discussed how the child in the latency period, through his love for and therefore his desire to identify with the teacher, over a period of years gradually develops an ideal and gets to a point where he learns in an attempt to fulfill the ideal rather than in order to please his teachers. He has developed an ego ideal to learn. The adolescent must and does dress exactly like his colleagues regardless of his parents' opinion of his wardrobe and he is terribly embarrassed if he is forced to dress differently from his companions. As an adult he may look back with embarrassment or with tolerant amusement on the way he dressed as an adolescent. The social ideal he had as an adolescent changes as he becomes an adult. My third example of the changes that occur in the ego ideal because of reality and the relation with other people is found in the familiar maxim, When in Rome do as the Romans. It is striking to see how people's ideals will change with a changed environment. Every traveler knows how those tourists who seem incapable of adjusting their ideals to those of another culture stand out like sore thumbs.

The superego is formed mostly during the prelatent period. The formation of the ego ideal occurs mostly in the latter part of latency and during adolescence. During the early part of the latency period the child has repudiated his infantile relationship with his parents and, in its place, desires to be one with the social organization, which for him consists of his peers. With his friends he develops a mutual ego ideal. This process can be seen in group formations, as Freud [2] has

[2] Sigmund Freud, *Group Psychology and the Analysis of the Ego*, London, International Psychoanalytic Press, 1922.

shown. A mob under the influence of an ego ideal common to the group and to the leader will commit crimes against which the superego of each individual member ordinarily would protest. An adolescent will alter his morals if he becomes a member of a delinquent group; a delinquent adolescent also may alter his morals if he becomes a member of a nondelinquent group. In all of these cases there is a change in the ego ideal which may be only transitory or may be more or less permanent. It is only in the latter case that the superego is influenced.

Not only does the adolescent make his ego ideal conform to that of his peers but he also constructs it through his devoted, if frequently shortlived, attachments to many of the adults with whom he comes in contact. These attachments are often as marked as crushes. As a result of these attachments, he takes over into his ego ideal certain characteristics of the particular adult, which he will retain as a part of his ego ideal throughout his life. All of us can look back on our lives during the latter part of the latency period and during adolescence and remember a number of instances where we have been associated with certain adults who have "influenced" our lives since then. This influence is usually greater than we are aware of consciously. These adults have become part of our ego ideal.

THE EDUCATION OF THE EGO IDEAL

Perhaps the most important principle in character education of which the professional educator should be aware is the matter of the formation of the ego ideal and the fact that many of the parts of the ego ideal are incorporated unconsciously and will remain unconscious in the mind of the child. Unconscious or not, they will serve constantly as a guide to him in his daily life, for he will attempt unconsciously to raise the functioning of his ego to correspond as closely as possible to his unconscious ideals.

In order that an individual may develop an ego ideal which will be adequate for a democratic way of life, it is essential that the growing child have many contacts with all kinds and conditions of people, both of his age and older, so that his ego ideal may be flexible and therefore better adapted to a democratic and international society. The fewer

Italy, and China, and how they could feel no revulsion and no desire to do anything about it. When I mentioned my puzzlement to a colleague, he replied that he thought their point of view was very realistic. I must violently disagree. Their attitude was realistic from a personal point of view, for no one wishes to undergo discomfort or to suffer pain or to die. It was realistic from the pleasure-pain point of view. But it was not realistic from the standpoint of happiness and success, even in personal life, because such happiness and success must be associated with ideals for the benefit of the group. The question is occasionally raised of whether a person who dies for his ideals is completely normal, but I think the evidence points to his really being so. It seems to me that these young Americans had some defect in the structure of the ego ideal part of their superego. Perhaps the ideal of the gentleman was too obsessional and too unrealistic, but I do not see any ideals being developed to replace it, and I shudder at what happens when the ideal is given up—with the results we all observed in Nazi Germany and, to a less extent, in fascist Italy and Spain.

It seems to me a sad commentary on the results of American education and the state of American ideals that in a country supposed to be one of the most literate in the world and famous for the fact that the new means of communication—newspapers, radio, and television—are in the possession of almost all the population, it should be possible for *Time*[4] to say, in regard to the Korean War: "The G.I. never quite understood what this particularly bewildering war was all about."

At this point the reader may exclaim, "From time immemorial old men have inveighed against the lack of manners, morals, and ideals in the younger generation. In horrified cries, they have protested that, to their eyes, youth is going to the dogs and the past was more wonderful than the present. However, mankind always has gone forward on the road to a better civilization and culture." Perhaps the reader is correct in leveling this charge against me. As I mentioned, I was appalled that the persons I questioned defined the ideals of democracy in terms of personal success. The purpose of ideals in a social organization is not to guarantee personal success, but to make it possible for the individual and for the social organization to continue to exist.

[4] *Time*, August 3, 1953.

There is no use teaching children that honesty is the best policy—because from a personal point of view it is not. Neither is there any use teaching that sympathy and pity and kindness will aid the accomplishment of personal ambition. Honesty, kindness, sympathy, and pity are very unrealistic from a personal point of view, but are very necessary ideals if we are to be able to continue to live in a social organization.

So far I have spoken about the disappearance of an ideal—the ideal of the gentleman—which seems to have had, and might still have, value. On the other hand, there are ideals which have become outworn and whose continuance causes trouble. During pioneer days it was necessary, in order to live, to work hard, to make what one could of oneself without expecting any help, and to have great courage in the face of real threats to life—from animals, people, and the wilderness itself. At least, looking back on these times, we believe that self-reliance and courage were the usual traits of our pioneer ancestors, although after reading the first two volumes of Freeman's life of Washington I am not sure that our belief that in those days men were men and women were women is correct. However, the tradition of those times gradually became an American ideal. Any man could be self-made. All he needed was industry, ambition, and courage, and he could climb the ladder of success. In fact, any man could become president if he so desired. This ideal was valid in its insistence that the pleasure principle must be replaced by the reality principle. This was true particularly under the conditions of pioneer life, where life and death were stark realities and where social life was not very important. But the pioneer ideal had less validity in situations where there was some social life, and it did not contribute to the ability to gratify an instinct through redirection. In pioneer times, the ideal was not too difficult to attain. Today, its attainment is not possible. To send a boy out full of hope, believing in this ideal and the results to be attained by it, into our highly mechanized, urbanized society with its periodic economic depressions and resulting unemployment, will result only in his discouragement and bitterness. Alexander has described, in fact, certain delinquents whose delinquency was an attempt to live up to the ideals of the self-made, courageous, ambitious man and who found success in this attempt possible only through delinquent behavior. It is no longer true that if I build a better mousetrap the world will make a path to my door. After building it, I had better arrange for a little radio and television advertising.

Here is an ideal that perhaps had better be discarded, but what are we developing to replace it? We say we subscribe to certain ideals called freedoms—freedom of speech (within limitations imposed by the code of the gentleman), freedom of worship, freedom from fear of want, insecurity, and danger. What are we doing to determine the basic meanings of these phrases so that we can construct ideals for ourselves and for the education of our children? With these as with other slogans, there is a tendency to try to establish ideals without an adequate understanding of what their basis is. I have been interested recently in the attempts made in certain excellent progressive schools to educate the pupils to be without irrational prejudices. The educators, however, do not understand all the components that go to make up irrational prejudices. Psychoanalytic observations have shown that part of the basic reason for such prejudices is the intolerance of the superego against certain unconscious representations of instinctual drives which, because of this intolerance, are denied by the individual as part of himself and are projected unconsciously onto other persons, whose differences in race, color, or religion render them suitable to be the object of the projection. Against them the combined ego and superego express intolerant prejudice. In this way, the ego itself is protected from the intolerant prejudice of the superego. Ignorance of these basic facts concerning irrational prejudices makes the attempts of these educators to remove prejudices much less successful than they would be if these facts were really understood. Unfortunately a similar lack of understanding of this part of the basis for prejudice is found among many sociologists, philosophers, and psychologists.

If we have rejected some of the codes of ideals of Western civilization, and if some of those remaining are so distinctly unrealistic that they are causing maladjustments for the adolescent and young adult, what are we evolving to replace them and what type of replacement are we teaching our children both by precept and by example? It may seem to the reader that like Toynbee [5] I am groping for a new religion. Toynbee points out that there has always been a conflict between

[5] Arnold J. Toynbee, *The World and the West,* New York, Oxford University Press, 1953.

Western culture and the rest of the world. Up till recently, Western culture seemed to be triumphant because it had a religion and had developed mechanization. Now the rest of the world has adopted the Western mechanization, but it has not adopted the Western religion. He believes that the conflict will continue until a new religion arises, which will be adopted by both the West and the rest of the world, and that under its auspices the conflict will cease. This view shows him to be looking for a father under whose guidance all people will find security. I do not believe I am looking for the same thing, but I do believe that new ideals will have to be evolved to replace those that are being lost.

Being only a psychoanalyst, whose task is to study the workings of the human mind, of which so little really is known at present, I have no answer to this question, nor am I in a position even to suggest one. It is a question which should be under consideration by educators. It seems to me that the answer will come only from the combined careful thinking and planning of educators, psychologists, statesmen, and historians, for I would take issue with the extremely progressive educators who seem to believe that the lore of the past has no importance for the child in the present. Just as in the consideration of prejudice, so in attempting to verbalize new ideals, this group should have available the information obtained through psychoanalytic researches. It is the task of the educator to learn these facts so that they may be added to the other facts at his disposal, in order that he may plan how they can be used to the most advantage in the field of education.

CHAPTER XVI

Some Suggestions on the Relationship between Psychoanalyst and Educator

A FEW years ago, the headmaster of a progressive school [1] told me that he believed progressive education had ceased to progress and had reached a plateau. He thought that the next impetus to forward movement would come through the addition of relevant knowledge concerning psychical processes gained through psychoanalytic research to the existing principles of progressive education. This book has attempted to present this knowledge. In no sense can it be said to do so in a very complete way, because I am sure that I have neglected to discuss many facts which are pertinent to the field of education. What I have presented is only an addition to the vast knowledge that has been obtained through the researches of educators and of educational and academic psychologists. It is in no way intended to supersede their data. Their researches have been largely concerned with the nonconflictual part of the ego and with the application of this knowledge in the education of children. This educational psychology has not yet been really synthesized with the psychoanalytic psychology of the ego and with what is known about the important role played by the instincts in all phases of human behavior. Such synthesis will be important, particularly, in increasing our knowledge of the dynamics and technics of the learning process. Just as important will be the synthesis of the psychoanalytic knowledge of the superego and ego ideal with

[1] Mr. Charles Clisby, Headmaster of the Miquon School, Miquon, Pennsylvania.

the well-established technics of education and training of the child.

Let me repeat. Psychoanalysts do not believe that they hold all or even many of the keys to the better education of the child. They believe only that they have a real contribution—even if just a small one—to make to the field of education. It would seem desirable for the educator, the educational psychologist, and the psychoanalyst to confer together frequently for the purpose of synthesizing and integrating the knowledge gained independently by the three disciplines. This will require an increasing amount of toleration on the part of each of the three groups. The educational psychologist is often intolerant of, and sometimes prejudiced against, discoveries by the psychoanalysts and considers their researches unscientific to the point of viewing them with considerable disdain. The educator, often, has a similar opinion, or if not, he believes that adequate educational procedures can cure the intrapsychic disorders of any child, and so psychoanalytic therapy is unnecessary except in very exceptional cases. The psychoanalyst believes that only through the knowledge of oneself gained through a personal psychoanalysis can any person really understand the dynamics of the mind. Therefore he sees no use in trying to convince a person who has not been psychoanalyzed of the validity of the knowledge gained by psychoanalytic researches. In fact, he often believes that such persons cannot be truly scientific and, like the educational psychologist, often looks down his nose at the attempts of others to understand his contributions, particularly when, as in most scientific discussions, the effort to reach understanding is made through intellectual argument. There are two reasons for this mutual distrust and disbelief. The conscious human mind universally feels repugnance and disbelief with respect to certain facts—the existence and powerfulness of the unconscious mind, the great importance of the sexual instincts in the life and development of the preschool child, and the subhuman primitiveness of the representations of the instincts in the unconscious—all of which have been well-established through psychoanalytic research. These universal resistances have been fully discussed by Freud in many places and actually form the basis for the watered-down concepts which are so frequently accepted by non-psychoanalytically oriented psychiatrists and by many intelligent lay people and which also form the real basis for the schools of thought among psychoanalysts themselves which have deviated from the well-known findings of psychoanalysis. Freud,[2] by the end of the first quarter century of psychoanalysis, was able to discuss very fully the reasons for the deviations which had occurred during that time, and when the more recent deviations are studied carefully it will be seen that the reasons he found at that time still hold good, as Lewy [3] recently has corroborated.

The training in these three disciplines has been distinctly different. The psychoanalyst usually has a medical background which makes communication between him and other physicians relatively easy but which hinders his ability to communicate with specialists whose background is nonmedical. The educator does not understand the increasing precision of diagnosis and psychopathology that exists in psychiatry today. The educational psychologist stands between the other two, so that he is affected more by his own resistances than by differences in his training. If the members of these three groups intend to try to pool their specialized knowledge in order to develop better educational procedures for the child, they will have to be aware of the existence of these reasons for mutual distrust and disbelief, so that the subject matter can be dealt with without too much intolerance and prejudice. I believe this can be done to a much greater extent than it has been so far.

The psychoanalytic contributions to the field of education, important as their effects may be when they are applied to the development of the child, are not a panacea through the application of which all neuroses, character neuroses, and psychoses, all maladjustments and all learning difficulties can be prevented. The causes of these conditions do not always lie in inadequate and improper education or in improper parent-child or teacher-child relationships. Frequently they result from traumatic accidents which, because they are acts of fate, cannot be foreseen and therefore are unpreventable or from differences in the strength of the instinctual drives.[4] The incidence of

[2] Sigmund Freud, "On the History of the Psycho-Analytic Movement," *Collected Papers,* Vol. I, London, Hogarth Press and the Institute of Psycho-Analysis, 1924.

[3] Ernst Lewy, "The Return of the Repression," *Bulletin of the Menninger Clinic,* 5, 1941.

[4] I have discussed this more fully in *Emotional Disorders of Children,* New York, W. W. Norton & Company, 1949.

such disorders can be decreased to some extent through better educational procedures, but regardless of what preventive measures are undertaken, intrapsychic disorders will be with us always. Public-health measures may reduce the incidence of disease, but regardless of the degree of efficiency of prevention, disease will continue to exist. This is a part of reality which few, if any, human beings really accept. All of us under the surface still (falsely) believe, and feel more comfortable when we believe, as our primitive ancestors did, that all disease and death is the result of malignant activity on the part of a human enemy. This belief tends to promote a feeling of safety because it implies that we need only destroy our enemy to live in health forever. It really is a form of this primitive concept which causes many intelligent educators to suppose that proper and adequate education for all children would not only prevent all intrapsychic disturbances but also cure those which have already developed.

The acceptance of the unpleasant reality that circumstances which cannot be prevented may cause a child or an adult to become ill emotionally or physically is an important part of the adjustment to reality, but it need not result in a laissez-faire attitude toward preventive measures. Instead, it should serve as an impetus to more research and to a better application of the knowledge we already have. To indicate how this knowledge may be applied has been the purpose of this book.

There are at least two practical measures for achieving this purpose. I have spoken of the need for educators, educational psychologists, and psychoanalysts to pool their specific contributions to the field of education. I believe, too, that schools might make more use of psychoanalysts who specialize in the psychoanalysis of children and adolescents. Perhaps this could be done in the following manner: When a teacher perceives that there is a child in his classroom who appears to be maladjusted—whatever the form of the maladjustment—he might take certain specific steps. First, he should devote several weeks—perhaps three or four—to the collection of observations of the child from as many different aspects as possible. In what particular subjects is the child interested or uninterested, and how successful is he in learning these various subjects? What is the attitude of the child toward the teacher, toward other teachers, and toward the school principal? What is his attitude toward the daily routines? How does he get on with his male colleagues and with his female ones? What is his attitude in sports and recreation and toward the child-imposed rules for games? What are his play interests? What is his attitude toward himself as a person and what are his personal habits, manners, and customs? What physiological disturbances does he show? What are the recurrent themes in his work and his compositions? What are his conscious daydreams and his dreams during sleep? (These could be obtained by asking the students once a week to write down their daydreams and their night dreams as part of their studies in English.) How has he behaved and what kind of work has he done in other classrooms and with other teachers? All these observations can be made without any direct questioning of the child. Having collected this mass of data, the teacher could confer either with the principal or with the school counselor (who should be equipped through special training to participate in such a conference) for the purpose of deciding whether the child has a personal problem or whether the teacher's attitude toward the child is the cause of the difficulty. If the latter is the case, the teacher need not feel chagrined, for no teacher can have an equally helpful attitude toward every child in his classroom. Perhaps he can change his attitude toward this particular child, perhaps it would be better for the child to have a different teacher.

If the child appears to have a problem of his own then the teacher and perhaps the principal, particularly if they can reach no decision in the first conference, could submit the data to and confer with a consulting psychoanalyst. I believe that every school—not school system—should have a consulting psychoanalyst, who should provide assistance in at least three ways.

First, he should know the preschool history of every child and should interview every child before the child enters the particular school. In this way, he will be in a position to advise whether this particular child should be enrolled in this particular school or whether another type of school would be more advantageous for him. There are some children who develop better in a more progressive type of school and some whose development is aided by a more traditional type of school.

Second, knowing the preschool history of the child, he will know whether the child has already been exposed to serious traumatic situations—parental deaths, divorces, or separations, or prolonged or painful illnesses of the child himself. He will be able to advise the teacher how to recognize early signs of the adverse results of such traumata, so that the child can have adequate care as soon as possible. Also, he may be able to determine the character type of a particular child and through this knowledge advise the teacher as to the best methods of education for this particular child.[5]

The consulting psychoanalyst's third task will be to take part in the consultations I have mentioned. The teacher, the principal, and the psychoanalyst will confer on the data which the teacher has collected, in order to try to answer several questions: Is this child himself suffering from an intrapsychic illness or is his present behavior a reaction to environmental pressures, and do these pressures exist in the school or elsewhere? If he has an intrapsychic illness what is its diagnosis and how serious is it? What treatment will be necessary? What are the next steps in the investigation of this case? At this point I may be asked if it is possible to answer any of these questions, even tentatively, from this small amount of data and without obtaining any history or seeing the child. I believe that very frequently it is possible to form conclusions from such data that will allow the teacher to suggest to the parent that the child is ill and needs psychiatric study and treatment. In other instances the data will be sufficient to indicate that a child does not have a serious intrapsychic problem, but that certain special studies—physical or psychological—are required. In many cases, of course, the conference will not reach any conclusions but will have to decide on what further methods of investigation are necessary. I believe that the percentage of cases in this last group will be decreased as both teacher and psychoanalyst obtain more experience in observing and weighing the results of the observations. After all, it is often

[5] It is possible that eventually he might be able to go further and on the basis of character types advise the teacher which particular children would have difficulty learning specific skills, such as reading or arithmetic, and therefore would require special methods of instruction. Children with predominantly anal characters might have difficulty in learning arithmetic, children who have repression of their scoptophilic impulses might have difficulty in learning to read. Children whose ego development generally was weak would require education of their ego defenses before they could learn any skills. One research project of the Miquon School for 1953–1954 is along these lines. The teachers will endeavor to correlate character types with the ability to learn specific skills. If this is possible, it will make an entirely new approach to the learning of skills, which, however, will require the help of a consulting psychoanalyst.

relatively easy for an experienced psychoanalyst to decide from a detailed description that a child has a serious intrapsychic illness and needs psychotherapy, and this is the important question to be decided at this conference. It is not important at this time to know whether the child has a specific type of neurosis, character neurosis, or psychosis, or what type of treatment will be necessary. These questions will be determined by the psychoanalyst to whom the child is referred.

If the conference decides that the child is ill and should be referred to a psychoanalyst for study, diagnosis, and treatment, then the next important question to be discussed is how the parents are to be told. This question is very momentous, and here the teacher's knowledge of the parents and the psychoanalyst's knowledge of approaches to parents about their children should be pooled, so that the parents' willing co-operation can be enlisted in getting help for the child. Unless this question is considered seriously and a definite plan of action mapped out, the parent may reject the whole idea, may become angry and resentful at the teacher and at the school even to the point of withdrawing the child, or may give lip service to the advice but either not carry it out or carry it out in such a way that no benefit is obtained. These disastrous results are well known to every teacher, to every school physician, and to every child psychoanalyst. They may occur even with the most careful technic, but if great care is used in approaching the parent, they will happen much less frequently. As any further studies—a physical examination, a psychological examination, obtaining the child's history, or a psychiatric study of the child himself—need the consent of the parents, the question of the approach to the parents is a vitally necessary one, to be discussed in every case where the problem is not obviously one for the school itself. I believe that it is in this area that the consultation with the psychoanalyst will be most valuable.

If a decision as to the presence of illness in the child is not reached, then the conference will decide what the next steps for investigation will be. After these are undertaken there will be another conference between the teacher, perhaps the physician, perhaps the psychologist, perhaps the school counselor, and the psychoanalyst. If the other professional people do not attend the conference personally, at least the teacher and the psychoanalyst will have the written reports of their studies, and on the basis of all of this data a valid diagnosis and recommendations can be made.

Two points should be discussed here. If the school already has a consulting psychologist, a school counselor, or a school social worker, could these not take the place of a consulting psychoanalyst? My experience has shown me that it is important that the school have a consulting psychoanalyst. He really is better equipped to perform such a function than members of the other professional groups. At the same time, through these frequent conferences the principal and teacher will gradually learn the application of the contributions of psychoanalysis to education and therefore will be more and more able to incorporate these contributions into their own thinking and thus into the field of education. Furthermore, if a child is referred for psychotherapy while remaining in the school, the teacher, having had personal contact with a psychoanalyst, will understand better the ways in which he can obtain the best help from the child's therapist in managing in his classroom the child who is under treatment. This co-operation between the teacher and the child's therapist will be of great benefit to both in their dealings with the child.

I have mentioned the referral of the child for treatment. The consulting psychoanalyst, of course, should be paid by the school for his conference time as well as for the other activities in which he participates. A certain number of parents who have sick children will be unable to pay for private treatment. The consulting psychoanalyst will know the reliable psychoanalytic clinics to which such children can be referred. For the parents able to pay for private therapy the consulting psychoanalyst should keep a list of those who have specialized in the psychoanalysis of children, and from this list the parents can make their choice. It is usually better for the consulting psychoanalyst not to take any of these cases into treatment himself unless the parents demand that he do so, and then only on mature consideration. The fact that he is consulting psychoanalyst to the school makes his therapeutic relation with the child more difficult for both the child and himself. I have not the time or space here to discuss the reasons for this, but they are well known to every psychoanalyst and have been borne out by my experience.

There are many problems of school children that do not require treatment by a psychoanalyst and many that he is by no means trained to treat. I[6] have tried in my article on learning difficulties in *The Psychoanalytic Study of the Child* to mention briefly the types of cases that can be treated best by the teacher, by the school counselor or social worker, by the psychologist, and by the psychoanalyst. The consulting psychoanalyst, in conference with members of the other professional groups, can help in deciding who is best trained to treat the particular child and his particular disability.

The question arises whether a really sick child, even though he is under psychoanalytic treatment, should remain a student in the ordinary school. I have seen a number of children who were unable to adjust in public school. The parents placed them in private school after private school until they ended up in the most progressive school the parents could find—to the despair of the teacher and the detriment of the group. A high percentage of maladjusted children is found in private schools, and the more progressive the school the higher the percentage of maladjusted children will be unless the intake committee exerts unusual vigilance. It is true, too, that educational psychologists, psychiatrists, and psychoanalysts put a great deal of pressure on the best schools to accept patients as students, because they know no other school will display a like degree of consistent understanding. These pressures are difficult for the intake committees and principals to resist. It is a question whether these good schools, or any schools, should be asked to put up with too many maladjusted children whose neuroses cause them to disrupt the group and who divert the teacher's attention from the group to the individual—which is upsetting to the working relationship within the group and therefore taxes the teacher excessively. It has been my experience that most cases of conversion hysteria, of anxiety hysteria, and of compulsion neuroses can attend the ordinary school while they are under treatment. The only difficulty is that the child patient may have to miss several hours of school a week in order to have treatment, and he is often reluctant and resentful if he has to use his free time to make up his work. This situation can be helped by a better understanding of therapy by the teacher. In certain cases, the neurotic illness interferes with the child's learning

[6] Gerald H. J. Pearson, "A Survey of Learning Difficulties in Children," *The Psychoanalytic Study of the Child,* Vol. VII, New York, International Universities Press, 1952.

ability at a particular time, so that the child will need special tutoring in the lost fundamentals as he begins to convalesce from the illness.

Similarly, some cases of character neurosis under treatment can get along all right in the ordinary classroom. In others, part of the secondary symptomatology is antisocial behavior. These children cause too much disturbance in the ordinary classroom and, for that matter, in their communities, and often their home situation is such that they should be removed from it.

There is a notable lack of proper day and boarding schools for such children and those that exist are usually quite expensive because of the high salaries needed to employ teachers highly trained for this type of work. Mrs. Rank's nursery school and kindergarten in Boston, the University of Chicago's Sonia Straubman Orthogenic School, under the direction of Dr. Bruno Bettelheim, the Southard School of the Menninger Foundation at Topeka, Kansas, the school conducted by Fritz Redl at Detroit, and the Emma Pendleton Bradley Home, Riverside, Rhode Island, are among the best boarding schools for severely disturbed children. The Devereux Schools at Devon, Pennsylvania, and Santa Barbara, California, are trying to develop units for such children, but so far have not been as careful in the selection of teachers and housemothers as have the schools I mentioned before—perhaps because they cannot afford high enough salaries and because only recently have they attempted to add the necessary therapy for such children.

There are in a few hospitals facilities for the diagnosis and treatment of severely disturbed and psychotic children, such as Dr. Lauretta Bender's department at Bellevue Hospital, New York, Dr. Leo Kanner's department at Johns Hopkins Hospital in Baltimore, and the Children's Department of the Western Psychiatric Hospital in Pittsburgh. There is some question whether psychotic children should be placed in boarding schools. Dr. Mary O'Neil Hawkins, who had considerable experience with such cases at the Southard School, believes they do better when their therapy is combined with living in a foster home.[7]

Day schools for these children are lamentably few and are generally disciplinary schools rather than therapeutic centers. There is an ur-

[7] Personal communication by Dr. Mary O'Neil Hawkins.

gent need for educators and foundations to develop more boarding and day schools for socially disturbed children, especially in the middle-income group, where education and therapy can go hand in hand. From the beginning, the organization and selection of personnel for such schools should be in the hands of a committee of educators, educational psychologists, and psychoanalysts.

The first reaction of the reader of this chapter will be that I am very far removed from reality and that although my idea of a consulting psychoanalyst for every school may be a good one, it is very impractical. Where are schools going to get enough psychoanalysts who have specialized in the psychoanalysis of children? They are too few in number even in the metropolitan areas, and in the smaller communities there are none. I realize this is so, but only as schools start to demand such services will the training institutes of the American Psychoanalytic Association and its subsidiary Committee on the Psychoanalysis of Children and Adolescents begin to consider the problem an important one. I believe the spread of this program will make necessary a relaxation of certain of the rules of the American Psychoanalytic Association—a relaxation which will mean not the lowering of standards but actually a heightening of them. At the present time, no institute in America may train a lay person in the theory and practice of psychoanalysis. This is not the case in Europe, and Freud [8] himself believed that this stand was not a wise or necessary one. Most psychoanalytic training institutes offer a few rather unorganized courses in psychoanalytic theory for teachers and the members of other professional disciplines. Except for the course given by the New York Psychoanalytic Institute and perhaps the course given by the Chicago Institute for Psychoanalysis, the instruction is too spotty to be of much value. It would seem to me that all psychoanalytic institutes which give instruction in the psychoanalysis of children and adolescents could increase their services to the community by carefully selecting certain teachers to be students in the institute. These teachers might be chosen partly from among instructors in the schools of education and partly from those in the school system itself. They should be given exactly the same instruction as are the psychiatrist students

[8] Sigmund Freud, *The Question of Lay Analysis,* New York, W. W. Norton & Company, 1950.

in the course on the psychoanalysis of children. They should have the same preliminary personal psychoanalysis and the same theoretical instruction, and should attend the same clinical and technical seminars. They should conduct a supervised psychoanalysis of at least one adult and three or four children. In this way they would learn by theory and practice the principles of psychoanalysis. When a teacher had successfully completed such a course, he could return to the school as a reputable consulting psychoanalyst. If after completing his course he should desire to devote himself entirely to psychoanalysis, as many pediatricians who have had psychoanalytic training have done, then the institute should demand that he limit his practice to the psychoanalysis of children in cases referred by a physician psychoanalyst and under his supervision. If the personal psychoanalysis has been really successful—and no such student should be permitted to complete his training otherwise—the teacher's increased ability to adjust to reality will enable him to accept these necessary restrictions with good grace and in good faith. There are relatively more teachers than physicians who show an intuitive ability to understand and work with children, and so the practice of the psychoanalysis of children would actually be benefited by this procedure. It would be hoped, however, that teachers with such intensive training would prefer to employ their knowledge of psychoanalysis in the field of education rather than in the practice of psychoanalytic therapy. As I said before, the procedure I have suggested would not lower but raise the standards of the American Psychoanalytic Association.

I realize that in this book I have only tapped the surface of the contributions of psychoanalysis to education but I am hopeful that as a result of this effort more psychoanalysts will consider the relation of their specialty to education and more educators will become interested in understanding and collaborating in the application of psychoanalytic knowledge to the field of education.

Index